Collaboration in Social Work Practice

Collaboration in Social Work Practice

*Edited by Jenny Weinstein, Colin Whittington
and Tony Leiba*

Jessica Kingsley Publishers
London and New York

First published in the United Kingdom in 2003
by Jessica Kingsley Publishers Ltd
116 Pentonville Road
London N1 9JB, England
and
29 West 35th Street, 10th fl.
New York, NY 10001-2299, USA

www.jkp.com

Copyright © Jessica Kingsley Publishers 2003

Library of Congress Cataloging in Publication Data
A CIP catalog record for this book is available from the Library of Congress

British Library Cataloguing in Publication Data
A CIP catalogue record for this book is available from the British Library

ISBN 1 84310 092 4

Printed and Bound in Great Britain by
Athenaeum Press, Gateshead, Tyne and Wear

Contents

EDITORS' PREFACE   7

PART I SERVICE USERS, PROFESSIONALS AND THE COLLABORATIVE CONTEXT   11

1 Collaboration and Partnership in Context   13
Colin Whittington, Independent Consultant

2 A Model of Collaboration   39
Colin Whittington

3 Who are the Participants in the Collaborative Process and What Makes Collaboration Succeed or Fail?   63
Tony Leiba, South Bank University, and Jenny Weinstein, Jewish Care

4 Shared Values in Interprofessional Collaboration   83
Jean Davis, South Bank University, and Dave Sims, University of Greenwich

PART II COLLABORATION IN PRACTICE   101

5 Allies and Enemies: The Service User as Care Co-ordinator   103
Christine Barton, Inclusive Living Sheffield Ltd

6 Collaboration or Confusion? The Carers' Perspective   121
Sonia Douek, Jewish Care

7 Working Together to Improve Children's Life Chances: The Challenge of Inter-agency Collaboration   137
Ruth Gardner, Royal Holloway College

8 Mental Health Policies and Interprofessional Working   161
Tony Leiba

9 Learning Disabilities: Effective Partnership and Teamwork
  to Overcome Barriers in Service Provision   181
  Tony Thompson, Independent Training Consultant

10 Social Work and Multi-disciplinary Collaboration
  in Primary Health Care   201
  Kirstein Rummery, University of Manchester

11 Collaborating for the Social and Health Care
  of Older People   219
  Mark Lymbery, University of Nottingham

THE CONTRIBUTORS   239

SUBJECT INDEX   241

AUTHOR INDEX   251

Editors' Preface

Collaboration in Social Work Practice argues that collaboration between professionals and with service users and carers is essential to the successful delivery of care services. The contributing authors, writing about care delivered in different contexts, take a positive approach but they also identify continued problems in achieving collaboration, despite myriad government policies, procedures and new forms of organization.

The urgency of addressing these problems is powerfully illustrated by two reports which appeared early in 2003, as *Collaboration in Social Work Practice* went to press. One, the report on *The Victoria Climbié Inquiry*, described in graphic detail the numerous breakdowns in communication within and between agencies in their failure to prevent the death of a young child (Laming 2003).

The other, written with contributions from people with learning disabilities, highlights some of the difficulties in achieving genuine involvement of service users. The White Paper *Valuing People* had advocated effective partnerships involving people with learning disabilities and their families as being 'key to social inclusion' (DoH 2001, p.106). Yet the *First Annual Report of the Learning Disability Task Force* (DoH 2003) says that the new partnership boards had found it difficult to include people with learning disabilities and 'the message "nothing about us without us" has not got through to most of Government outside those working with Disability' (DoH 2003, p.2).

Collaboration in Social Work Practice has been written primarily for social workers, and draws in particular on examples from social care and health, but its contents will be relevant to all who work in care services and at their interface. Each chapter offers both analysis and good practice guidance.

Part I, comprising Chapters 1 to 4, provides the policy, conceptual and ethical contexts for the seven chapters in Part II which focus on aspects of collaboration in practice. Key themes such as service-user and carer involvement, social inclusion, interprofessional relationships, barriers to effective collaboration, policies, structures, procedures and methods for collaboration, and interprofessional shared learning are introduced in Part I and exemplified in different settings in Part II.

In Chapter 1, Whittington explores the vocabulary and meanings of collaboration and partnership before demonstrating their significance in the
context of national social policy. Turning to the structure of agencies, he
describes areas for joint work at different organizational levels and outlines
degrees of service integration. He also shows that analysis must extend
beyond policy and organizational contexts or we miss the multi-dimensional
and sometimes contradictory nature of collaboration and partnership. These
twin concepts, Whittington concludes, have become essential to the practice
and organization of social workers and other care practitioners but require
reflective, critical application.

In Chapter 2, Whittington sets out a new model of collaboration. Illustrated with research from social work, social care, health and education, it is
essentially trans-disciplinary and therefore relevant across care professions
and related agencies. Service users and carers are at the heart of the model
and are represented collectively as one of five key 'spheres'. The other four –
the inter-personal, interprofessional, inter-disciplinary team and
inter-organizational spheres – are also described and the connection of all
five illustrated using a 'whole system' perspective.

In Chapter 3, Leiba and Weinstein introduce the participants in the collaborative process – service users, carers and professionals. They begin by
arguing the importance of collaboration with service users and carers, offering research evidence to illustrate good or poor practice. A brief review of
the literature about how professionals perceive each other is followed by a
critical discussion of key interprofessional structures and methods, including
child protection. The authors argue that while research is not yet conclusive
there is evidence to demonstrate that effective collaboration with users and
between professionals improves outcomes for service users and their carers.

Sims and Davis address interprofessional values in Chapter 4, comparing the values statements of social work with the ethical codes of nursing.
Sims and Davis have been involved for some years in delivering
interprofessional education for nurses and social workers. They were helped
in constructing the chapter by graduates who now hold a dual nursing and
social work qualification. The graduates participated in a discussion to
explore the similarities and differences in ethics and values between health
and care professions. A case study exemplifies some ethical dilemmas in
practice and the authors argue that a shared interprofessional values base is
needed.

The service users' perspective is the subject of Chapter 5 by Barton. She shares her own experience as a disabled woman and the stories of other service users, told in their own words, to demonstrate the negative impact on service users of professionals' failure to work in partnership with them. On the positive side, there are instances of how good practice can genuinely enhance service users' quality of life. In particular, she emphasizes the importance of focusing on the individual and not on the services available. Barton concludes with advice for social workers and other professionals about how they can work effectively in collaboration with service users.

In Chapter 6, Douek, who runs a carers' service, pursues many of the points raised by Barton: the importance of listening, the importance of providing relevant information and the need to provide flexible services. Douek reviews the research on carers' opinions about working with professionals and illustrates some of the findings in four case studies from her own practice. The case studies demonstrate good practice in different contexts – mental health, dementia care, disability, and addiction – showing how genuine partnership between professionals and carers can ameliorate carers' stress, improve outcomes for users and, in some cases, prevent family breakdown.

Gardener focuses on child-care practice in Chapter 7. The emphasis of this chapter is on the prevention of family breakdown and the promotion of social inclusion for children who may be at risk. The author describes a wide range of innovative social community and education projects; she argues that the direct involvement of children and families in the management of the projects is a crucial success factor. She draws on relevant evaluative research both in the UK and the USA which leads her to conclude that, although costly in time and resources, effective collaboration can improve children's life chances.

In Chapter 8, Leiba discusses collaboration in mental health. He focuses on three aspects – a critical evaluation of the implementation of relevant legislation and policy; the relationships between mental health professionals and how they perceive each other; and the importance of interprofessional education and training, particularly on subjects such as anti-discriminatory practice and the management of conflict. Leiba argues that while legislation that prescribes collaboration can provide a framework, the crucial factor determining success or failure for partnership working is the way in which professionals relate to each other and to service users and carers.

Thompson argues in Chapter 9 that learning disability services have been in the forefront of initiating interprofessional collaboration and working practices. However, in spite of progressive legislation and some leading edge projects, research indicates that systematic collaboration has not been achieved and this has led to variable and sometimes poor outcomes for service users and their carers. Thompson considers the potential impact of recent government initiatives to address the problems but concludes that insufficient resources have been devoted to achieve the necessary changes. Like Leiba, he advocates improved teamworking and more comprehensive interprofessional education and training.

Rummery, in Chapter 10, explores the barriers and benefits of collaboration for the main parties in primary care – namely, the service users and carers, social workers, GPs, community nurses and managers. She also reports research on the experience of the social services representatives involved in primary care groups (PCGs). Rummery notes evidence of significant gains to primary care professionals from collaboration but cautions that the challenge is to translate them into demonstrable benefits to service users and carers. She also observes that there may be losses as well as gains for social workers from joint working and suggests lessons to strengthen their contribution.

In Chapter 11, Lymbery states the case for a central contribution by social work to the policy and practice of collaboration in the care of older people. This flows, he argues, from social work's commitment to collaborative values and the understanding of the person that social workers can bring. Lymbery recognizes obstacles to his goal, related partly to the marginalization of older people and of social work with them, but responds by illustrating how an active presence of social work professionals can enhance quality when implementing cornerstone collaborative policies on assessment and intermediate care.

References

DoH (2001) *Valuing People: A New Strategy for Learning Disability for the 21st Century.* Cm 5086. London: Stationery Office.

DoH (2003) *Making Things Happen: First Annual Report of the Learning Disability Task Force.* London: Department of Health.

Laming, Lord (2003) *The Victoria Climbié Inquiry.* London: HMSO.

PART I

Service Users, Professionals and the Collaborative Context

Chapter 1

Collaboration and Partnership in Context

Colin Whittington

Introduction

On each working day, and at night too, social workers will be found busily in discussion with colleagues from their own teams and organizations and from other agencies. The discussion does not take place *instead of* professional practices, but as *an essential part of it*. The colleagues involved may be other social workers, or nurses, personal care staff, therapists, doctors, housing staff, lawyers, police officers, administrators or one of the many other occupations who together make up the multi-disciplinary network of contemporary care.

Their discussion may be focused on trying to understand the nature of a social care problem, to determine a course of action, to secure a service for someone in need or to re-establish help that has broken down. A kaleidoscope of factors enters the exchange: the views of service users and carers, service policies and structures, inter-agency agreements, professional cultures and methodologies, power and status, budgets and care resources, time, priorities and personal styles. The parties may reach agreement quickly, spend time negotiating or find themselves working to resolve real differences of view. This is collaboration with other professions and agencies, in action.

The scenario is not new (Whittington 1983, 1998) but one thing certainly is. For the first time, there is a declared belief at virtually all points of the social care spectrum, from government (DoH 1998d), through the organizations that review services and their performance (Audit Commission 2000), to training and the front line (Whittington and Bell 2001), that:

- *partnerships* between agencies are essential to delivering the objectives of care services

- skilled *collaboration* between the staff who deliver the services is indispensable in making those partnerships work.

It is also recognized that the ideas of partnership and collaboration must condition the relationship of agencies and care professionals with service users and carers, by putting service users at the 'heart of the enterprise' (SSI 2001, paragraph 1.10). Service users and carers and their representatives are pressing for more direct influence and involvement both in the decisions that affect them individually and in decisions about services (Beresford 2002). They also wish services to work in partnership and professionals to collaborate, and they seek this with good reason (Audit Commission 2002). Service isolation and fragmentation can result in lack of co-ordination, poor communication with service users, users spending longer periods away from home and increased service costs (Audit Commission 2000; Nuffield 1997).

In the early 1990s, social workers were already reporting in detail the great importance they attached to skills in working with other professions and organizations (Whittington and Bell 2001). There is still some way to go, but the wider system is at last catching up with them by promoting the systematic learning opportunities and service structures that collaborative practice requires and by making co-operation with other professionals an explicit expectation (DoH 2002c; GSCC 2002).

The aim of this book is to respond to and support these developments and the objectives for significantly improved care services that they embody. Our purpose is to contribute to more effective collaboration by social workers with other professionals, agencies and service users by offering analysis of collaboration and partnership, exploring their policy and practice contexts and sharing evidence and examples of good practice. This first chapter will:

- say what we mean by collaboration and partnership and some related concepts

- review the foundation and progress of collaboration between services and their staff in the context of national policies

- outline some dimensions of collaboration and partnership in care services

- reflect on some further dimensions of collaboration and partnership and, in the process, signal possible directions for future critique and development.

What is meant by collaboration and partnership?

The terms 'collaboration' and 'partnership' are often used together in ways that assume common agreement on their meaning and are sometimes treated as interchangeable. This need not be especially problematic during day-to-day practice, or even in an edited collection on the subject; the editors here have not insisted on a single usage. However, an attempt to distinguish them and to clarify their meaning does help to detect dimensions that may otherwise be lost. The terms also tend to be used as if their purpose and beneficiaries are always clear and self-evident. It will become apparent later that the position is more complicated than that.

To begin with 'partnership', there are no absolutes, but *working in partnership* tends to be the formal, institutional-level label attached to the idea of 'working together'. It is how government policies express the expectation of so-called joined-up services (DoH 1998e) and what the Audit Commission calls 'mandatory partnership working' (1998). Second, it is how agencies and professionals describe what they are doing together to respond to service users, carers and communities whose requirements extend beyond the responsibilities or resources of one professional group or agency. Third, it refers to arrangements between a service or services and representatives of service users and carers involved, for example, in planning, delivery or monitoring of services.

Turning to *collaboration*, this may be thought of as the more active form of 'working together'. Collaboration is the collection of knowledge, skills, values and motives applied by practitioners to translate the following into effective practice:

- formal systematic joint working arrangements (such as inter-disciplinary or integrated teams)

- less formalized joint work between different professions and agencies arising in the course of assessing for, arranging,

  providing and evaluating services (sometimes called multi-agency
  or multi-professional networks)

- the goals of participation, empowerment and social inclusion of
  service users and carers.

In summary, the following usages are suggested:

- *Partnership is a state of relationship, at organizational, group, professional
  or inter-personal level, to be achieved, maintained and reviewed.*

- *Collaboration is an active process of partnership in action.*

The lexicon of partnership and collaboration contains a number of other
terms. They fall into two sub-sets and both imply degrees of shared purpose
(Barton and Quinn 2001; Lupton 2001). The first sub-set is concerned with
organizations and includes terms such as *multi-agency* working and
inter-agency or *inter-organizational* working. Sometimes the word 'team' is
appended as in *multi-agency team.* Government policies have placed particular
emphasis on the importance of effective partnership *between agencies.* This
stance has real strengths since *organizational* and *inter-organizational* dimensions are too easily overlooked. Professionals are naturally concerned with
their relationships with service users and with one another, yet *organizations*
frame much of what takes place in those relationships.

  However, the establishment of inter-agency partnership policies will not
automatically lead to effective front-line partnerships between separate professions (Hudson 2002b). This is where the second sub-set of terms assists. It
is concerned with the professions or disciplines involved and with types of
collaboration variously described as *multi-professional* or *multi-disciplinary*
practice and *interprofessional* or *inter-disciplinary* practice. Again, the word
'team' may be added, as in *inter-disciplinary team.*

  A key difference within the two sub-sets is found in the prefixes 'multi'
and 'inter'. The term 'multi' tends to be used where agencies, professions or
team members work in parallel, maintaining distinctive organizational,
intellectual and professional boundaries. The prefix 'inter' is associated with
greater interaction, integration and adaptation, the merging of ideas and creation of new practices. In actuality, forms of professional and agency
co-operation vary around these two types, multi and inter, and it helps to be
clear in any particular case which of them, or some hybrid form, applies.

  All of the terms in the two sub-sets above convey important dimensions,
yet each represents only part of the collaborative enterprise. Terms con-

cerned with profession and discipline tend to overlook the many unqualified staff of care services and to exclude, as we have seen, the agency dimension, while none directly encompasses collaboration with service users and carers (Nolan and Badger 2002). Some of these limitations can be overcome by thinking more broadly of 'collaborative practice', an idea that unifies many of the terms. There are also advantages in using models that connect the key terms and dimensions of collaborative practice. A model of collaboration is described in Chapter 2.

The national policy context of collaboration and partnership

During the late 1980s and the 1990s, after countless false starts and decades of legislative lip-service (Loxley 1997), questions of inter-agency and interprofessional working began to move up the national policy agenda. The Thatcher Conservative government of the 1980s, worrying about spiralling costs, service fragmentation and inefficient use of resources in community care, sought solutions with the radical reforms of the NHS and Community Care Act 1990 (DoH 1989; Griffiths 1988). This made local authorities responsible, in co-operation with medical, nursing and other interests, for assessing individual need, designing care arrangements and securing their delivery.

The Act introduced three central changes to community care: first, an assessment and care management system intended to be needs-led and to implement effective inter-agency co-ordination; second, demarcated purchaser and provider functions within and between local social service agencies and others; and, third, the goal of more effective joint planning (Lewis and Glennester 1996). The aim was to achieve what the Minister of Health Virginia Bottomley had called a seamless service for users (Bottomley 1991).

Each change depended in part on collaboration for its achievement. Hence, the White Paper *Caring for People* (DoH 1989) described an essential skill of care managers as the ability to 'manage the involvement, contribution, co-operation and partnership between the local authority and the other authorities and professions involved in providing services' (paragraph 3.2.7). Similar collaborative principles were expressed in other social legislation on disability, child protection and criminal justice in the period and were part of a widening belief in the importance of 'working together'.

The events of the preceding decade had supplied a powerful policy case for collaboration and partnership (Whittington 1983). The case, elaborated and repeatedly invoked since, includes the following factors:

- a history of inquiries where failures of inter-agency co-ordination and communication were publicly blamed for the death or harm of children or adults

- a desire to overcome fragmentation caused by recurrent reorganization and to manage the endemic change in the wider system

- the drive for effective, efficient and economic services, rooted in the intention of successive governments to provide care and control, contain or target public expenditure and secure value for money

- the movement for consumer rights and empowerment of service users and carers

- the influence of management theories that view services as part of a system which should be planned and managed corporately or as a 'whole system'

- attempts to produce models of social work practice that extend beyond the focus on direct work with individual clients to encompass systems thinking and social care planning

- growing recognition by practitioners themselves that providing care services necessarily involves working with other professionals and agencies.

The impact of the community care policies of the late 1980s and early 1990s in stimulating interprofessional perspectives was unprecedented and pivotal (Biggs and Weinstein 1991; DoH 1990a, 1990b, 1990c). Collaboration between agencies and their staff was put clearly on the political agenda. There are repeated references to inter-agency collaboration in Audit Commission reports addressing community care, probation and child care and the connections with housing and the voluntary sector (Audit Commission 1992a, 1992b, 1995). This collaboration must be developed and strengthened, the Commission said, at both the strategic and operational levels. Front-line operational staff like care managers would 'broker services' across the statutory and independent sectors. Staff resistance and service fragmentation must be overcome and, the Commission warned darkly, there may be severe consequences for those groups and services who do not co-operate.

These reports connected with guidance on community care, child care and mental health and were buttressed by evidence on the contribution of co-operation in delivering services, including services to black and other minority ethnic groups (Barnes, Bowl and Fisher 1990; Bowl and Barnes 1990; Home Office *et al.* 1991; Mental Health Act Commission 1991).

The period between the roll-out of the reforms of the early 1990s and the election of the New Labour government in 1997 saw an acceleration of research interest in collaboration within teams and between organizations. This included studies of community mental health teams (McGrath 1993; Onyett 1995; Øvreteit 1997), the care programme approach and care management (SSI 1995), service commissioning (Hancock and Villeneau 1997) and primary care (Nuffield 1997).

These studies revealed the many complexities and obstacles to collaboration built into the professional and organizational identities of the parties and in the structures within which they worked. Collaboration between professions and agencies could be accomplished but it would take time, skills, motivation and creativity as well as significant change at professional and organizational levels. It seemed that Virginia Bottomley's vision of a seamless service had greatly oversimplified the task and underestimated the level of change required to achieve it.

By the arrival of the New Labour government in 1997, ideas of service partnership, co-ordination and joint commissioning were no longer new, and growing numbers of advocates of interprofessional and inter-agency training and practice were entering the lists. The Prime Minister Tony Blair made it clear straightaway that collaboration was central to his government's plans to modernize care services: 'Barriers between GPs, social services and hospitals must be broken down,' he said (Blair 1997). The stance was reiterated more colourfully by members of his cabinet. The Home Secretary Jack Straw reportedly promised criminal justice agencies a 'rocket up the backside' and financial penalties for failure to collaborate (BBC 1997a), and Frank Dobson, the Secretary of State for Health, repeated his intention 'to break down the Berlin Wall between health and social services' (BBC 1997b).

This shift of vision from the Tories' seamless fabric of services to New Labour's barrier-free terrain left some care professionals, then and since, uncertain how the Labour project saw them: were they an unwillingly divided and estranged people whom New Labour would first liberate and then unite, or separate camps to be coerced from their outdated attachment to one side of a divided domain? Both are stereotypes and both are invoked in political debate. In the event, New Labour has sought to facilitate and to coerce (DoH 2000a, 2000b; Hudson 2002a).

The idea of partnership ran through New Labour's entire modernization agenda (Cabinet Office 1999). In policies that advocated 'whole system' development, the aim was to move from the Conservatives' internal market system towards one based more on partnership (DoH 1998e). This was a shift by New Labour but not a complete reversal of Tory objectives. Partnership should be adopted to improve services to users, certainly, but also to eliminate wasteful duplication and to ensure the best use of public funds (DoH 1998e). Furthermore, while the Prime Minister had a broad vision of the sectors that should be involved in partnerships, New Labour also shared the Tories' particular interest in the relationship of health and social care. This would resurface repeatedly.

Growing devolution under New Labour increased the prospect of variations in care policies and legislation across the UK, and some have proved significant, but there are core themes. Tony Blair's defining slogan for his first period in office was 'education, education, education'. For those toiling in care services it might have been: 'collaboration, collaboration, collaboration', as the following review will show.

The government's publication of *Better Services for Vulnerable People* in 1997 introduced the idea of *joint* investment plans (JIPs) and foreshadowed *multi-disciplinary* assessment of older people (DoH 1997a). In the same year the NHS White Paper (DoH 1997b) set out health improvement programmes (HimPs) as key vehicles for local joint work. It also signalled both a new strategic structure for primary care (the service provided through GP practices), beginning with primary care groups (PCGs) of GPs working with nursing, social services and lay representatives, and new cross-service, standard-setting 'national service frameworks' (NSFs).

In 1998, the *Modern Local Government* White Paper advocated local partnerships and, in a nod towards a more co-operative approach to the goal of cost-effective services, replaced compulsory competitive tendering (CCT) with best value (DETR 1998). In care services, government papers on mental health and older people registered the centrality of partnership and the latter paper specifically set out to test inter-agency strategies (DoH 1998a,

1998c). Action on drug abuse established multi-agency drug action teams (Home Office 1998) and the Crime and Disorder Act 1998 initiated multi-agency youth offending teams (YOTs).

In the same year the Quality Protects programme was launched to transform services to vulnerable children and their families (DoH 1998f, 1999b) and included strengthened multi-agency requirements of children's service plans and targets (DoH 1998d; DoH/DfEE 1996). In 1999, new guidance was issued on inter-agency co-operation and training in child protection (DoH/Home Office/DfEE 1999) and, a year later, further guidance on Quality Protects included a substantial chapter on inter-agency assessment (DoH/DfEE/Home Office 2000, Chapter 5).

Amid those multiplying developments, the government issued the first national priorities guidance for the modernization of health and social services (DoH 1998b). This promoted partnership via mechanisms introduced in other policies such as JIPs, HimPs and health action zones (HAZs) and allocated areas of lead and shared responsibility between the NHS and social services for developing particular programmes. At the end of that year, social services were given their own White Paper, *Modernising Social Services* (DoH 1998d). This major document promised accessible, user-centred services, gave notice of a national carers' strategy and announced partnership grants. It also promised to legislate for better joint working by acting on *Partnerships in Action* (DoH 1998e) to remove barriers to co-operation between social services and health in the use of funds.

The focus of *Modernising Social Services* on partnership was primarily strategic, identifying grants, service policies and legislation to make joint working easier. It resisted the temptation of major reorganization of service boundaries, seeking instead a new spirit of flexible partnership (DoH 1998d, paragraph 6.3). It was at pains to point out that these partnerships should extend across the range of statutory agencies such as housing, education, employment and the voluntary sector. Yet the importance of social services' collaboration with the NHS continued to occupy a special place in the government's thinking and became more acute with each successive skirmish over hospital waiting lists and claims that older patients were ready to leave hospital but lacked suitable local authority care arrangements (Health Committee 2002).

The subsequent 1999 Health Act established a statutory duty of partnership between NHS bodies and local authorities (Section 27). The chief vehicle of co-operation became the Act's Section 31 'flexibilities' promised in the social services White Paper. These optional powers allowed pooled budgets, delegation of commissioning responsibilities to a single 'lead' organization and integration of aspects of health and social care services within a single provider organization (DoH 2000b).

The NHS Plan (DoH 2000d) shifted the collaborative strategy up several gears. Its vision was to repair the 'fault line' laid down in the financial and structural separation between health and social services when the original services were established in 1948. These had inhibited both partnership and patient-centred services (paragraph 2.23). One set of solutions was to give a leading role in integrated services to primary care trusts (PCTs). All primary care groups (PCGs) in England would become PCTs by 2004 (paragraph 7.8). The optional Health Act flexibilities would become a requirement (paragraph 7.3) and a new relationship between health and social care would bring about a radical redesign of the whole care system. PCTs would commission social care services for older people and those with mental health problems and the delivery of social services in new settings; social care staff would work alongside GPs and other primary and community health staff, forming part of a single local care network, enhancing joint assessment and personal care plans.

This vision promised significant change and showed that the government's earlier resistance to the temptation to reorganize was weakening. If the vision did not quite match the level of seismic shift suggested by the 'fault-line' metaphor, the tremors from the government's announcement of care trusts registered them immediately. These new multi-purpose trusts can commission and deliver primary and community health care and social care, which will be delivered 'under delegated authority from local councils' (paragraph 7.10). Care trusts will 'usually' be established locally where there is joint agreement that this is the best model but, the NHS Plan warns, where there is a failure to establish effective joint partnerships, the government will take powers to impose them (paragraph 7.11).

Responses to the NHS Plan from social care ranged from broad welcome, through fears that a medical model would dominate, to heated protest at the wider subordination of social services to health (*Community Care* 2000; *Guardian* 2000). The government lowered the temperature a little when it set aside plans for powers to impose care trusts while leaving in place promised incentive payments to encourage and reward joint working (paragraph 7.7). The first four care trusts were established in April 2002 (DoH 2002a).

Alongside the NHS Plan, other 'modernization' processes continued. There were reforms under the Care Standards Act 2000, to improve training, practice and regulation in social work and social care (DoH 2000d) and further significant service developments, all with expectations of strategic or operational collaboration. These had appeared in the *National Service Framework (NSF) for Mental Health* (DoH 1999a) and were now reiterated in the *NSF for Older People* (DoH 2001) and in the promotion of inter-agency working in the family justice system (Lord Chancellor's Department 2002). Similarly, they had been expressed in the 'compact' on relations between government and the voluntary and community sector and were now developed in the Treasury's 'cross-cutting review of the role of the voluntary sector in public services' (NCVO 2002; Secretary of State for the Home Department 1998).

Expectations of collaboration also permeated the government's long-term spending reviews for the NHS and social services (HM Treasury 2002) and preoccupied the Health (Select) Committee (2002) which repeated a call for piloted integration of services. In the wake of the Victoria Climbié inquiry the government again courted reorganization to achieve better co-ordination, this time promising to pilot children's trusts to unify the work of local agencies (HM Treasury 2002, paragraph 28.5). Meanwhile, organizational change was spreading among local authorities. More than 20 per cent of social services departments in England had combined with other services while some social services departments had been replaced by separate structures for the care of adults and children, respectively (Revans 2002).

The resulting picture was of care service structures in flux, of widespread recognition that the needs of service users cut across the services of different agencies and of attempts by a growing number of agencies to respond by creating new forms of strategic partnership and new mixes of staff collaboration. The staff of the services faced many uncertainties but one thing was clear: the future would demand, more than ever, skills in collaboration with other professions and agencies.

Dimensions of collaboration and partnership in care services

The preceding discussion of care trusts and other structures can be summarized in the form of a continuum of service partnerships in social care and health as shown in Figure 1.1. This locates arrangements for delivering services by their degree of organizational integration. It runs from the *ad hoc*

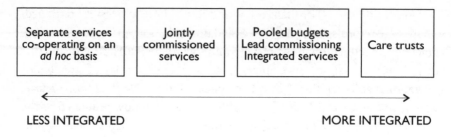

Figure 1.1 A continuum of service partnerships in social care and health

co-operation of separate services where there is little or no integration of policy, funding or personnel, through to the care trust model where all of these are integrated into one organization and service. A similar figure could be created to illustrate other areas – for example, services to children and families.

The organizations and systems that provide care services are typically large and complex. If services are to be joined up, it will take more than collaboration by staff at a single level – that is, partnerships must be developed at multiple levels between these organizations and be held together by multiple acts of collaboration.

Users and carers are plainly affected by the nature and quality of inter-agency partnerships but they are not alone. Social workers and other front-line professionals and managers are themselves affected by the strategic collaboration undertaken by senior managers, directors, chief executives, boards and elected members of partner organizations. 'Strategic' is used here to mean the level at which service and other corporate goals are clarified and resources are marshalled, organized and allocated to achieve them. Social workers are also participants in operational collaboration. 'Operational' is used to mean the delivery of services to users and carers. We are concerned in this book particularly with the latter but it is important to be aware of the strategic levels as well.

Since organizational structures vary, it may help to think of them on three levels, from strategic through intermediate to operational (Figure 1.2) and to consider the areas necessary for collaboration if partnership is to be achieved between agencies. To start at the upper level, there needs to be *strategic* joint planning and management of: service goals; acquisition and deployment of the major resources the services require, including the

Level	Areas of partnership and collaboration
Strategic	Planning and management of: • Service goals. • Acquisition/deployment of resources, including the workforce. • 'Whole system' review, learning and development.
Intermediate	• Joint and lead commissioning. • Management of pooled budgets. • Management of integrated provision. --- • Quality assurance, governance, regulation and standards, and participation of service users and carers. • Focused review, research and service development. • Planning and delivery of workforce learning and development. • Development of information and communications systems.
Operational	• Service delivery in multi inter-disciplinary settings and services. --- • Service delivery working across departmental and agency boundaries by staff and teams of non-integrated services/multi-agency networks. --- • In both scenarios, contribution to service review, organizational learning and development.

Figure 1.2 Organizational levels and areas of partnership and collaboration

'workforce'; and 'whole system' review, learning and development. At the *intermediate* level, two sets of joint activity are needed. One involves joint or lead commissioning of services and the management of pooled budgets and integrated services. The other involves joint work to assure quality and the participation of service users and carers, to review and develop services and staff, and to ensure effective information and communications systems.

At the *operational* level there are two broad scenarios. In the first, joint work takes place within multi-disciplinary service teams and settings, inter-agency groupings and projects, or integrated services. Staff members at this level are at the front line with service users and have a key joint contribution to make to organizational review and learning about the service (Pedlar and Aspinwall 1998).

Examples of multi-disciplinary, or in some cases the more integrated inter-disciplinary teams, include community mental health teams (CMHTs), community teams for learning disabilities (CTLDs), primary health care teams (PHCTs), rapid response teams, palliative care teams, community drugs teams, youth offending teams (YOTs) and other specialist teams for particular disabilities and clinical need (Miller, Freeman and Ross 2001). New forms are emerging as the provisions of the Health Act 1999, the NHS Plan (DoH 2000d) and national service frameworks take effect.

In the second scenario, the cross-agency boundaries are highlighted more than the professional ones, although again both are present. Here, collaboration takes place between separate (that is, non-integrated) teams, departments and agencies by front-line staff and managers, for instance in child protection. This is sometimes described as a multi-agency network. Increasingly, the separate teams and agencies in these networks, such as assessment and care management teams of local authorities, employ staff from different professions although they may not be recognized as multi-disciplinary teams. Again, the staff involved are at the front line with service users and have a key contribution to make to 'organizational learning' about the service.

The two scenarios described above suggest a picture of convergence and that, whether we are thinking of staff who work in inter-disciplinary teams or in multi-agency networks, most if not all will be involved in collaborative working in some way. Working with people from other disciplines and across agencies is not the rare exception or specialist case but a core activity of the competent social and care worker (Whittington 1999).

The two dimensions from Figures 1.1 and 1.2, respectively, of 'more and less integrated' and 'strategic and operational' can be brought together to give an illustrative matrix of collaborative structures, as shown in Figure 1.3. An example is included in each quadrant.

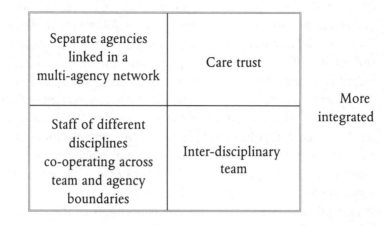

Figure 1.3 A matrix of collaborative structures

Critical reflections on collaboration and partnership

Earlier sections of this chapter defined collaboration and partnership and described the growing significance of collaboration between professions and agencies in care policies. Left there, the analysis may seem to confer on these ideas an aura of neutrality or perhaps of unquestioning approval. Yet if they are considered in the context of a wider set of reference points than are offered by the earlier definitions or by government policies, they become multi-dimensional, taking on some altogether different and perhaps unexpected features. This final section will reflect on these other dimensions, signalling possible directions for future critique and development.

To take up the earlier discussion, collaboration and partnership are *instruments of policy*, chosen to achieve particular social and political goals, such as supporting independence of older people by seeking an effective blend of social and health care and thereby reducing waiting lists. Underlying this and wider policies – say, on care trusts – is an implicit *theory about how to organize* in order to improve system effectiveness and efficiency – that is, a relationship is being assumed between a way of organizing services and a result, such as better client care or value for money.

The confident thrust of policy and its taken-for-granted theory also masks the double-edged nature of the policies – that is, the *outcomes of collaboration and partnership are not uniformly good or bad for service users and may be contradictory*. They may give clients access to services not previously available (Atkinson *et al.* 2002) yet submerge genuine professional differences that would offer alternative outcomes to a service user (Anderson 2000; Biggs 1993). They may improve prevention by early intervention (Atkinson *et al.* 2002) but result in the care-oriented practices of one agency being overridden by the control policies of the partners (Barton and Quinn 2001). They may also improve service access by bringing social care and health into closer partnership but, where health dominates, risk the loss or dilution of social models of care, health and disability.

Growing formal partnerships and opportunities for collaboration may be double-edged for professionals too. Social workers are reported as finding great satisfaction in multi-disciplinary working (SSI 2001) but others are cautious about the spread of multi-disciplinary training and practice and the prospect of flexible job roles. In the latter context, ideas of collaboration and partnership may be seen as *mechanisms of workforce control* in which professional boundaries and skills of distinct professions are dismantled, reducing the power of the occupations involved and their ability to resist restructuring according to market pressures (Webb 1992).

Collaboration and partnership also occupy a place in a wider domain of ideas which connects the local and the global and sees public services, companies and governments as operating in environments of continuous local, national and international change which require more adaptive leadership, flexible governance and fluid boundaries (Giddens and Hutton 2001; Warwick University 2002). Here, collaboration and partnership are aspects of a *strategic response to an increasingly global strategic analysis* and gain in persuasiveness from the weight and variety of their advocates. Alliance strategies are advocated as the key to success in global business, as the foundation of a national renaissance of public services through the Labour government's public private partnership schemes (PPP) and, as we have discussed, as the solution to multiple failings in the delivery of care services (Audit Commission 1998; Doz and Hamel 1998; Freidheim 1998). The more widespread the ideas, the more they may seem self-evidently correct, especially if they carry a business pedigree.

It appears so far, then, that while the rhetoric of collaboration and partnership may appeal to an unquestioning commonsense acceptance of these
ideas, they are anything but neutral. But what if their supposedly benign
appearance actively served to conceal potential harm to the supposed beneficiaries, the service users and carers? Critical language study (CLS)
(Fairclough 2001) alerts us to the potential of collaboration and partnership
to function as *ideology* by concealing and perpetuating unequal power relations, disadvantage and benefits to sectional interests. The ideas of
collaboration and partnership would be ideological in CLS terms if used to
obscure the chronic underfunding and inadequacies of social care services
described by the King's Fund (Henwood 2001), by implying that more
effective organization of partnerships alone will deliver good services and
that service failures caused by lack of funds are the result of
non-collaboration by the professions and agencies involved.

As the imperatives of collaboration and partnership have become ever
more firmly embedded in policy and visions of practice, the demand has
grown for *sets of professional competencies* that will help to realize them and for
learning and teaching to develop them (Barr 2002; Whittington 2003). In
social work education these competencies are expressed at the qualifying (or
pre-registration) level in requirements, benchmarks and occupational standards (DoH 2002c; QAA 2000; TOPSS 2002a, 2002b).

If the idea of collaboration and partnership as competencies is
unpacked, a further aspect is revealed, namely that they are a particular blend
of *professional values and practice techniques*. In this incarnation, they are found
in a wide spectrum of methods that emphasize self-determination, empowerment or liberation, such as therapeutic counselling, solutions-focused
techniques and some forms of group and community work. The common
thread is that participation is both desirable in its own right and fosters motivation in creating the necessary conditions for development. Yet it is here
that practitioners and their managers must also confront *the limits of collaboration*, where the voluntaristic values and techniques of care meet the
imperatives and authority of control.

This arises most starkly where vulnerable children, older people or other
adults are at risk of abuse or self-harm (DoH 1999b, 2000c). The identification, assessment and management of risk and direct action to protect must
progressively qualify and displace collaborative values and techniques. This
goes not only for the relationship of the social worker with the service user
or carers but with the partner agencies and professionals too. There is stark

evidence that agencies may not act to make good the misjudgements of other services (Newham ACPC 2002). A commitment to collaborative values and a desire not to disrupt co-operative relations could conceivably act as a further brake on necessary action. This reminds us that collaboration and partnership with other professions are, ultimately, means not ends: relationships must be service-user-centred not partner-centred.

Lastly, collaboration and partnership have become identified as *fields of research*. This is exemplified in many of the citations in the present collection, which cover areas typical of what has become known as evaluation research (Shaw 1999), namely studies of policies, implementation programmes and practice. In viewing the findings of that research, it is important to look out for the paradigm or world-view within which the researcher or evaluator is operating. Some ask 'what works' or comparative 'what works best' questions ('postpositivist' paradigm). Others ask about how ideas of collaboration are constructed and negotiated by those involved and how working together is accomplished ('constructionist'). A third group raises questions about collaboration and partnership as ideology, about the possible concealment of power relations and, perhaps, about the potential for the evaluation itself to contribute to emancipatory goals ('critical'). Governments, managers and care professionals tend to be interested particularly by the postpositivist type of enquiry, although it may leave many important questions unasked and faces many complex methodological problems in testing what leads to better outcomes for service users (Levin *et al.* 2002).

These reflections on collaboration and partnership support the case for a critical and analytical approach. This is needed if we are to reach beyond a passive acceptance of the versions we are offered and gain a wider understanding of our subject. The ethical responsibility of social workers and other care professionals is not only to 'do' as effectively as their skills will allow, but also to 'reflect' as rigorously as possible both on what they are doing and what is being offered as evidence to justify it. This is required especially when ideas, like collaboration and partnership, carry a huge weight in policy objectives and official rhetoric, yet remain in development, and when focused evaluation of core policies takes time to deliver (DoH 2002b; Hudson *et al.* 2002).

The question now arises, in the light of the preceding analysis, what stance should the social worker take on collaboration and partnership? Two related positions are proposed:

- first, recognition that they have become essential elements of practice and require competent, constructively critical application (which this book seeks to assist)

- second, recognition that they converge with user-centred social work values.

This convergence supplies part of the case for building them into one's practice, but there is more. We have already seen the powerful imperatives of government policy. Collaboration and partnership are also now the subject of growing empirical evidence. While comparative findings on their effectiveness in improving services is slow to accumulate, there are other kinds of account. Action research and case studies report the experience of staff and service users, identifying service benefits and how to achieve them (Audit Commission 2002). Interviews and case studies involving professionals and their managers also report gains to service users, to agencies and to professionals themselves from working together (Atkinson *et al.* 2002; Nolan and Badger 2002). In addition, there is good evidence that where services and their professional staff *fail* to work together, harmful effects can and do follow (Audit Commission 2000; Laming 2003; Newham ACPC 2002; Nuffield 1997).

These findings, and others reported in later chapters, give empirical support to the case for building collaboration and partnership into the practices, and organization, of social workers and other care workers. That case, which needs substantially more empirical evidence to inform it, is strengthened meanwhile by the convergence of values already described. Finally, the twin strands of empirical evidence and user-centred values come together in the clear and compelling message from service users heard earlier: professionals and their agencies, they say, should work with them, and with one another (Audit Commission 2002; Beresford 2002).

Key points

Collaboration and partnership:

- are closely related concepts – partnership is a state of relationship; collaboration is the active process, that is, of partnership in action

- apply to relationships with service users and carers, and with other professions and agencies

- became instruments of policy under the Conservatives, especially in community care in the early 1990s, and later took a central place in the New Labour government's 'modernization' of public services

- are advocated across sectors but have received particular attention in social care and health, and in child and adult protection

- may be found in strategic, intermediate and operational co-operation between agencies, which vary in the degree to which their services and professionals are integrated

- have multiple and sometimes contradictory dimensions that need to be recognized as part of a critical and reflective understanding

- must not override the professional's responsibility to act in cases involving risk of abuse or self-harm

- are closely congruent with user-centred social work values and are found, in some types of evidence, to bring service, and other, benefits

- are sought by service users in the relationship that professionals and agencies have with them and with one another

- have become essential to the practice and organization of social workers, and others in care services, and require competent, constructively critical application.

Acknowledgement

I am indebted to Margaret Whittington for advice and discussion on this chapter which benefitted from her first-hand professional knowledge of the policy and practice of collaboration.

References

Anderson, S. (2000) 'Disagreement Can Be a Good Thing.' *Community Care*, 1 June, 11.

Atkinson, M., Wilkin, A., Stott, A., Doherty, P. and Kinder, K. (2002) *Multi-Agency Working: A Detailed Study*. LGA Research Report 26. Slough, Berkshire: National Foundation for Educational Research.

Audit Commission (1992a) *Community Care: Managing the Cascade of Change*. London: HMSO.

Audit Commission (1992b) *Community Revolution: Personal Social Services and Community Care.* London: HMSO.

Audit Commission (1995) *Improving Value for Money in Local Government.* London: Audit Commission.

Audit Commission (1998) *A Fruitful Partnership: Effective Partnership Working.* London: Audit Commission.

Audit Commission (2000) *The Way to Go Home: Rehabilitation and Remedial Services for Older People.* Promoting Independence 4. London: Audit Commission.

Audit Commission (2002) *Integrated Services for Older People: Building a Whole System Approach.* London: Audit Commission.

Barnes, M., Bowl, R. and Fisher, M. (1990) *Sectioned: Social Services and the 1983 Mental Health Act.* London: Routledge.

Barr, H. (2002) *Interprofessional Education: Today, Yesterday and Tomorrow. A Review.* Health Sciences and Practice/LTSN. 12 July. http://www.health.ltsn.ac.uk/miniproject/HughBarrFinal.htm.

Barton, A. and Quinn, C. (2001) 'The Supremacy of Joined-Up Working: A Pandora's Box for Organizational Identity?' *Public Policy and Administration 16*, 2, 49–62.

BBC Radio 4 (1997a) *The World at One*, 15 October.

BBC Radio 4 (1997b) *Today* Programme, 29 December.

Beresford, P. (2002) 'Making User Involvement Real.' *Professional Social Work*, June, 16–17.

Biggs, S. (1993) 'User Participation and Inter-professional Collaboration in Community Care.' *Journal of Interprofessional Care 7*, 2, 151–159.

Biggs, S. and Weinstein, J. (1991) *Assessment, Care Management and Inspection in Community Care: Towards a Practice Curriculum.* London: CCETSW.

Blair, T. (1997) 'Speech to the Labour Party Conference 30th September.' *Guardian*, 1 October, 8.

Bottomley, V. (1991) *Oral Answers to Questions: NHS and Community Care Act 1990.* Hansard HC, 18 June, col. 130. Norwich: Stationery Office.

Bowl, R. and Barnes, M. (1990) *Approved Social Worker Assessments, Race and Racism.* Birmingham: Social Services Research Group.

Cabinet Office (1999) *Modernising Government.* Norwich: The Stationery Office.

Care Standards Act (2000) London: Stationery Office.

Community Care (2000) 'Letters.' 3–9 August, 26.

Crime and Disorder Act (1998) London: Stationery Office.

DETR (1998) *Modern Local Government.* London: Department of the Environment, Transport and the Regions.

DoH (1989) *Caring for People. Community Care in the Next Decade and Beyond.* Cm 849. London: HMSO.

DoH (1990a) *Assessment and Care Management: Draft Guidance.* London: Department of Health, Caring for People Implementation Documents.

DoH (1990b) *Policy Guidance: Community Care in the Next Decade and Beyond.* London: HMSO.

DoH (1990c) *Training for Community Care: A Strategy.* London: SSI, Department of Health.

DoH (1997a) *Better Services for Vulnerable People.* London: Department of Health.

DoH (1997b) *New NHS: Modern, Dependable.* Cm 3807. London: Stationery Office.

DoH (1998a) *Better Government for Older People.* London: Department of Health.

DoH (1998b) *Modernising Health and Social Services: National Priorities Guidance 1999/00–2001/2.* London: Stationery Office.

DoH (1998c) *Modernising Mental Health Services: Safe, Sound and Supportive.* London: Department of Health.

DoH (1998d) *Modernising Social Services: Promoting Independence, Improving Protection, Raising Standards.* Cm 4169. London: Stationery Office.

DoH (1998e) *Partnerships in Action: New Opportunities for Joint Working between Health and Social Services.* London: Department of Health.

DoH (1998f) 'Quality Protects: Transforming Children's Services.' LAC (98) 28. London: Department of Health.

DoH (1999a) *National Service Framework for Mental Health.* London: Department of Health.

DoH (1999b) 'The Quality Protects Programme: Transforming Children's Services.' LAC (99) 33. London: Department of Health.

DoH (2000a) *A Quality Strategy for Social Care.* London: Stationery Office.

DoH (2000b) *Guidance on the Health Act Section 31 Partnership Arrangements.* London: Department of Health.

DoH (2000c) *No Secrets: Guidance on Developing and Implementing Multi-agency Policies and Procedures to Protect Vulnerable Adults from Abuse.* London: Department of Health.

DoH (2000d) *The NHS Plan: A Plan for Investment. A Plan for Reform.* Cm 4818–1. London: Stationery Office.

DoH (2001) *National Service Framework for Older People.* London: Department of Health.

DoH (2002a) 'Care Trusts.' Department of Health, 20 December. http://www.doh.gov.uk/caretrusts/.

DoH (2002b) 'Health and Social Care: Effective Partnerships.' Policy Research Programme, Research Specification. London: Department of Health.

DoH (2002c) *Secretary of State's Requirements for Social Work Training.* London: Department of Health.

DoH/DfEE (1996) *Children's Service Planning Guidance.* London: Department of Health.

DoH/DfEE/Home Office (2000) *Framework for the Assessment of Children in Need and their Families.* London: Stationery Office.

DoH/Home Office/DfEE (1999) *Working Together to Safeguard Children.* London: The Stationery Office.

Doz, Y.L. and Hamel, G. (1998) *Alliance Advantage.* Boston, Mass: Harvard Business School Press.

Fairclough, N. (2001) *Language and Power,* 2nd edn. Harlow, Essex: Pearson Education.

Freidheim, C. (1998) *The Trillion Dollar Enterprise.* Reading, Mass: Perseus.

Giddens, A. and Hutton, W. (eds) (2001) *On the Edge: Living with Global Capitalism.* London: Vintage.

Griffiths, Sir Roy (1988) *Community Care: Agenda for Action, a Report to the Secretary of State for Social Services.* London: HMSO.

GSCC (2002) *Code of Practice for Social Care Workers.* London: General Social Care Council.

Guardian (2000) 'Letters.' 31 July.

Hancock, M. and Villeneau, L. (1997) *Effective Partnerships: Developing Key Indicators for Joint Working in Mental Health.* London: Sainsbury Centre for Mental Health.

Health Act (1999) London: Stationery Office.

Health Committee (2002) *Third Report: Delayed Discharges.* Press Notice No. 27 of Session 2001–02, 24 July.

Henwood, M. (2001) *Future Imperfect: Report of the King's Fund Care and Support Enquiry.* London: King's Fund.

HM Treasury (2002) *Opportunity and Security for All: Investing in an Enterprising, Fairer Britain.* New Public Spending Plans 2003–2006. London: HM Treasury.

Home Office (1998) *Tackling Drugs for a Better Britain.* London: Home Office.

Home Office, Department of Health, Department of Education and Science and Welsh Office (1991) *Working Together under the Children Act 1989.* London: HMSO.

Hudson, B. (2002a) 'Delayed Reactions.' *Health Service Journal,* 22 August, 18.

Hudson, B. (2002b) 'Interprofessionality in Health and Social Care.' *Journal of Interprofessional Care 16,* 1, 7–17.

Hudson, B., Hardy, B., Glendinning, C. and Young, R. (2002) *National Evaluation of Use of the Section 31 Partnership Flexibilities in the Health Act 1999. Final Project Report.* Manchester: National Primary Care Research and Development Centre and Nuffield Institute for Health.

Laming, Lord (2003) *The Victoria Climbié Inquiry.* Norwich: HMSO.

Levin, E., Davey, B., Illiffe, S. and Kharicha, K. (2002) 'Research Across the Social and Primary Health Care Interface: Methodological Issues and Problems.' *Research Policy and Planning 20,* 3, 3–29.

Lewis, J. and Glennester, H. (1996) *Implementing the New Community Care.* Buckingham: Open University Press.

Lord Chancellor's Department (2002) *Promoting Inter-agency Working in the Family Justice System: Consultation Paper.* London: Lord Chancellor's Department.

Loxley, A. (1997) *Collaboration in Health and Welfare: Working with Difference.* London: Jessica Kingsley Publishers.

Lupton, C. (2001) 'Interdisciplinary Practice.' In M. Davies (ed) *The Blackwell Encyclopaedia of Social Work.* Oxford: Blackwell.

McGrath, M. (1993) 'What happened to teamwork? Reflections on CMHTs.' *British Journal of Social Work 23,* 15–19.

Mental Health Act Commission (1991) *Fourth Biennial Report 1989–1991.* London: HMSO.

Miller, C., Freeman, M. and Ross, N. (2001) *Interprofessional Practice in Health and Social Care: Challenging the Shared Learning Agenda.* London: Arnold.

NCVO (2002) *The Report of the Treasury's Cross Cutting Review of the Role of the Voluntary Sector in Public Services.* London: NCVO.

Newham ACPC (2002) *Chapter 8 Review (The Death of Ainlee Labonte).* December. London: Newham Area Child Protection Committee.

NHS and Community Care Act (1990) London: Stationery Office.

Nolan, P. and Badger, F. (eds) (2002) *Promoting Collaboration in Primary Mental Health Care.* Cheltenham: Nelson Thornes.

Nuffield Institute for Health (1997) *Inter-agency Collaboration: Links between Primary Health Care and Social Services.* Research Update Issue 3. Leeds: Nuffield Institute for Health, Community Care Division.

Onyett, S. (1995) *Making Community Mental Health Teams Work.* London: Sainsbury Centre for Mental Health.

Øvreteit, J. (1997) 'Evaluating Interprofessional Working – A Case Example of a Community Mental Health Team.' In J. Øvreteit, P. Mathias and T. Thompson (eds) *Interprofessional Working for Health and Social Care.* Basingstoke: Macmillan.

Pedlar, M. and Aspinwall, K. (1998) *A Concise Guide to the Learning Organization.* London: Lemos and Crane.

QAA (2000) *Social Policy and Administration and Social Work, Subject Benchmark Statement.* Gloucester: Quality Assurance Agency for Higher Education.

Revans, L. (2002) 'Social Services take on Wider Role as Councils Combine Departments.' *Community Care,* 15–21 August, 6.

Secretary of State for the Home Department (1998) *Getting It Right Together: Compact on Relations between Government and the Voluntary and Community Sector in England.* Cm 4100. London: Home Office.

Shaw, I.F. (1999) *Qualitative Evaluation.* London: Sage.

SSI (1995) *Social Services Departments and the Care Programme Approach: An Inspection.* London: Social Services Inspectorate.

SSI (2001) *Modern Social Services: A Commitment to Deliver.* The 10th annual report of the Chief Inspector of Social Service 2000/2001. London: Social Services Inspectorate.

TOPSS (2002a) *Draft National Occupational Standards for Social Work.* Leeds: Training Organization for the Personal Social Services.

TOPSS (2002b) *National Occupational Standards for Social Work Values and Ethics Statements: Working Copy.* May. Leeds: Training Organization for the Personal Social Services.

Warwick University (2002) 'Beyond the boundaries.' Warwick conference on governance and public management. November.

Webb, D. (1992) 'Competencies, Contracts and Cadres: Common Themes in the Social Control of Nurse and Social Work Education.' *Journal of Interprofessional Care 6,* 3, 223–230.

Whittington, C. (1983) 'Social Work in the Welfare Network: Negotiating Daily Practice.' *British Journal of Social Work 13,* 265–286.

Whittington, C. (1998) 'Readiness for Organisational and Interprofessional Practice in Social Work: A Sociological Study of Key Contexts and Their

Relevance for Qualifying Education and Training for Social Workers.' Unpublished PhD Thesis. London: King's College.

Whittington, C. (1999) *In Support of Partnership of Social Care and Health – Supplementary Report for the National Training Strategy for Social Care.* Leeds: TOPSS England.

Whittington, C. (2003) 'Learning for Collaborative Practice: A Study to Inform Development of the Degree in Social Work.' A research project commissioned by the Department of Health.

Whittington, C. and Bell, L. (2001) 'Learning for Interprofessional and Inter-agency Practice in the New Social Work Curriculum: Evidence from an Earlier Research Study.' *Journal of Interprofessional Care 15*, 2, 153–169.

Chapter 2

A Model of Collaboration

Colin Whittington

The goal of collaborative practice is to enhance care services. To do this, it has to take place on a number of levels and between a range of different participants. This chapter develops a model of collaboration that describes and links key participants, the service users, carers and professionals, and the teams and organizations to which they relate.

The world of care practice is complex and becoming more so. There are new kinds of organization and there are changes in established relationships between care professionals, agencies and those who use and participate in care services (see Chapter 1). The model aims to lend order to that complexity. Its objective is to assist both the practice and analysis of collaboration by providing a framework that addresses separately, and in a connected way, the people and groups involved and their interactions.

The model is built in two stages. The first stage (illustrated in Figure 2.1) provides a baseline for identifying and reviewing key parties and systems implicated directly both in care services and in collaboration. The second stage (illustrated in Figure 2.2) builds on this baseline to describe the parties and systems as they actively engage in collaboration and partnership. As in Chapter 1, 'partnership' is used to refer to a state of relationship and 'collaboration' is partnership in action.

The first stage of the model consists of five spheres representing the main participants. Underlying the model are two sets of ideas, 'system' and 'identity', and a perspective known widely as 'the social construction of reality' (Berger and Luckman 1967). The idea of system enables us to think of each sphere as being real in the sense of having dynamics and characteristics that are experienced as independent of any of the individual people involved. The idea of identity refers to the way in which individuals define themselves personally and in relation to particular groups (Abrams and Hogg 1999). As well as humanizing the otherwise abstract notions of 'sphere', identity provides us with a link to the theoretical concept of socially constructed reality. In this perspective, identity (the sense of one's self) is constructed through participation in significant relationships and through the mediation of group membership. Furthermore, in a process that is, variously, conscious and unconscious, pragmatic and habitual, we socially construct our wider social world, and the systems that make it up, by our participation in its rules and relationships. The systems are sometimes also challenged, or even changed, through our collective critical reflections and the movements they may engender. The notion of 'spheres' is used in the model to encapsulate identity and system and the processes that bind them.

The model, stage 1: key spheres in care practice and collaboration

There are five interconnected spheres represented in the model:

- service users and carers
- personal
- professional
- team
- organizational.

If we adjust the order and embolden particular initials of **S**ervice **U**sers and Carers, **P**ersonal, **P**rofessional, **Or**ganizational and **T**eam, we get a mnemonic, SUPPORT. Each sphere and the reason for including it in the model are described below.

Figure 2.1 locates the participants within a flow model to convey that, in such complex systems, the start and finish of influence and response cannot be confidently determined (Pedler, Burgoyne and Boydell 1997). Hence, arrows are shown circulating and connecting the outer and all four inner spheres with one another. There is no single departure or end point. It is not a hierarchy, except that in terms of outcomes, the interests of service users and carers *should* be primary.

There are also wider contexts, of course, but those shown are intended to represent the personal and social dimensions that the practitioner will most

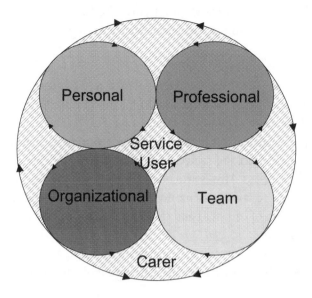

Figure 2.1 Key spheres in care practice and collaboration

directly encounter. Indeed, practitioners themselves may carry identities related to some or even all of the spheres. As well as having my own personal identity that connects with, but is not the same as, my professional identity, I have myself been concurrently a user of medical services, a carer for my elderly mother and part of a team and a wider organization.

It is not suggested that these identities are all equally in play simultaneously, or all of the time, but that they should be on the agenda whenever we are thinking about our own practice, the actions of others and collaboration and partnership with them.

The service-user and carer sphere

Service users and carers are grouped together in the model as a way of representing their centrality, although this does not imply that needs or interests among and between them are identical. In locating them at the centre, the model reflects that the primary purpose of care services from the practitioner's perspective is, or should be, the service to users and carers. Similar analyses may not in the past have located users and carers *inside* the boundary sphere (Figure 2.1) with direct connections to the others. They have been thought of as categories that are fundamentally different from and outside the professional and organizational systems. The position has changed with the widening commitment to empower and legitimate service-user involvement.

This has come with the growing legal and policy mandate for involvement, the increasing articulation of the voice of service users and carers, and the convergence in social work of traditional and radical segments around the values of respect and empowerment (Braye 2000). There has been a corresponding drive to establish new roles and conscious identities among service users and carers themselves and to shift how they are perceived by the staff of the services. This is articulated in national level developments by the primacy given to lay representation in the General Social Care Council's (GSCC) regulation of care staff and the centrality of service users and carers in the *Code of Practice for Social Care Workers* (GSCC 2002). Hence, Figure 2.1 shows service users and carers very clearly as part of the system, and seeks to place them at its heart. In this respect, the model is prescriptive as well as descriptive.

The personal sphere

The personal sphere is included in the model to recognize that people experience and represent themselves as having characteristics and a biography which is not denoted adequately by their professional self alone, or by their membership of a team or organization. This goes for the service user or carer too, since each person is plainly more than these generalized role labels can convey.

Encompassed within this 'personal sphere', and sometimes overlooked in textbook discussions of professional practice, are our own personal and social characteristics and experience: for example, our gender, 'race', religion and sexuality, our health, our commitments and responsibilities to partners, children, parents and others, our political preferences and our financial circumstances. These affect our perceptions and experience of our work and the energies we have available for it.

The personal sphere also covers characteristics such as our talents, interests and aspirations and our ways of responding to success, disappointment, stress and change. It also includes our preferred or typical styles in learning and decision-making. These different aspects will play, to a greater or lesser degree, into our working situation, relationships and interactions with others, including collaboration.

The professional sphere

The staff of care services come from many occupations. All have contributions to make to collaborative practice and the model of collaboration could be extended to encompass them. However, its formulation here pays particular attention to those staff whose occupational membership, and the significant identity that it typically represents, is reinforced by 'professional' structures; these include a formal training, a qualification and registration with a national professional or regulatory council such as the GSCC.

Let us look briefly at what happens to social workers, and other professionals, when they train, and the relationship to identity. They are selected, follow programmes of learning in academic and practice settings and are assessed. The process conveys and reinforces which behaviours are approved and disapproved (DoH 2002, paragraph K). Students are exposed to, learn, modify, practise, test, and accept or reject models of practice and associated knowledge, skills and values (Milner and O'Byrne 1998). They do this through interaction with, and influence by, course and agency staff, service users and fellow students (Dominelli 1997), against a backdrop of government and media pronouncements. In this 'socialization' process they form their professional identity. It is not that learners are simply programmed into sets of behaviours or all come out the same. Learning and the acquisition of identities is an interactive, partly structured and potentially inconsistent process in which the learner adopts some parts of what is available and may reject others (Brockbank and McGill 1998).

Nevertheless, over time, assimilation takes place into varying degrees of identification with what it means to be a social worker or, say, a nurse, doctor or psychologist. This does not end at the completion of training since agencies induct the newly trained, adding to or sometimes seeking to modify aspects of the socialization process. And the process is set to continue in social work, as with other professions, with post-qualifying study increasingly expected, the enforcement of codes of conduct and the formulation of qualifying conditions for re-registration with the GSCC or equivalent national body. The overall processes are broadly similar for most professions who come together in the provision of care services, although content and outcomes may differ. For example, the identities and models of practice they acquire (such as 'medical' and 'social' models, 'traditional', 'radical' and 'feminist' models) and their different philosophies of teamwork will shape how they define and participate in collaboration (Adams, Dominelli and Payne 1998; Miller, Freeman and Ross 2001).

The team sphere

The team or work group represents for many social workers, and some other professionals, the most tangible connection between their personal and professional self and the organization in which they work. For some, the team provides the human face of an otherwise large and impersonal organization. It may help them in locating a real sense of membership and with it an important identity.

The influence of the work group on the motivation of members and the meaning of their work has been a major strand of organizational research and development since the 1920s (Mayo 1949) and teams have long been recognized as significant in social work (Stevenson and Parsloe 1978). Indeed, so commonplace has the idea become that it is possible to take for granted, and overlook, the pervasiveness of team-related ideas in care services. We speak of team members and team managers, team meetings, teamwork, team building and team development (Belbin 1993; Walton 2002). And there are specialist and generic teams, multi-disciplinary teams, project teams and even 'virtual' teams (Dearling 2000).

Teams claim a place in the model of collaboration because they are so widespread in contemporary practice, and because social workers attach high levels of importance to teamworking skills (Whittington 1998). They are also key arenas for collaboration, which occurs both within particular teams and between them (Miller *et al.* 2001; Payne 2000).

The organizational sphere

The primary preoccupation of professionals, during their training and subsequent practice, is on skills in direct work with service users. Yet a year after qualifying, a large majority of surveyed social workers reported that knowledge of organizations and skills in working in them are also an indispensable part of performing their job (Whittington 1998).

Social work in the UK is carried out in voluntary and private sectors as well as the statutory sector, yet it remains a largely state-sponsored activity. This means that many social workers are employed in or otherwise connected to large administrative organizations. Old-style, allegedly mechanistic public bureaucracies have been widely rejected but they have not been replaced either by models delivering the independence congenial to professional practitioners or by liberal models achieving comprehensive staff participation. Two other approaches have held the ring: the business-led, market-inspired 'new managerialism' (Farnham and Horton 1996; Lawler and Hearn 1995) developed in the 1980s and, growing from it, the performance-management and efficiency models promoted for governments by the Audit Commission (Audit Commission 1989, 1995).

Under New Labour's modernization agenda, aspects of the earlier competitive organizational models of services have given way to more co-operative ones (see Chapter 1). Furthermore, a mission to shape services and organizations around the needs and wishes of service users has been more extensively articulated. This has come with a commitment to work environments that are more staff-friendly and that foster involvement and development by adopting the principles of the 'learning organization' (DoH 2000; SSI 2001).

Yet government-driven managerial methods and their effects often seem to contradict these liberalizing goals. The inspection regime of assessment frameworks and external reviews continues to employ many centralized criteria to define local performance and has come under challenge (King 2003), while the graded results are used in league tables to publicly reward or disgrace the organizations they measure. And reports on why public sector staff leave single out complaints of lack of autonomy, excessive paperwork, inadequate resources and too many targets that seem unrelated to what really matters (Audit Commission 2002b).

In the midst of this, levels of organizational change remain high, with new structures reported or promised across health and social care (George 2002; Hudson *et al.* 2002; Laming 2003). Many of them aim to improve collaboration and partnership. Whatever their precise impact on care services and staff, we can be confident that the significance of the organizational sphere will remain high.

The model, stage 2: collaboration – spheres of interaction

Using the first stage (Figure 2.1) as our baseline, the model can now be extended to the second stage (Figure 2.2). As this is done, the model shifts from a description of key parties implicated in practice to the collaborative processes between them. Accordingly, the terminology also shifts from:

- the personal to the *inter-personal*
- the professional to the *interprofessional*
- the team to the *inter-disciplinary team*

- the organizational to the *inter-organizational*

- and, in each case, to *collaboration with service users and carers.*

The model represents the main spheres of *interaction* that are involved or likely to be implicated in collaboration and partnership. It uses the prefix 'inter' to denote the aim of a more *inter*active and integrated level of collaboration than would be indicated by the use of the term 'multi' (see Chapter 1), although the latter will be used where it is the preferred term of a cited author.

As before, the flow of arrows indicates that in the 'real world' these spheres are experienced in a more fluid, diffuse and inter-connected way than their separate labels suggest. The following section will look at aspects of each of the spheres.

Figure 2.2 Collaboration – spheres of interaction

Collaborating with service users and carers

It was said earlier that grouping service users and carers together should not imply that their needs or interests are identical or are never in tension. However, aspects of the developing analysis of user involvement do apply to both. For example, there has been a shift from questions about *whether* users and carers should be involved to *how* to ensure that they are involved, both at the level of practice and at the level of strategic policy-making. (other chapters explore this in more detail.) Beresford (2002) highlights four issues: inclusion, diversity, impact and location (IDIL).

Inclusion can take place in a number of ways and they may be broadly distinguished on two dimensions (Carter and Beresford 2000). The first contrasts a consumerist philosophy, which tends to concentrate on consultation about the service and system, with a democratic philosophy which aims to focus more directly on people's lives and how they define the issues. The second concerns whether involvement is led by the organization or professional, or by the service user.

Beresford's second issue in his IDIL list is *diversity*. He reminds us that, like any group, service users reflect social divisions and hierarchies. Involvement should address these as in other areas of social work practice, ensuring that people participate on equal terms irrespective of their age, gender, race, disability, health status, sexuality, culture or religion. This requires underpinning policies by the agency and team covering the provision of access and support and stating the expected collaborative approach of the practitioner.

The third issue of *impact* refers to the expectation that involvement of service users as partners with agencies and in collaboration with their staff will make a positive difference to their lives.

The final issue of *location* indicates the priority areas in which service users themselves believe they can make the biggest difference. They are involvement in:

- professional practice, where they must have the opportunity to contribute, influence and negotiate
- training
- policy development, connecting with the team and organizational spheres of the model and with the wider policy framework
- developing quality standards and outcome measures and
- monitoring, evaluation and research. (Beresford 2002)

Beresford's five areas effectively set the wider agenda for collaboration and partnership with service users and carers and connect directly to all four of the spheres of activity that are set out below.

Inter-personal collaboration

The earlier discussion of the personal sphere noted that people bring a range of personal characteristics and styles to their work. This reminded us to 'humanize' our understanding of work encounters; that they are, for us and for others, *personal* encounters as well as professional and organizational ones. One aspect of those encounters deserves special attention here because it is recurrently cited as central to the success of collaboration: it is *trust* (Child and Faulkner 1998; Hardy, Hudson and Waddington 2000; Lane and Backmann 1998).

Child and Faulkner describe trust as based on three types of involvement: 'calculation', 'mutual understanding', and 'identification' or 'bonding' (1998). In the first type, the relationship is typically new or relatively undeveloped and regarded as trustworthy because it is calculated that the benefits to ourselves and our collaborator outweigh the costs of breaking trust. In the second, trust rests in the perception that the other person shares with you ways of thinking, that you hold common assumptions and that you are likely to act in mutually predictable ways. The third type is based on the perception among those involved that they share a personal or professional identity, with common values and norms of obligation.

Child and Faulkner's analysis reminds us that not only is the conduct of collaboration reliant on a measure of trust but that 'this comes down to trust *between the individuals involved*' [italics added] (1998, p.61). The point is every bit as true for collaboration with service users as it is with others. This discussion serves to underline that the personal and *inter*-personal spheres are fundamental to our understanding and practice of collaboration.

Interprofessional collaboration

This sphere represents, along with collaboration with service users and carers, core subject matter of this book. It is defined in Chapter 1 and other chapters cover a range of its dimensions. This section will therefore focus on just two aspects: first, particular sets of understanding that practitioners appear to bring into play when they engage in effective interprofessional collaboration; and, second, the paradoxical implications that face social workers as they learn about and engage in the collaborative process.

Effective *interprofessional* collaboration appears to require practitioners to learn (Whittington 2003), negotiate and apply the following:

- what is *common* to the professions involved
- the *distinctive contribution* of each profession
- what may be *complementary* between them
- what may be in *tension or conflict* between them

and

- *how to work together.*

Being able to work together encompasses many skills, and underpinning knowledge, and there is good evidence that social workers place great store in them (Whittington and Bell 2001). These skills include:

- use of formal and informal networks
- communication
- managing confidentiality
- forming co-operative working relationships
- negotiating working agreements with other professions
- the ability to challenge discrimination by other professions
- ensuring the social worker's professional point of view is heard
- conducting multi-disciplinary meetings
- conveying the agency's policies
- handling conflict
- adapting to change.

Similar sets of skills are embodied in the requirements for the degree in social work and underline the expectation in government policy that social workers will actively engage in learning for and development of collaborative practice (DoH 2002; Quality Assurance Agency for Higher Education 2000; Training Organization for the Personal Social Services 2002).

The use of the knowledge and skills described above in effective interprofessional working is said to promise real satisfaction for social workers (SSI 2001) and anecdotal experience supports this. They also appear to face social workers (and other care professionals) and their teachers with a number of paradoxical demands that have to be worked out and managed in the process of collaboration, namely:

- Develop and sustain your professional identity but stay flexible and 'unfinished'.

- Recognize where you are the same as other care professions and where you are different and have confidence in your distinctiveness but don't use it as a boundary or barrier – either to other professions or to collaboration with users and carers.

- Know how to distinguish between differences that are legitimate for you to defend, even in the face of conflict, and those where you are being professionally insular and must give way.

- At the same time, know, keep to and represent correctly the agency's policies and priorities, reconciling them, as you have always had to do, with your professional values and deciding your stance when the two conflict.

These injunctions represent real challenges for social workers and their teachers and managers in their task of defining, developing and sustaining professional, and interprofessional, identities of social workers. They indicate instability of roles amid the organizational change described earlier, in which agency and practice boundaries move about and the staff try to adapt. Theories of self-identity suggest that these developments may disrupt the processes in which identity is produced and reproduced (that is, socially constructed), by multiplication of competing and possibly conflicting versions (Giddens 1991; Kasperson 2000). The result may place real strain on social workers (and other similarly placed care professionals) and necessitate considerable support. As we shall see in the discussion below, getting the team philosophy right may play a crucial part in this.

Collaboration in inter-disciplinary teams

Members of inter-disciplinary teams have a growing literature to inform them, ranging from practice guides to reports of original research (Gorman 1998; Miller *et al.* 2001; Onyett 1995; Payne 2000). This section will pay particular attention to the findings of two pieces of case-study-based research.

Miller and colleagues (2001) gathered evidence from case studies of six health-related 'multi-professional teams' in neuro-rehabilitation, child development assessment, diabetes, general practice and community mental health. They found that individual members can make or break the capacity of the team to work effectively together (Miller *et al.* 2001, Chapter 4). Beliefs about teamwork shape what to do and how to do it and stem largely, they say, from two sources: professional socialization and previous experience of working in teams.

The study identifies three main philosophies of 'multi-professional' working which are analysed for their impact on types of teamworking. A *directive* philosophy was most frequently held by doctors and some non-specialist nurses. It assumed that the team would be led hierarchically. Control was vertical and communication was initiated from above. The (medical) director's aims determined the framework of tasks and staff were defined by their contributions to these tasks. Learning flowed from those above to those below.

The *elective* philosophy represented 'anti-teamwork' and was closer to a system of liaison. The parties preferred to work autonomously and thought of other professionals as points for case referral. Their working style was insular, emphasized distinctive roles, kept communication brief and informational, and valued learning only from those who held equal or higher status.

An *integrative* philosophy was expressed most often by therapists and social workers and among health visitors and some nurses. They sought to practise collaborative care and to be team players. This required a 'team understanding' of the patient and necessitated discussion, negotiation and an acceptance that communication may be complex. Core role distinctions were recognized but with flexibility at the boundaries. They accorded equal value to each contribution and saw learning from one another as important in developing the individual and the team. When translated into integrated teamworking, this kind of philosophy promised continuity, enhanced communication, referrals that were timely and appropriate and a holistic basis for decisions, with consequent benefit to patients.

Another report by Molyneux (2001) relates her experience of work in an interprofessional team assisting stroke patients with discharge and home-based rehabilitation. The team (two occupational therapists, two physiotherapists, a speech and language therapist and a social worker) had no opportunity for team building or discussion prior to taking referrals and, at first, worked from different sites. Team members reported working well together, without obvious conflict or problems; working relationships became closer over time while professional boundaries lessened; and all members contributed fully to the development of innovation.

She interviewed team members and searched the related literature, finding that three broad groups of factors were important to successful interprofessional team working. First, the team structure and attitudes consisted of equality of status and grades among members, shared values of flexibility, openness and adaptability, confidence in sharing roles, and a commitment to the group. Second, communication was given priority and fostered by a move to a common work-base and by allowing plenty of time for regular meetings and case discussions based around a single set of shared case notes. Third, there was scope and stimulus for innovation; in the absence both of a predetermined model for teamworking and of doctors who might expect to lead, members felt empowered to be creative.

It is tempting to offer Molyneux's description and the integrated philosophy identified by Miller and colleagues as yardsticks, especially as the integrated type appeared in particular to be associated with benefits to patients. However, Miller and her fellows are determined not to offer it as the only way to operate since some teams have neither the required time nor necessary conditions. Notably absent for many teams is the organizational stability that provided the conditions for developing the integrated team. Instead, she and her colleagues recommend some underpinning requirements for getting the right team approach. They are:

- a means for ongoing discussion and agreement about a system that is appropriate to the team concerned

- a shared understanding of *what* they want to achieve and *how*

- support for collaborative working by the organization

- capacity among the professionals to learn how to overcome problems of professional culture and for reflection on individual beliefs about working with others

- capacity among team members to understand and cope with group processes as they are affected by power, authority and professional culture.

To this may be added the characteristics of successful inter-disciplinary teams that Miller and colleagues found in other research (Miller *et al.* 2001, p.24). The members of these teams:

- have a central purpose, goal or model that transcends disciplinary boundaries

- understand one another's roles and recognize areas of overlap
- appreciate others' cognitive maps and their different interpretations of the same phenomena
- value different perspectives, accepting challenges and changes in authority and status
- are able to manage and use conflict for growth and integration.

The list mentions 'difference' and two specific aspects deserve mention. First, teams must be able to value and benefit from diversity among members, managing issues related, for example, to the race and sex of members (Walton 2002). At the same time, members have to be able to overcome protection of professional difference in the interest of building interprofessional connections and commitment to 'multi-disciplinary' teamwork (Gulliver, Peck and Towell 2002). The underlying challenge of inter-disciplinary teams is that members of different professions are asked to share or defer autonomy (Molyneux 2001, p.33) and to move partly outside of their respective cultures to engage in the development of an inter-disciplinary team culture (Miller *et al.* 2001, p.110). The combined message in the cited studies is that professional allegiances have to make room for team membership while the power held by particular individuals and groups has to be kept in check to enable team members to engage in genuinely collaborative practice.

Inter-organizational collaboration

As well as working with other *professions*, social workers work with other *organizations* (Whittington and Bell 2001). While there is clearly overlap between the two, everyday distinctions are nevertheless made between working with a nurse, doctor or lawyer on the one hand, and dealing with the benefits agency, housing agencies or the courts on the other. In this sphere of collaboration, people may well see the social worker in terms of his or her role of agency representative while any perception of professional identity is secondary.

Research among social workers after a year in practice found that they placed great importance on the knowledge and skills they required to work effectively with other agencies (Whittington and Bell 2001). They needed, for example, to know about the structure and services provided by those

agencies, how to access them and the right organizational level for communication.

In this sphere, we see the social worker working across boundaries,
involved in multi-agency networks and engaged in inter-organizational collaboration. Typically, the level of collaboration described has been
case-based: that is, related to the day-to-day work of practitioners in
response to a range of service-user needs and requirements. But increasingly
agencies, their social workers, other professional staff and managers are
engaged in more planned and formalized arrangements: that is, in joint projects, multi-agency teams and integrated services (see Chapter 1). It is here
that we see a shift to the terminology of 'partnership' as a state of relationship to be achieved, maintained and reviewed. Nevertheless, collaboration
remains an active element since it is the process that puts partnership into
action (see Chapter 1).

'Partnership' is used particularly in government policy and in the
research and development literature to describe inter-organizational relationships. The concept is used across services and sectors and there has been
particular interest in discovering the factors that lead to successful partnership (Geddes 1999; Hutchinson and Campbell 1998). The results of two
studies will be given. Finally, an approach to service development will be
described that takes partnership as its foundation, namely 'whole system'
working.

Drawing on the in-depth experience of partnership working in care services of staff at the Nuffield Institute for Health, Hardy and colleagues
researched and identified six partnership principles in a detailed guide for
inter-organizational projects. The principles contain many echoes of the preceding discussion and foreshadowed later findings on the importance of
local commitment, leadership and trust (Hudson *et al.* 2002). In outline, they
are (Hardy *et al.* 2000, p.9):

1. 'Recognize and accept the need for partnership', learning from
    local achievements, past successes and barriers encountered.

2. 'Develop clarity and realism of purpose', involving a clear vision
    and values and agreed service principles.

3. 'Ensure commitment and ownership', especially at senior levels
    among participating organizations, give leadership and recognize
    and reward people with networking skills.

4. 'Develop and maintain trust', by ensuring equal status for participants and fairness in sharing benefits or gains.

5. 'Create robust and clear partnership working arrangements', ensuring openness over the financial contributions brought by partners, clear accountabilities and a focus on outcomes.

6. 'Monitor, measure and learn', using agreed methods and success criteria, revising the partnership approach as findings suggest and celebrating successes.

In another project, Atkinson and colleagues studied 30 'multi-agency' initiatives involving education, health and social services and interviewed nearly 140 staff before undertaking case studies of six of the initiatives (Atkinson *et al.* 2002). Their findings identified five types of multi-agency activity differentiated by function and location.

The key perceived success factors were:

- commitment or willingness to be involved
- understanding of roles and responsibilities of the different professionals and agencies
- common aims and objectives
- effective communication and information sharing
- leadership or drive
- involving the relevant personnel
- access to and sharing of funding and resources.

Other key factors highlighted by interviewees included good working relationships, time, flexibility, trust, honesty, and review and development. It is clear that there is a good deal of overlap of the Nuffield principles, the factors identified by Atkinson and colleagues, and earlier discussion of teams and other spheres.

Finally, we turn to an Audit Commission study of an approach to inter-organizational development that 'always rests on a foundation of partnership', namely 'whole system' working (2002a, paragraph 19). This looks explicitly beyond particular teams and agencies to the wider systems. It is advocated as especially relevant to services for groups such as older people who may have multiple needs and who frequently experience difficulties at the interface between the different agencies. The approach pays as much attention to the space between services as to the structure of the individual services themselves.

As well as a vision of the interconnections of the wider system, the approach requires recognition of the complexity and unpredictability of the system and a correspondingly flexible, more loosely planned strategy in getting the system to work better. The aim is to allow those involved at strategic and at operational levels to operate within broad, simple rules that encourage creativity and enable change.

The study says that in practice this means that senior managers must engage directly with service users to enable them to shape the services. Managers must develop a strategic vision that is held in common with others and understand the parts of the service system and how they fit together.

The approach also means enabling front-line workers to identify the full range of service users' needs and to understand comprehensively what other help is available in the system. Service users must be provided with clear information about services and how to access them and given guidance and support in moving between them. These are plainly roles suited to social work practitioners, who can bring additional skills of emotional support and problem-solving to people who are making difficult decisions in their lives. The approach also requires effective collaboration between professional groups and each worker to accept responsibility for bringing in the right care or service, or for finding someone who can.

This is precisely the kind of system in which many professional social workers would be delighted to work, and may seek in vain. However, the 'good practice' case studies in the report claim progress among some agencies in using whole system ideas to develop integrated inter-agency networks.

The whole system approach is not a quick or cheap fix. We know from a number of studies that joining-up services can be complex and needs investment of finance, time and staff to make it work (Atkinson *et al.* 2002). Given this investment, however, the whole system approach described in the Audit Commission study promises a strategy for services that resonates closely with the model of collaboration developed in this chapter. *Service users and carers* are at its heart. Their needs and perspectives are central both to service design and process and must inform training and development. *Inter-personal* trust is required in establishing a common vision and in leaving sufficient flexibility in roles and structures to allow creative development. The professionals involved have a shared responsibility to know the range of services and to work *interprofessionally* to ensure that users are guided and supported in accessing them. *Inter-disciplinary teams* are given particular importance in delivering integrated care and the entire approach relies on *inter-organizational* partnership. This is realized by involvement of service users and by the collaboration of organizational leaders, middle managers and front-line staff across the shifting boundaries of professions and organizations, and in the spaces between.

Key points

- Care practice has been made more complex by new kinds of organization and by changes in established relationships between care professionals, agencies and those who use and participate in care services.

- A model of collaboration is developed here to lend order to that complexity, providing a framework that addresses key participants and their interactions.

- There is widening professional and political commitment to empower and legitimate involvement of service users and this is reflected in their place at the heart of the model.

- Key spheres are implicated in care practice and in collaboration: the *service users* and *carers*, the *personal*, the *professional*, the *team* and the *organizational*.

- Each sphere has a specifically collaborative form: the *inter-personal*, the *interprofessional*, the *inter-disciplinary team*, the *inter-organizational*, and collaboration of each sphere with *service users and carers*.

- Maximum gains of collaboration with *service users* come from practices of active inclusion, recognizing diversity, facilitating access, involving them comprehensively and ensuring that collaboration makes a positive difference to their lives.

- Provision of care services means *inter-personal* level encounters as well as professional and organizational ones, and *trust* between individuals is central to the success of collaboration in these encounters.

- Effective *interprofessional* collaboration appears to require practitioners to learn, negotiate and apply understanding of what is *common* to the professions involved; their *distinctive contributions*; what is *complementary* between them; what may be *in conflict*; and *how to work together.*

- There are rewards but also paradoxical demands in developing and enacting an *interprofessional*, as well as professional, identity.

- *Inter-disciplinary team* practice requires that professional allegiances make room for team membership and that the power of particular individuals and groups is kept in check.

- Factors leading to successful *inter-organizational* partnerships include clarity of purpose, realism, shared commitment, leadership, trust, clear financial and working arrangements and methods for monitoring and learning.

- Finally, 'whole systems' working offers an approach for translating the multi-level model of collaboration described here into a strategy for integrating the delivery of care services.

References

Abrams, D. and Hogg, M. (1999) *Social Identity and Social Cognition.* Oxford: Blackwell.

Adams, R., Dominelli, L. and Payne, M. (1998) *Social Work: Themes, Issues and Critical Debates.* Houndmills, Basingstoke: Macmillan.

Atkinson, M., Wilkin, A., Stott, A., Doherty, P. and Kinder, K. (2002) *Multi-agency Working: A Detailed Study.* LGA Research Report 26. Slough: National Foundation for Educational Research.

Audit Commission (1989) *Managing Services More Effectively – Performance Review.* London: Audit Commission.

Audit Commission (1995) *Calling the Tune: Performance Management in Local Government.* London: Audit Commission.

Audit Commission (2002a) *Integrated Services for Older People: Building a Whole System Approach in England.* London: Audit Commission.

Audit Commission (2002b) *Recruitment and Retention: A Public Service Workforce for the 21st Century.* London: Audit Commission.

Belbin, M. (1993) *Team Roles at Work.* Oxford: Butterworth Heinemann.

Beresford, P. (2002) 'Making User Involvement Real.' *Professional Social Work*, June, 16–17.

Berger, P. and Luckman, T. (1967) *The Social Construction of Reality: A Treatise on the Sociology of Knowledge*. New York: Doubleday.

Braye, S. (2000) 'Participation and Involvement in Social Care: An Overview.' In H. Kemshall and R. Littlechild (eds) *User Involvement and Participation in Social Care*. London: Jessica Kingsley Publishers.

Brockbank, A. and McGill, I. (1998) *Facilitating Reflective Learning in Higher Education*. Buckingham: SRHE and Open University Press.

Carter, T. and Beresford, P. (2000) *Age and Change: Models of Involvement of Older People*. York: Joseph Rowntree Foundation.

Child, J. and Faulkner, D. (1998) *Strategies of Co-operation*. Oxford: Oxford University Press.

Dearling, A. (2000) *Effective Use of Teambuilding in Social Welfare Organisations*. Lyme Regis: Russell House.

DoH (2000) *The NHS Plan: A Plan for Investment, A Plan for Reform*. Cm 4818-1. London: Stationery Office.

DoH (2002) *Secretary of State's Requirements for Social Work Training*. London: Department of Health.

Dominelli, L. (1997) *Sociology for Social Work*. Houndmills, Basingstoke: Macmillan.

Farnham, D. and Horton, S. (1996) *Managing the New Public Services*, 2nd edn. Houndmills, Basingstoke: Macmillan.

Geddes, M. (1999) *Achieving Best Value Through Partnership*. London: Department of the Environment, Transport and the Regions.

General Social Care Council (GSCC) (2002) *Code of Practice for Social Care Workers*. London: GSCC.

George, M. (2002) 'Under the Knife.' *Care and Health 24*, 13–26 November, 6–9.

Giddens, A. (1991) *Modernity and Self-Identity: Self and Society in the Late Modern Age*. Cambridge: Polity Press.

Gorman, P. (1998) *Managing Multi-disciplinary Teams in the NHS*. London: Kogan Page.

Gulliver, P., Peck, E. and Towell, D. (2002) 'Balancing Professional and Team Boundaries in Mental Health Services: Pursuing the Holy Grail in Somerset.' *Journal of Interprofessional Care 16*, 4, 359–370.

Hardy, B., Hudson, B. and Waddington, E. (2000) *What Makes a Good Partnership: A Partnership Assessment Tool.* Leeds: Nuffield Institute for Health and NHS Executive, Trent.

Hudson, B., Hardy, B., Glendinning, C. and Young, R. (2002) *National Evaluation of Use of the Section 31 Partnership Flexibilities in the Health Act 1999. Final Project Report.* Manchester: National Primary Care Research and Development Centre and Nuffield Institute for Health.

Hutchinson, J. and Campbell, M. (1998) *Working in Partnership: Lessons from the Literature.* Research Report No. 63. London: DfEE.

Kasperson, L.B. (2000) *Anthony Giddens: An Introduction to a Social Theorist.* Oxford: Blackwell.

King, C. (2003) 'Challenging Positions.' *Care and Health 28,* 29 January–11 February, 24–25.

Laming, Lord (2003) *The Victoria Climbié Inquiry.* Norwich: HMSO.

Lane, C. and Backmann, R.E. (1998) *Trust Within and Between Organizations.* Oxford: Oxford University Press.

Lawler, J. and Hearn, J. (1995) 'UK Public Sector Organizations: The Rise of Managerialism and the Impact of Change on Social Services Departments.' *International Journal of Public Sector Management 8,* 7–16.

Mayo, E. (1949) *The Social Problems of an Industrial Civilization.* London: Routledge and Kegan Paul.

Miller, C., Freeman, M. and Ross, N. (2001) *Interprofessional Practice in Health and Social Care.* London: Arnold.

Milner, J. and O'Byrne, P. (1998) *Assessment in Social Work.* Houndmills, Basingstoke: Macmillan.

Molyneux, J. (2001) 'Interprofessional Teamworking: What Makes Teams Work Well?' *Journal of Interprofessional Care 15,* 1, 29–35.

Onyett, S. (1995) *Making Community Mental Health Teams Work.* London: Sainsbury Centre for Mental Health.

Payne, M. (2000) *Teamwork in Multiprofessional Care.* Houndmills, Basingstoke: Macmillan.

Pedler, M.J., Burgoyne, J.D. and Boydell, T.H. (1997) *The Learning Company: A Strategy for Sustainable Development,* 2nd edn. Maidenhead: McGraw Hill.

Quality Assurance Agency for Higher Education (2000) *Social Policy and Administration and Social Work, Subject Benchmark Statement.* Gloucester: QAA.

SSI (2001) *Modern Social Services: A Commitment to Deliver.* The 10th annual report of the Chief Inspector of Social Service 2000/2001. London: Social Services Inspectorate.

Stevenson, O. and Parsloe, P. (1978) *Social Services Teams: The Practitioner's View.* London: HMSO.

Training Organization for the Personal Social Services (2002) *Draft National Occupational Standards for Social Work.* Leeds: TOPSS.

Walton, J. (2002) *Team Development Programme.* Lyme Regis: Russell House.

Whittington, C. (1998) 'Readiness for Organisational and Interprofessional Practice in Social Work: A Sociological Study of Key Contexts and Their Relevance for Qualifying Education and Training for Social Workers.' Unpublished PhD thesis. London: King's College.

Whittington, C. (2003) 'Learning for Collaborative Practice: A Study to Inform Development of the Degree in Social Work.' A research project commissioned by the Department of Health.

Whittington, C. and Bell, L. (2001) 'Learning for Interprofessional and Inter-agency Practice in the New Social Work Curriculum: Evidence from an Earlier Research Study.' *Journal of Interprofessional Care 15*, 2, 153–169.

Chapter 3

Who are the Participants in the Collaborative Process and What Makes Collaboration Succeed or Fail?

Tony Leiba and Jenny Weinstein

Introduction

This chapter is underpinned by a set of ideas and beliefs about collaborative working that have been developed by the authors – by background a nurse and a social worker – after a decade of working together on interprofessional education projects. Our overarching belief, formed over many years of meeting and talking with different interprofessional groups, is that where the expressed needs of the service users are central to the aims of the different professionals who work with them, effective ways of working together will be achieved.

Our second premise is that effective collaborative practice will benefit service users and carers. Evidence to prove this assertion is still not conclusive but there are growing numbers of studies, some of which are discussed later in the chapter and in other parts of the book, which support it. Nevertheless, it is important to acknowledge that some commentators (Biggs 1997; Pollitt 1995) warn that close collaboration with each other may distract professionals from meeting the needs of users.

From our perspective, therefore, service users are the most important participants in the collaborative process. The first section of this chapter sets out some good practice principles for working in partnership with service users and discusses the extent to which these are implemented. The second section deals with professional participants in the collaborative process. It reviews their inter-relationships, explores the reasons why they sometimes break down, and critically appraises some of the structures and processes that have been established to enhance interprofessional working.

Service users and carers as participants in the collaborative process

This chapter will consider service user involvement under three headings:

1. involvement of users and carers in decisions about the services that they receive

2. involvement of service users and carers in the strategic planning of new services

3. involvement of service users and carers in research (Kemshall and Littlechild 2000).

Involving users and carers in the services they receive

We share the view of Evers and colleagues that service users are the experts on their own needs and must therefore be fully involved with health and care professionals in decisions about their care (Evers, Cameron and Badger 1994). Meanings and beliefs about health, illness and social care need can vary considerably between cultures. Users' perceptions of need may be very different among white, black and other minority groups (Rehman and Walker 1995). It is therefore vital for professionals to listen to users rather than making assumptions about what they need. Service users' health and social care problems often have implications for other areas of their lives so that the relationships between health, social need, housing, employment and income are also crucial (Solancke 1996).

We also have to think carefully about whether closer collaboration between the services may lead to a loss of choice for users and carers (Pollitt 1995). It can be difficult for them if their view of a course of action differs from the view taken by individual health or social care professionals. The fear of being labelled troublemaker discourages many users and carers from raising issues of concern (Harding and Beresford 1996).

It may be doubly difficult for them to alter or challenge professional decisions that have been made by an interprofessional team. In addition, if the service user seeks action that conflicts with the conclusions of professional assessments, professional staff may be reluctant to comply (Glendinning 2002). Furthermore, if the service user is unhappy with the professional response to his or her wishes, the interprofessional dimension may result in uncertainty about how or to whom to complain. Is there a single complaints procedure or must the different complaints procedures of the collaborating agencies be used? Professionals must therefore always keep in mind the daunting nature of the health and welfare system from the users' perspective and the possibility that collaboration between professionals and agencies may, paradoxically, intensify this. These are additional reasons for working in partnership with service users and carers.

The following quotation from an annual report of the South London and Maudsley NHS Trust (2002) exemplifies an organization's good practice approach for working with users and carers:

> Over the past year the Trust has been developing a service user involvement and advocacy strategy. The backbone of this strategy is the idea that service users have involvement in their own care, accompanied by timely and sensitively given information, advice and education from professionals. This can build capacity within service users to regain self determination and autonomy. Such interventions can also assist service users to self manage their own mental health.

We believe that service users should be able to expect:

- to be treated as someone who is an expert about themselves and their own mental health

- that staff are aware of all the elements of distress and anxiety that can accompany entry or re-entry into services

- to be asked their opinion

- to have their views taken into account in the decisions made about them and their care

- to be fully informed and involved in the plan that is made for their care.

It is not only the 'what' but the 'how' that is important to service users. Feedback given to Beresford (1994) indicates that service users and carers seek courtesy and respect and to be treated as equals, as individuals and as people able to make their own decisions. Service users value health and social care workers who are well informed, reliable and able to explain clearly, to listen and to make practical help actually happen. A big problem is language that excludes service users and carers. This may occur when the language is technical, because of different cultural vocabularies or because the service users' first language is not English.

The involvement of carers is crucial because they play a key role in the well-being of the service user (see Chapter 6). One way of preventing carers from feeling marginalized and to make good use of the special understanding they have of the situation is to engage them fully in assessment and care planning. If service users agree, carers can be given access to the written records kept by professionals and can contribute to them. A system whereby carers were enabled to hold the records themselves was evaluated by Simpson (1997) who found a positive outcome for service users as well as a feeling among carers of being valued by health and social care providers.

Involving service users in the strategic development of services
Legislation and social policy referenced in Chapter 1 of this collection requires that service users and carers are involved in the development of new services. Drawing on the work of Harding and Oldman (1996), we understand user involvement in terms of developing relationships with professionals through the building of trust, respect and empowerment. This means that in consultations about the development of new services, professionals and service users should get to know one another, talk frankly and develop mutual understanding.

Beresford (1994) brought together a group of service users to prepare some good practice guidelines for user involvement which are adaptable to different contexts. The group recommended that users and carers should be involved on an equal basis from the start of any initiative. Plans for meetings and events must ensure that users and carers may genuinely participate. This means attending to accessible venues, transport, times of meetings, crèche facilities and other practical issues such as reimbursement or substitute carers. People need to be given space and opportunity to talk, at their own pace and in their own way; advocates or interpreters should be provided where necessary.

Professionals sometimes find the idea of working in partnership with service users threatening and users themselves can feel uncomfortable. These anxieties must be recognized and opportunities provided to talk them through, if they are not going to become barriers to change. Ascertaining users' views on a broader basis through surveys, focus groups or citizens' juries (Chambers 2000) may put less pressure on individuals although they require adequate time and resources to be effective.

Involving service users in research

Evidence-based practice is now at the heart of effective planning and delivery of health and social care (Macdonald 1997). Some researchers are beginning to involve service users as active participants rather than simply as the subjects of research. Within social work, this approach has been driven by a strong anti-oppressive agenda (Evans and Fisher 1999). For example, Fenge suggests that participatory research can be used to encourage older people, including older people from minority groups, to have a voice in defining their needs and experiences (2002).

The 'survivor movement' in mental health has developed a strong voice, and this may explain why user participation has gained a place on the mental health research agenda for some years (for example, Beresford and Wallcraft 1997). User involvement is necessary for responsive service development (Hickey and Kipping 1998) and service users have a right to contribute because they are best placed to advise, shape and develop services (Chamberlain and Rogers 1990). In the experience of Truman and Raine (2001), user participation in the research process led to changes in how research was commissioned and assessed and enabled user involvement to become more viable.

Participatory research provides a means of shifting the balance of knowledge production back in the direction of service users. It provides those who take part in it with a greater sense of ownership over the findings, and at the same time alerts the powerful research commissioning bodies such as the Department of Health to the necessity for service-user involvement from the outset.

How well are service users and carers being involved?

There is little detailed evidence to demonstrate the outcomes of service-user involvement. The few studies summarized below indicate that genuine user involvement is patchy and very much dependent on individual champions or local circumstances. Progress is being made and most agencies have stated policies and procedures for user involvement, although these vary in the comprehensiveness of their aims and in the extent of implementation in practice. In a study of user involvement, Bowls (1996) found that some social services departments had developed comprehensive user involvement strategies covering the availability of information, involvement in the planning, assessment and evaluation of services, and a commitment to power sharing rather than merely consultation. One department with a detailed document entitled 'Strategy for Users of Services and Carers', prepared by users and carers themselves, had found that involving users in staff selection was a particularly effective way of enabling people to be directly involved in decisions that affect their lives.

An extract from a social services user involvement policy is reproduced below.

Definition:

For the purposes of this policy service users include: 'individuals who use, or may use, social services'.

Policy aims:

- That service users' involvement becomes a central part of all activities that are concerned with community care and child care.

- That a range of types of involvement are encouraged relating to individuals participating in decisions which affect their own lives and collective involvement in planning, development and monitoring.

- That things are organised (structures) and done (processes) in ways that make user participation both possible and a positive experience.

- That the development of independent organisations of service users is actively encouraged and supported.

- That there are clear mechanisms for service user involvement activities to influence decisions making.

- That service user involvement has an identifiable impact on how community care and child care services are organised and delivered.

- That service users who are involved should wherever
  practicable receive feedback on what happens to their
  contribution and what effect it has had.

(Knowsley Council 2002)

The task of implementing policies of involvement seems to require major shifts that present difficulties to mainstream agencies, with their established culture, complexity and many preoccupations. A funded project that enabled service users and carers to be involved in all aspects of local authority services – planning, delivery and evaluation – made great strides in developing equal partnerships between service users and the professionals. However, the evaluation indicated problems in translating the learning from leading-edge projects into mainstream practice because genuine service-user involvement requires a significant input of time and resources (Office for Public Management 1993).

After a decade and a half of rhetoric about service-user and carer involvement, uncertainty remains as to whether involvement is working and is benefiting users and carers. Evidence on consultation and representation, such as that provided in the user and carer chapters in this book, suggests a continuing concern about quality of involvement, tokenism and lack of resources.

Most initiatives involving service users, carers, service providers and professionals have been carried out under the banners of common interests, partnership, collaboration and working together. These words provide only the starting point for projects which must also manage key realities such as resource limitations, the different agendas of the participants and the imbalances in power. Where service users and carers are always invited but never invite, the true nature of the collaboration must be questioned.

Health and social care professionals as participants in collaboration

If we listen carefully to service users and carers (see Chapters 5 and 6 in this collection) one of the things they tell us is that professionals should collaborate more effectively with each other. Absence of interprofessional collaboration causes breakdown in communication, delays in service delivery and general confusion and frustration for service users (Foote and Stanners 2002). Outlined below are some of the common conflicts and differences identified in the literature as causing barriers between different health and care professions.

In our view, the continuation of uni-professional education serves to reinforce these barriers and we welcome attempts to address them at an early stage through joint training and shared learning (Glen and Leiba 2002; Low and Weinstein 2000). We also welcome, with caution, some of the new structures and ways of working summarized later in the chapter that are aimed at facilitating more effective collaboration between professionals.

Social workers in the UK probably work most closely with the nursing profession across its different branches in health visiting and community nursing. A number of studies highlight the differing approaches of the two professions. Dalley (1991) found ideological and cultural differences between nurses and social workers in relation to the degree of risk that should be permitted to enable self-determination by a client or patient. Nurses saw themselves as having to 'protect' patients while social workers saw their role as enabling people to take the risks required to lead independent lives. District nurses and social workers undertaking assessments of older people were interviewed by Worth (2001). She found that although both groups claimed to undertake 'holistic' assessments, nurses were much more thorough about the health aspects of the person's needs while social workers concentrated on social and emotional issues. Differences in values and attitudes were also highlighted in research by Birchall and Hallett (1995) which found that although social workers and health visitors were the professions who worked most closely on child protection, they were highly likely to differ in their approaches to cases.

General practitioners (GPs) and social workers have traditionally been viewed as mutually antipathetic. Social workers are frustrated by the reluctance of GPs to engage in case conferences in child protection (Birchall with Hallett 1995; Lupton *et al.* 1999). Lupton's study found that most front-line professionals in child protection felt that GPs performed their role in assessing and reporting on child abuse less well than any other professional group. One possible explanation for this is that 'medical know-how' has become less important in the management of child protection, which has become more dominated by the legal process and by social models of assessment (Lupton, North and Khan 2001, p.129). For their part, GPs become frustrated by the bureaucracy and length of time taken to access social services whether it is for an assessment by an approved social worker or a package of care for an older person (Mathers and Gask 1995).

Significant work has gone into embedding anti-racist and anti-discriminatory practice (ADP) into social care services (although full implementation has been hard). These shifts in attitudes have been much slower in the health service (Baxter 1997; Kai 1999; Torkington 1991) and some social workers believe that to embrace the role of social care agencies within the NHS could lead back to a 'medical model' (*Guardian Society* 2001). We share the more optimistic view expressed by Statham (*Community Care* 2000), who saw the move toward closer collaboration as an 'opportunity for social work values to go mainstream'.

Overcoming the barriers to interprofessional collaboration
The barriers to interprofessional collaboration have been rehearsed many times in the literature, but it is useful to reiterate them here because, as illustrated in some of the examples provided later in the chapter, they are still impeding progress. Commonly found difficulties (Hudson 2002; West and Poulton 1997) include: status differentials, uni-professional education which socializes professionals into different language and different values; a lack of understanding about each other's roles; employment by different organizations with different cultures and in different locations; and fear of 'dilution' and associated professional protectionism. In most cases, professionals or their employing agencies insist on keeping separate records, in different formats, on clients they share with others and they 'will not entrust their work to others without retaining direct supervisory control' (Foote and Stanners 2002, p.306). Shared records will be encouraged through the introduction of a single assessment process (DoH 2002).

In addition to understanding the obstacles, it is important to be aware of the positive factors that enhance collaboration. Partnerships work best when each party to the arrangements has a clear sense of and confidence in their own unique identity and contribution (Weinstein 1998). Positive attitudes and communication within or between organizations are an essential prerequisite to effective collaboration with service users and with other agencies (Loxley 1997). Participants need to share the same goals: a survey jointly undertaken by the *Local Government Chronicle* and the *Health Service Journal* (2000) found that while well over 80 per cent of chief executives from NHS and local government welcomed the notion of closer partnership, over half on each side acknowledged that they had competing priorities. This could explain why many health and social services departments have joint plans that are not always implemented in practice.

Mechanisms for interprofessional collaboration

In the light of a better understanding of the barriers and of the dynamics of interprofessional collaboration, a range of initiatives has been developed to promote it.

Examples include:

- the establishment of care trusts, primary care groups and primary health care teams

- the care programme approach in mental health

- interprofessional child protection procedures and area child protection committees

- looked-after children procedures

- single assessments for older people

- key working (i.e. the identification of a key worker, who may be someone from a range of different professions, whose role is to co-ordinate the care of an individual and ensure communication between all the professions/agencies who are involved)

- multi-disciplinary teams – for example, youth justice, child and adolescent mental health teams (CAMHS), learning disabilities

- CARTs – community assessment and rehabilitation teams (nurses, therapists, social workers or care managers and medical support).

Collectively, these structures, procedures or methods of working bring a huge range of professionals together in different combinations, in different models of collaboration and in different specialties, including police officers, GPs, medical specialists, health visitors, school and community nurses, therapists, teachers, lawyers and magistrates. Social workers are likely to be participants in most of the systems that result – often as the professional with the key role for co-ordinating and implementing interprofessional plans or package of care. In Chapter 2 Whittington develops a multi-level model to assist our understanding of this complex environment and other chapters in this book will explore some of the specific mechanisms in more detail. In the next section we will focus on three of the examples above: multi-disciplinary teams, the care programme approach, and child protection. We wish to highlight some key components of collaboration in practice:

- focusing on the service user
- key working and involving users and carers in the interprofessional team
- blurring role boundaries and sharing case records
- open and clear communication between agencies
- understanding each other's roles
- not 'dumping' a multi-professional problem on one agency.

Multi-disciplinary teams

One of the positive outcomes of the development of well-functioning primary health care teams (PHCTs) is that a top-down GP-dominated approach has been replaced by a more collegial way of working. Health care is less disease-focused and more holistic; and the patient's experience of his/her care is listened to and taken into account (Billingham, Flynn and Weinstein 1999). Social workers have been welcomed as members of many PHCTs because health professionals recognize the valuable role that they play in co-ordinating the contribution of different professionals.

The importance of sharing knowledge and skills, and the consequences of not doing so, are well illustrated in a comparative study of multi-disciplinary teams undertaken by Miller and colleagues. They compare community mental health teams (CMHTs), where referral and allocation of clients was done via mono-professional systems, with a multi-disciplinary rehabilitation team where there were shared meetings and sharing of cases through one management and recording system. In the former, community psychiatric nurses (CPNs) tended to be appointed the key workers for more severely ill service users and it was felt by managers that social worker involvement would be 'duplication'. However, the CPNs did not feel comfortable dealing with some of the social issues and this led to 'professional defensiveness between social workers and CPNs' (Miller, Ross and Freeman 1999, p.104).

In the team where work was shared, professionals from different disciplines learnt from each other, thus increasing their own range of skills. As the team matured, all members could work with all service users as long as they were able to consult regularly with each other. Being able to exchange roles in this way is not professional dilution or 'watering down' as some fear but about increasing and enhancing professional knowledge and competence.

The care programme approach

The care programme approach (CPA) (DoH 1990) for mental health services arose because of serious concerns about lack of co-ordination for mentally ill people leaving hospitals. CPA requires the following: the assessment of the users' health and social care needs by a multi-disciplinary team; an agreed plan of care and treatment; the allocation of a key worker with responsibility for maintaining contact and monitoring the implementation of the plan; and regular reviews.

Care planning and review meetings must always involve users, carers and, when necessary, family, friends, care staff of residential homes, independent advocate if requested, and mental health professionals. Users' and carers' views on their involvement with the mental health services and admission to hospital are recorded separately from the professionals' views, clarifying disagreement, needs and aims. Action plans are formulated to meet the needs and a contract, signed by all parties, is negotiated and includes monitoring and review arrangements. Information has to be provided to service users and carers about rights and services including medication management and how to complain.

Procedures for child protection

Since the first area child protection committees were established in the 1980s, child protection procedures and legislation have placed the focus on the child and urged professionals to work together. This perspective set the tone for subsequent government guidelines and inter-agency policies and procedures (see Chapter 1). However, in 2002 the Victoria Climbié inquiry heard about yet another catalogue of breakdowns in inter-agency communication that led to the death of a young child. *Community Care* suggested that: 'Proof of a willingness to communicate and learn across agency boundaries is desperately needed if we are to be given the remotest chance of arguing against the creation of a new, national child protection agency' (*Community Care* 2002, p.5). In the event, the *Victoria Climbié Inquiry* report by Lord Laming (2003) advised against a separate Child Protection Agency on the basis that it would be unwise to separate child protection issues from those of support for children and families. Although he concluded that the report demonstrated poor practice within and between professions and agencies, Lord Laming found that the problems did not lie so much with legislation and procedures as with poor practice and lack of accountability. He recommended the replacement of area child protection committees with local management boards for children and families which would have influence over resources, policy and practice. The boards would be chaired by the chief executive of the local authority and comprise senior officials from all the key local agencies. The board would oversee the budget contribution of each service as well as ensuring effective inter-agency training and proper co-ordination and monitoring of services. Accountability at government level should be invested in a Children's Commissioner of ministerial rank who would be in charge of a new National Agency for Children and Families. This agency would regularly review relevant legislation and work through regional structures to ensure monitoring of services at local level.

Reviews of previous child abuse inquiry reports throw some light on where collaboration breaks down. Reder, Duncan and Grey (1993) found that lack of clarity between staff from different agencies about professional tasks played a key part in the breakdown in eight cases. In a review of 40 reports of serious incidents of child abuse undertaken by Bullock and Sinclair (2002), lack of inter-agency working and inadequate sharing of information were still identified as two out of the six most common practice shortcomings. Only in three of the 40 studies could the fault be laid at the door of one single individual or agency. The authors suggest that, within and between agencies, there is no common understanding of the family circumstances or evidence regarding a child at risk that would lead to an assessment of need or risk of significant harm. Furthermore, they question whether agencies have a common understanding of the response required to a given assessment. As mentioned above, previous research by Birchall and Hallett (1995) indicates that professionals will often have a different response to the same set of circumstances in relation to children and their families. One of the recommendations of Lord Laming's inquiry (Laming 2003, recommendation 13) is that the guidance, *Working Together to Safeguard Children* (DoH and DfEE 1999) and the *Framework for the Assessment of Children in Need* (DoH 2000), should be reproduced as one document to ensure a common language across agencies.

Bullock and Sinclair (2002) identified 34 different professionals who had been involved with one or more of 40 children who were seriously abused. In trying to understand why communication breaks down, they suggest that one of the difficulties may be a misunderstanding by some professionals about the rules on confidentiality. The Data Protection Act 1998 addresses this by specifically exempting the sharing of 'confidential' information between agencies for the purpose of protecting children and recommends the establishment of explicit protocols for this purpose. Lord Laming (2003) recommends more training for staff in all agencies about the implications of this legislation.

Lord Laming's (2003) position that ever more prescriptive procedures and protocols will not necessarily ensure effective working together to protect children is supported by Lupton and colleagues (Lupton *et al.* 2001) in their book on the role of the NHS in child protection. Their research indicates that different organizational structures, the different status of various professions, separate regulation and accountability of different professional groups and ideological dissonance in approaches to practice are all barriers to effective collaboration. It is interesting that in his recommendations about inter-agency child protection training, Laming (2003) stresses the importance of enabling professionals to have the confidence to challenge each other if they are really concerned about a child, regardless of respective status or role.

Doctors interviewed in a research study by Lupton *et al.* (1999) acknowledged that they keep their distance from child protection because they are wary of the strict procedures and protocols that they feel undermine their professional autonomy. Although many of the professionals who attend protection conferences are employed by the NHS or other agencies they perceive the process as being led by social services. This was graphically illustrated in the *Victoria Climbié Inquiry* report (Laming 2003) which described how a paediatrician examining Victoria had decided not to talk with the child on a one-to-one basis about her injuries for fear of jeopardizing a future joint investigation by police and social services. Lord Laming characterized the general attitude of health professionals as one that expected another agency, at some unspecified time in the future, to take on the responsibility for the problem. There is a lesson here for social workers who, while they do ultimately carry responsibility for children at risk, must find ways of engaging health, police and teaching colleagues as collaborators and not bystanders.

Evidence that collaboration benefits users

There is plenty of evidence that breakdowns of communication between professionals or between service users and professionals can harm users. It is more difficult to show that user involvement and multi-professional working benefits users and carers although some studies, examples of which are offered below, begin to provide some evidence.

Milewa *et al.* (2002) argue that user involvement has resulted in changes in the organization of some primary care groups. Improvements include: resources for the relocation of physiotherapy sessions from a community hospital to a general practice; procedures for medical outreach for homeless people; advice to teenagers on sexual health and contraceptives; reviews of local mental health strategies; and prescription patterns and procedures. While this demonstrates the potential advantages of user involvement, effective collaboration is highly dependent on how individual clinicians and managers in primary care groups choose to prioritize the views of local service users and carers.

Dowling and Hatfield (1999) evaluated multi-professional working between health and social care professionals and their collaboration with users and carers. They investigated whether multi-professional continuity of care reduces hospital re-admissions. The study reveals benefits for users and carers whereby the interventions were associated with lower re-admissions rates. They cite the importance of multi-professional planning and continuity of care, along with securing active collaboration with users and carers.

Carpenter and Sbaraini (1997) worked with a health trust and the local social services department to set up a care programme system and evaluated it in collaboration with service users and carers. They found that users with a care programme felt more involved in planning their own care and treatment, had more choice and were better informed about rights and services; most service users were positive about their relationships with their key worker, who was either a psychiatric nurse or social worker. The findings indicated that the professional staff were committed to the involvement of users but many thought the process very time-consuming and difficult to implement within existing resources.

An innovative project to develop an elderly persons integrated care system brought together health, social services, voluntary agencies and older people themselves. It was managed by a project board on which all the stakeholders, including the older people, were represented at senior management level and had decision-making powers (Foote and Stanners 2002). The aim was to maintain older people within the community and to prevent inappropriate admissions to health or social care institutions. A thorough evaluation was undertaken which incorporated care outcomes, service users' satisfaction and comparative costs. The savings made by keeping older people within their own homes were significant. More importantly, the analysis found a high rate of service-user satisfaction, easier and quicker access to services and more effective use of professional time by using single assessments and one set of records.

Summary and conclusion

Collaboration and working in partnership are essential roles for social workers, no matter which agency they work for or which client group they serve. Their primary partners in any collaboration are the service users who should be involved in the planning, delivery, evaluation and research into services they receive. In order to ensure service users have a straightforward pathway between the different services, professionals must share information, clarify their respective roles, and overcome barriers caused by differences in status, training, values, organizational culture and defensiveness. New structures and new ways of working have been developed to promote effective collaboration and social workers have a vital role to play in all these new models of collaboration to which they bring distinctive and essential skills.

Learning points for practitioners

Collaborating with service users

- Treat users as equal partners.
- Acknowledge and respect difference and diversity.
- Communicate clearly, paying careful attention to language and culture.
- Involve service users in assessment, care planning and reviews.
- Share records with users and carers, while taking care with necessary permissions.
- Pay users who are helping with strategy, planning, evaluation or research.
- Ensure venues for meetings are accessible and appropriate.

Collaborating with other professionals

- Utilize opportunities for joint training and shared learning.
- Develop trusting relationships by listening and understanding each other's roles.

- Respect differences but do not let differences of status get in the way of communication.

- Take pride in one's own distinctive contribution but do not be territorial.

- In multi-disciplinary teams, share roles and records and learn from each other to augment skills.

- Respect confidentiality but not if it risks the safety of the service user, the worker or the public.

- Develop clear inter-agency protocols but do not allow them to impede necessary informal communication and professional skills.

References

Baxter, C. (1997) *Race Equality in Health Care Education.* London: Baillière Tindall.

Beresford, P. (1994) *Changing the Culture: Involving Service Users in Social Work Education.* London: CCETSW.

Beresford, P. and Wallcraft, J. (1997) 'Psychiatric System Survivors and Emancipatory Research Issues, Overlaps and Differences.' In C. Barnes and G. Mercer (eds) *Doing Disability Research.* Leeds: Disability Press.

Biggs, S. (1997) 'User Voice, Interprofessionalism and Postmodernity.' *Journal of Interprofessional Care 11*, 195–203.

Billingham, K., Flynn, M. and Weinstein, J. (eds) (1999) *Making a World of Difference: Developing Primary Health Care.* London: Royal College of General Practitioners.

Birchall, E. with Hallett, C. (1995) *Working Together in Child Protection, Report of Phase Two: A Survey of the Experience and Perceptions of Six Key Professions.* London: HMSO.

Bowls, R. (1996) 'Involving Service Users in Mental Health Services: Social Services Departments and the National Health Service and Community Care Act 1990.' *Journal of Mental Health 5*, 3, 87–303.

Bullock, R. and Sinclair, R. (2002) *A Review of Serious Case Reviews.* London: Department of Health.

Carpenter, J. and Sbaraini, S. (1997) *Choice Information and Dignity: Involving Users and Carers in the Care Programme Approach in Mental Health.* Bristol: Policy Press.

Chamberlain, J. and Rogers, J.A. (1990) 'Planning a Community Based Mental Health System: Perspectives of Service Recipients.' *American Psychologist 45*, 11, 1241–1244.

Chambers, B. (2000) *Involving Patients and the Public: How to Do It Better.* Abingdon, UK: Radcliffe Medical Press.

Community Care (2000) 'We Will Survive.' *Community Care,* 31 August–6 September, 16–17.

Community Care (2002) Editorial Comment 'Met's Step is a Start.' *Community Care,* 11–17 July, 5.

Dalley, G. (1991) 'Beliefs and Behaviour, Professionals and the Policy Process.' *Journal of Aging Studies 5,* 2, 163–180.

Data Protection Act (1998) London: Stationery Office.

DoH (1990) *The Care Programme Approach for People with a Mental Illness Referred to the Specialist Psychiatric Services.* HC 23 LASSL. London: Department of Health.

DoH (2000) *Framework for the Assessment of Children in Need and their Families.* London: Department of Health.

DoH (2002) *The Single Assessment Process – Key Implications for Social Workers.* London: Department of Health.

DoH/DfEE (1999) *Working Together to Safeguard Children.* London: Department of Health and Department of Education and Employment.

Dowling, A. and Hatfield, B. (1999) 'The Care Programme Approach: Dimensions of Evaluation.' *British Journal of Social Work 29,* 841–860.

Evans, C. and Fisher, M. (1999) 'Collaborative Evaluation with Service Users.' In I. Shaw and J. Lishman (eds) *Evaluation and Social Work Practice.* London: Sage.

Evers, H., Cameron, C. and Badger, F. (1994) 'Interprofessional Work with Old and Disabled People.' In A. Leathard (ed) *Going Interprofessional: Working Together for Health and Welfare.* London: Routledge.

Fenge, A.L. (2002) 'Practising Partnership: Participative Inquiry with Older People.' *Social Work Education 21,* 2, 172–181.

Foote, C. and Stanners, C. (2002) *Integrating Care for Older People. New Care for Old – A Systems Approach.* London: Jessica Kingsley Publishers.

Glen, S. and Leiba, T. (2002) *Multi-professional Learning for Nurses: Breaking the Boundaries.* Basingstoke: Palgrave.

Glendinning, C. (2002) 'Partnership between Health and Social Services: Developing a Framework for Evaluation.' *The Policy Press 30,* 1, 115–127.

Guardian Society (2001) 'Forward Together.' *Guardian,* 28 February (consulted 7 November 2002). www.societyguardian.co.uk/healthandsocialcarebill/story/0,7991.443818,00.html.

Harding, T. and Beresford, P. (1996) *The Standards We Expect*. London: National Institute for Social Work.

Harding, T. and Oldman, H. (1996) *Involving Service Users and Carers in Local Services*. London: National Institute of Social Work.

Hickey, G. and Kipping, C. (1998) 'Exploring the Concept of User Involvement in Mental Health through a Participation Continuum.' *Journal of Clinical Nursing 7*, 83–88.

Hudson, B (2002) 'Interprofessionality in Health and Social Care.' *Journal of Interprofessional Care 16*, 1, 7–17.

Kai, J. (ed) (1999) *Valuing Diversity: A Resource for Effective Health Care of Ethnically Diverse Communities*. London: Royal College of General Practitioners.

Kemshall, H. and Littlechild, R. (2000) *User Involvement and Participation in Social Care*. London: Jessica Kingsley Publishers.

Knowsley Council (2002) Extract from Service User Policy for Older People implemented in 1996 (consulted 7 November 2002). www.knowsley.gov.uk/social/older_people/suserpolicy.html.

Laming, Lord (2003) *The Victoria Climbié Inquiry*. Norwich: HMSO.

Local Government Chronicle and Health Service Journal (2000) '"So How Are You Two Getting Along?" Patient:Citizen Partnership Working between Local Government and the NHS.' *Local Government Chronicle and Health Service Journal*, 8–10.

Low, H. and Weinstein, J. (2000) 'Interprofessional Education.' In R. Pierce and J. Weinstein (eds) *Innovative Education and Training for Care Professionals*. London: Jessica Kingsley Publishers.

Loxley, A. (1997) *Collaboration in Health and Welfare*. London: Jessica Kingsley Publishers.

Lupton, C., Khan, P., North, N. and Lacey, D. (1999) *The Role of Health Professionals in the Child Protection Process*. Portsmouth: Social Services Research and Information Unit, Report No. 41, University of Portsmouth.

Lupton, C., North, N. and Khan, P. (2001) *Working Together or Pulling Apart? The National Health Service and Child Protection Networks*. Bristol: The Policy Press.

Macdonald, G. (1997) 'Social Work Research: The State We're In.' *Journal of Interprofessional Care 11*, 1, 55–65.

Mathers, N.J. and Gask, L. (1995) 'Surviving the "heartsink" experience.' *Journal of Family Practice 12*, 176–183.

Milewa, T., Harrison, S., Ahmad, W. and Tovey, P. (2002) 'Citizens' Participation in Primary Healthcare Planning: Innovative Citizenship Practice in Empirical Perspective.' *Critical Public Health 12*, 1, 39–65.

Miller, C., Ross, N. and Freeman, M. (1999) *Researching Professional Education. Shared Learning and Clinical Teamwork: New Directions in Education for Multiprofessional Practice.* London: English National Board for Nursing, Health Visiting and Midwifery.

Office for Public Management (1993) *User and Carer Involvement in Community Care: From Margin to Mainstream.* Briefing Paper. London: Office for Public Management.

Pollitt, C. (1995) 'Justification by Works or Faith? Evaluating the New Public Management.' *Evaluation 1,* 2, 133–154.

Reder, P., Duncan, S. and Grey, M. (1993) *Beyond Blame, Child Abuse Tragedies Revisited.* London: Routledge.

Rehman, H. and Walker, E. (eds) (1995) 'Researching Black and Ethnic Minority Groups.' *Health Education Journal 54,* 4, 489–500.

Simpson, R.G. (1997) 'Carers as Equal Partners in Care Planning.' *Journal of Psychiatric and Mental Health Nursing 4,* 345–354.

Solancke, A. (1996) 'Focus on Black Women's Health.' *Health Line,* February, 5.

South London and Maudsley NHS Trust (2002) Extract from 2001 Annual Report (consulted 7 November 2002). www.slam.nhs.uk/news/anreport2001/14asp.

Torkington, N.P.K. (1991) *Black Health: A Political Issue.* Liverpool: Liverpool Institute of Higher Education.

Truman, C. and Raine, P. (2001) 'Involving Users in Evaluation: The Social Relations of User Participation in Health Research.' *Critical Public Health 11,* 3, 216–229.

Weinstein, J. (1998) 'The Professions and their Interrelationships.' In T. Thompson and P. Mathias (eds) *Standards and Learning Disability,* 2nd edn. London: Baillière Tindall.

West, M.A. and Poulton, B.C. (1997) 'A Failure of Function: Teamwork in Primary Health Care.' *Journal of Interprofessional Care 11,* 2, 203–216.

Worth, A. (2001) 'Assessment of the Needs of Older People by District Nurses and Social Workers: A Changing Culture?' *Journal of Interprofessional Care 15,* 3, 257–266.

Chapter 4

Shared Values in Interprofessional Collaboration

Jean Davis and Dave Sims

Introduction

The term *social work values* has special resonance for members of a profession which has been under continual public scrutiny – notably through a long series of inquiries into failures to protect children and other vulnerable people – for half a century. Aspects of the values of social work, particularly those which derive from a consideration of the structural context in which people live their lives and inform the notion of *anti-discriminatory practice*, have been subjected to what has been called 'the political correctness backlash' (Aymer 2000, p.123), alleging that blackness is unconditionally valued over whiteness, female over male, and so on. 'Political correctness' when used in this way is a pejorative label, implying a commitment to extremist, anti-establishment politics.

The idea that social workers should promote individual well-being and autonomy in a context of social justice remains, however, at the heart of the profession. But how far can these values be said to be exclusive to social work? Could it be that a key barrier to collaborative working is the belief that different professions 'own' distinctive sets of values and ethics, whereas there can in reality be only one set that should be shared by all?

In considering how to chart a way through the complex issues of values and ethics in relation to social work and interprofessional collaboration, the authors were greatly helped by a group of health and social care practitioners who had all qualified on South Bank University's joint degree course which combined social work and learning disability nursing (Davis, Rendell and Sims 1999).

This programme emphasizes integration of learning for the two disciplines with the objective of developing practitioners who are:

- able to develop a model of joint practice between nursing and social work which transcends the traditional professional demarcations between health and social workers

- fully aware of the integrity of two professional disciplines and their respective roles and responsibilities

- committed to developing an integrated approach to their practice recognizing the totality of people's needs.

An integrated competency framework (agreed at validation by the relevant social work and nursing professional bodies) is used to assess the quality of the student's practice whether he or she is in either a nursing or a social work placement. The framework rests on what is effectively a shared values base which, although derived from social work, was subscribed to by the professional nursing bodies involved in setting up the course.

We were confident that graduates from this programme would have important perspectives on values in interprofessional collaboration. The group agreed to assist us by attending a one-day meeting. We recorded and transcribed the discussion, which was structured through a series of broad questions delimiting the ground we wished to cover. We asked and obtained the permission of the group to quote anonymously from their contributions to the discussion, and some of these are included in the chapter in the form of quotations. All the participants were also offered the opportunity to read and comment on the draft of the chapter.

We should add that the authors were both involved with the delivery of this joint training programme over several years and had substantial experience of the assessment of practice, including the practice values formulated as part of the competency framework for the course.

In this chapter our first aim is to consider some of the terminology which can in itself lead to misunderstandings between professionals and to interprofessional stereotyping. It is clear from only a brief study of the literature that professionals use different words to describe similar concepts and principles that underpin their practice. We will then go on to consider where values may differ between two professional groups – social work and nursing – in order to explore the interprofessional awareness and understanding that must emerge if collaboration is to be effective. As a part of this we will also consider the shared ground between these groups that needs to be expanded to enhance that understanding. In our experience of practitioners who have been trained on an interprofessional course it would be possible to arrive at a shared values base across the professions and this would promote collaboration to the optimum degree. Through a case study of an actual ethical dilemma from practice, we will seek to explore the benefit to the assessment process of subjecting professional decision-making to holistic critical appraisal. In conclusion we will argue that effective collaboration is an essential component of good practice and must be underpinned by a set of shared values.

Terminology and definitions

If we are aiming to identify what is sound, ethical, collaborative social work practice, let us start by offering some definitions as a working basis for differentiating between values and ethics:

- **Values** are about *beliefs* and they contain *moral judgements*: 'Value-beliefs are beliefs about *morally* good (or bad) ways of living with and treating others in the world' (Clark 2000, p.29). 'A value-system is an enduring organisation of beliefs concerning preferable modes of conduct or end-states of existence along a continuum of relative importance' (Rokeach 1973, p.5 quoted in Clark 2000, p.27).

- **Ethics** are about *behaviour* and are derived from values. Ethical practice is practice that embodies core values. Professional ethics may be defined as '*a specific prescriptive scheme of obligations*' (Clark 2000, p.25) which is applied to professional practice.

The essential relationship between values and ethics may be illustrated with reference to the five basic values contained in BASW's *Code of Ethics for Social Work* (British Association of Social Workers 2002). These are: human dignity and worth; social justice; service to humanity; integrity; and competence. Each basic value is held to yield principles which should be exemplified in practice. In terms of our definition, professional ethics would embody these principles and they would be expressed in rules for good practice.

One of the most significant developments in recent years in defining professional values for both health and social care has undoubtedly arisen from the involvement of service users and carers in the assessment of need and the provision and evaluation of services. This is epitomized in the 2002 *Code of Ethics for Social Work* published by BASW and referred to above. Sections 5 and 6 of the code set out in detail the rights of and responsibilities to service users, including self-determination and autonomy, informed consent, privacy, confidentiality and care of records.

To consider further the difference between values and ethics, let us take as an example with a direct bearing on social work practice the value of *social justice*, from which a number of principles are derived. These principles would include such elements as the fair and equitable distribution of resources, fair access to public services and benefits, equal treatment, and protection under the law.

Ethical practice would seek to express the basic value of social justice and apply the principles derived from it to areas of social work practice, such as advocacy on behalf of people with learning difficulties. We do not suggest that this proposed distinction between values and ethics is the only one that can be drawn, but we have found it useful as a working tool, provided always that it is used consistently. It has to be said that the distinction is sometimes blurred by the rather free and inexact use of terminology; for example the 'values of social work' put forward by CCETSW (1995, p.18) really describe behaviour rather than beliefs.

Social work values – how particular to social work?

The frequently used term *social work values* could be problematic for collaboration between professionals if it implies that social workers have exclusive ownership of principles which should be shared across the professions.

We have stated above that social work values are of primary importance to practitioners in defining the relationship between the individual and their social context. In establishing the values of social work for social work education programmes to implement, CCETSW (1995) expected that qualifying social workers would be able to make an understanding of this relationship a central part of their practice. This connection between the person and his/her social context has been underpinned theoretically through the incorporation of anti-discriminatory practice into social work teaching in a way that has not generally been the case in pre-qualifying nursing programmes. As one of the students in our reference group commented:

> I think there is great difference between nursing and social work val-
> ues…the nursing programme had no lecture on anti-discriminatory
> practice. This was amazing as social workers thought this was a very
> important value. If you consider that one of the groundings of social
> work is anti-discriminatory practice, then there is a massive difference.

It is significant to note that in 2000, nurse education was changed to incor-
porate anti-discriminatory practice into its new competency framework
(UKCC 1999). This should have the effect of bringing nursing and social
work training closer together. But, as the above quotation suggests, it is certainly possible that the different emphasis in training set up real potential for
misunderstanding between professionals in the past.

The convergence of the social work and nursing curricula around
anti-discriminatory practice clearly provides an opportunity for shared values to underpin collaborative practice between the two professions. If this
opportunity is to be grasped, there is a need for the development of literature
and training materials around the application of anti-discriminatory practice
to nursing. On the shelves of libraries and bookshops this literature is still
predominantly found under social work titles although texts are beginning
to emerge that look at equalities issues across the health and social care spectrum (Thompson 1998, 2001).

It is encouraging that a shared commitment to anti-discriminatory practice is emerging. However, at the heart of anti-discriminatory practice is an
awareness of structural oppression, which has been an important development in social work education and its values base (Banks 1995). How
different, then, are social work and nursing in respect of structural issues? A
historical comparison of the codes of conduct/ethics of nurses and social
workers may help to shed light on this question. Wilmott (1995) compared
the 1992 UKCC statutory *Code of Professional Conduct* for nurses with the
1986 *Code of Ethics* of the British Association of Social Workers
(non-statutory). He found that the codes differed in three important respects,
which gave nurses a different orientation to their practice from social workers.

First, while the UKCC required the nurse to serve the interests of society
and justify public trust and confidence, the BASW code gave a more active
dimension to the social worker's role in terms of social policy planning and
action. The relationship between the state and society appeared to be a legitimate area for action by social workers but not by nurses.

The second area of difference between the roles of nurses and social workers related to response to risk, hardship or suffering. Nurses were required to report to an appropriate person (or authority) circumstances which could jeopardize standards of practice and care, while social workers were expected to bring to the attention of those in power (or in government) public situations where government, society or agency created or contributed to hardship and suffering. This lent an overtly political and challenging dimension to the social worker's responsibility.

There is a third point of difference between the messages of these codes to their respective professionals. This is regarding how the traditional value of respect is enshrined within them. The UKCC (1992) code referred to the client's uniqueness and dignity and stated that care should be provided irrespective of a patient's ethnicity, religious beliefs, personal attributes and so on. The BASW (1986) code embraced these individual differences, but required that group-based differences were not denied. The social worker was therefore more explicitly required to locate people in their collective and cultural context. (This comparison raises the interesting debate as to whether respect means treating everyone the same irrespective of their identity or treating them differently because of it.)

Although individual practitioners will by no means fall neatly into two professional stereotypes reflecting the two codes, comparing them does help to shed light on possible different orientations towards practice. From the comparison, there appears consistently to have been a more proactive position for social workers in respect of rights and discrimination. Thus the subsequent BASW code published ten years later in 1996 required social workers to:

- help clients to obtain not only services but rights to which they are entitled

- seek to ensure that services are ethnically and culturally appropriate

- challenge actions of colleagues or others which may be racist, sexist or otherwise discriminatory. (BASW 1996)

The most recent revision of the BASW code, published in 2002 and referred to earlier, continues to reflect a significant emphasis on the context in which social workers operate. If social workers were to claim exclusive ownership of this political dimension to professional practice, this would be to aspire to an unhelpful 'cognitive exclusiveness' (Larson 1977), marking out their professional identity as substantially different from that of other health-care professionals.

As mentioned above, the more recent BASW code (2002) places important emphasis on the involvement of service users and carers in partnership with professionals, reflecting a significant shift in attitudes to practice in social care and redefining the responsibilities of social workers. A similar principle of partnership with patients and clients is reflected in the new revised *Code of Professional Conduct* for nurses, midwives and health visitors (NMC 2002). Service-user involvement is therefore emerging as a common key element in ethical practice.

Collaborative practice

One of the practice rules that is material to the present discussion is that good practice must be collaborative and accountable. We can state as axiomatic that good practice is collaborative practice. It encompasses:

- working with other professions and occupations in the interests of service users

- working across and ultimately breaking down barriers of status, organization, method and professional ethos

- being accountable to colleagues to complement and reinforce each other's efforts. (Clark 2000)

The enhanced emphasis on service-user involvement must be reflected in the way in which accountability is interpreted; health and social care professionals should be accountable not only to each other (as Clark suggests) but in a fundamental sense to the people whose interests they are serving. This underlines the fact that collaborative practice is not only about different professions working together, but also implies a shared commitment to work with and on behalf of service users and carers (see Chapter 3).

Why, then, is collaboration frequently so difficult to achieve? The evidence has stacked up over many years and many inquiries into failures in practice, especially into cases where the statutory protection of children has broken down. Although blame is frequently attributed to particular individuals and agencies, inquiries into child deaths (see Chapter 3) demonstrate that the failure of collaboration is an exceedingly complex business. Do professionals attach insufficient weight to the ethic of collaboration, despite the fact that this can be a life-and-death matter in some cases? In the light of these questions it is quite surprising that the most recent version of the BASW *Code of Ethics for Social Work* (BASW 2002) has not included collaborative practice as one of its key principles.

However, the new *Draft Code of Conduct for Social Care Workers* published by the General Social Care Council (GSCC) in preparation for the professional registration of social workers does require them to work 'openly and cooperatively with colleagues and other professionals, recognising their roles and expertise and treating them with respect' (GSCC 2002, p.8).

We may compare this with the NMC's 2002 revised *Code of Professional Conduct* for nurses, mentioned earlier, in which a section of the code is given over to the requirement to co-operate with others in the team, explicitly stating that 'the team' includes social care professionals in the NHS, independent and voluntary sectors (but not, apparently, in local authority social services departments!). When comparing these two codes and considering that they have been drafted and finalized in the same year, it is clear that an opportunity has been lost to identify some common aspects to a values base that could be shared across at least some of the caring professions.

Different ground – shared ground

Before we move on to look at the shared ground for collaborative practice, it is as well to recognize that different ethical dimensions in practice may be expressed in different models of care. Our case history below is an example of the same situation being viewed (and judged) from different viewpoints based on differing professional perceptions. As one of our group of jointly trained practitioners said:

> I think the principles behind the disciplines of nursing and social work are different. Nursing ethics are run by the medical model of care, reflected in the code of practice. Social workers don't have an equivalent to 'uphold life at all costs'. Social workers have more of a focus on welfare. For example, some medical professionals would think unhygienic home conditions should lead to the withdrawal of the children. Some social workers would not want to do this.

The example given in this passage reflects a familiar dilemma: it is not a matter of one party being right and the other wrong; it is often in fact a difference of emphasis, a different weight put on the various factors involved in a situation that leads to a different conclusion being drawn. Our case history suggests that such a dilemma may be capable of resolution if there is mutual respect and understanding; but only too often perceived differences of viewpoint may exacerbate personal difficulties in working together.

Different value systems – different models of care

We have had to acknowledge the different value systems that are reflected in different models of care. A good example can be drawn from the development of work with people with learning difficulties over many years, where medical and social models have competed for predominance (Davis, Rendell and Sims 1999 and see Chapter 9). However, in spite of their tendency to solidify, value systems are not static entities, and there is a process of change and development that can be charted; after all, social workers and health professionals have discovered and practised on common ground over many years now, working together in multi-disciplinary teams.

This experience has to be set in the context of wider societal change in terms of value shifts. The death of Stephen Lawrence and the subsequent inquiry (Macpherson 1999) were an important turning point in changing public awareness of racism and institutional discrimination, and engendering an official commitment to combating it.

An example of the potential for clash of values between nursing and social work arose between social work and nursing lecturers on our joint training programme. This concerned the approach taken to the allocation of placements and the different needs of students. Should a student's child-care arrangements be considered when allocating a placement (so that the student would have less distance to travel)? Social work lecturers generally felt that they should because an individual student's success on the programme might depend on it. Nursing lecturers were sometimes more inclined to the opposite position on the basis that what was ultimately fairer was to treat everyone the same. Here the clash of values was about the very meaning of 'fair and equal treatment'.

Clearly we need to study professional and occupational cultures in order to understand why professionals may think and behave as they do, and in doing so we uncover some of the historically and socially determined differences between the professions. It cannot be too strongly emphasized that where there are interprofessional conflicts in practice, where there are failures in communication and the co-ordination of services, where there is mutual recrimination and attribution of blame, it is above all the service user and carer who loses out. This is seen in its starkest form in cases such as that of Victoria Climbié (Laming 2003) where children have been abused and killed.

Values and ethical practice in interprofessional working: a case history

The following case history was presented to the discussion group brought together to look at issues of values and ethics in interprofessional working by a jointly trained practitioner employed as a care co-ordinator for people with learning difficulties (referred to here as 'Cathy').

It concerns a white British middle-aged woman with learning difficulties and mental health problems (referred to as 'Beverley') who had lived for the past five years with an African family in London. The family consisted of two parents, both of whom were nurses (one a staff nurse and one a ward manager) in the local hospital, and a child of seven. Beverley had become a virtual member of the family, accompanying them on holidays abroad and becoming well known to family members in Africa.

Beverley's own mother was elderly and lived in a different part of London. She remained in close contact with Beverley and her substitute family and was happy with her daughter's living arrangements.

Since Beverley had gone to live with her substitute family, she had been diagnosed with breast cancer and had been successfully treated in the sense that the illness had been in remission for approximately four years. Beverley had some difficulties with communication and often found it hard to verbalize her needs in a coherent manner, especially when she was agitated. She often repeated what was said to her but, interestingly enough, only repeated those things that she agreed with or was happy to do. Her level of understanding of the spoken word was high. She would generally make her feelings on particular issues known through her carers.

At the time under consideration, a multi-disciplinary meeting (consisting of the care co-ordinator from the provider organization, care manager, psychiatrist, psychologist, community psychiatric nurse and community nurse) had been called to discuss Beverley's future care in the light of the fact that her carers were expecting a second child. This caused concern to some of the professionals involved, who questioned the carers' ability to continue to provide the same quality of service to Beverley when the new baby arrived. The majority view in the team was that it would not be feasible for Beverley to remain with the family; this judgement revolved around risk, in terms of her potential need for increased health care should the cancer recur.

Cathy felt that the team was reaching a decision about an individual's life without considering all the relevant factors, especially the contribution of the family's care to Beverley's good health status over recent years. Most importantly, the proposal to move Beverley did not properly take into account her own wishes and those of her carers.

It is important to emphasize that throughout the placement Cathy had had regular contact aimed at fully involving Beverley and her carers in all aspects of Beverley's life with her substitute family. Cathy normally met with Beverley at least once a fortnight on a one-to-one basis, and also with the principal carer once a fortnight for supervision and update of the progress of the placement.

At the time under discussion, there was extensive consultation with Beverley and her carers. Beverley was involved in a three-way meeting with Cathy and her principal carer to discuss the proposed changes in her care arrangements. She expressed happiness about the fact that her carer was going to have another baby, but when told she might have to move house replied emphatically, 'No! Stay here with nurse' (as she called her carer). On another occasion her care manager met her and explored the possibility of her moving, but Beverley was equally adamant that she wanted to stay with the family.

The carers' views when consulted on the proposed move were similar to Beverley's own. They did not see the arrival of the new baby as posing difficulties, but rather as a challenge to the whole family (including Beverley herself). The principal carer was also involved in meetings with health and social services in which she came up with positive suggestions, including the idea of a move to a larger house, as well as asking for additional support hours as part of the service user's overall care package so that Beverley could get out to pursue various activities.

The outcome of all this consultation was to strengthen Cathy's conviction that there was not a case for moving Beverley. Moreover, she felt that insufficient consideration had been given to the potential impact of a decision to move her.

As the person responsible for the co-ordination of Beverley's care, Cathy seized the opportunity to act as her advocate, and presented the case from a different viewpoint based on her assessment of Beverley's needs. She was able to help the other members of the team to understand the family dynamics and to appreciate how well the carers had done in meeting Beverley's needs over a period of five years. It was no coincidence that both parents in the family were themselves nurses. Cathy stressed that Beverley had now become an accepted member of the extended family, and to move her could have a detrimental effect on her physical and mental well-being.

After further debate in the team, which brought into play issues of social versus medical models of care for people with learning difficulties, it was agreed that Beverley should remain with her substitute family. The team was able to accept that the arrival of a new baby or other addition to a family was a normal and regular occurrence, and that the professionals needed to support the family in managing it.

The ethical dilemma

There was general agreement in this case that the service user's interests must come first; what was not at first apparent to most members of the team was how they would be best served in the given situation.

On the one hand, Beverley's needs would have changed once she was diagnosed with and treated for breast cancer. This would have affected the actual tasks involved in caring for her through the stages of treatment for cancer, as well as coping with the emotional impact. The demands on her carers must have substantially increased at this time. The possibility of recurrence of the disease would inevitably involve additional stress, and Beverley might well need a lot of extra care should this happen. On the other hand, the disease had reportedly been in remission for four years and the prognosis would normally be seen as favourable.

Given all the circumstances at the time of the review of the placement, it is understandable that some of the professionals involved (especially, perhaps, those coming from a medical background) might feel that the arrival of a new baby in the family could militate against the carers giving Beverley the level of care she needed (or might need in the future).

It had, however, to be recognized that the family had been conspicuously successful with Beverley's care over a number of years. Furthermore, the new baby would be only the second child, and the first was already well beyond infancy. The quality of family life that Beverley enjoyed with them appeared to be particularly good. Cathy, as care co-ordinator, saw these considerations as of overriding importance.

Discussion

There is an underlying question in a case such as this: how can a judgement be based on the assumption that the present carers might not be able to cope with Beverley's care in future? In arriving at a judgement in a complex situation, there is of course always more that needs to be known. There may be no conclusive information in the present state of knowledge, for example, about a possible relationship between remission and recurrence in malignant disease and the patient's contentment or otherwise with her living situation. Conversely, can the idea that moving her from her substitute family might actually affect her prognosis be supported by any research findings? Such questions underline the relationship between full and accurate information and ethical judgements in real-life situations.

We may often need to know more in particular cases before we can arrive at a balanced judgement that reflects best ethical practice. Judgement has always to be informed by professional values, and in interprofessional working, these have to be agreed values.

If we identify some of the principal underlying values on which practice needs to be based in a case such as Beverley's, we would have to include:

- respect for the person and her life choices
- upholding of her right to care suited to her needs (including her medical needs in the case of a cancer patient)
- fairness and equity in assessing the needs of a person with a learning disability
- the right of a vulnerable person to protection
- respect for those who care for vulnerable people and acknowledgement of the value and validity of their lifestyle.

If this particular case example were to be used for teaching and learning purposes, a number of questions could be addressed:

1. What would have happened in this situation had Cathy not been there?

2. Would anyone else have put a contrary view to that of the necessity of moving Beverley from her substitute family?

3. What might have happened had she been moved?

It is instructive to reflect that in the event a sound decision was made, but only after a challenge to the majority view and a resolution of conflicting stances. It is fair to say that in the circumstances, both stances had some force; otherwise there would have been no dilemma.

Lessons

The story involves the intervention of one practitioner in a multi-disciplinary team whose outlook had been shaped in the course of joint training as a social worker and learning disability nurse. It is arguable that her outlook was qualitatively different from that of colleagues trained in a single professional context, that she had been socialized into a professional identity that transcended the limits of either separate profession and which enabled her to take a truly holistic view of Beverley's needs. It should also be noted that her training and experience had given her the confidence to challenge the majority view in the team, some of whose members were from 'higher status' professions than hers.

For best practice to prevail, however, it is important to go beyond the characteristics of individual practitioners trained to work interprofessionally. The goal should surely be to develop a shared perception of people's needs as the basis for interprofessional working. In a case such as that recounted above, the decision about a service user should reflect the shared values of the team, rather than the triumph of one view over others.

This is an easy goal to annunciate, but not to achieve. We have to take into account the power relations inherent in the professional hierarchies represented in a multi-disciplinary team.

Endpiece

In this chapter we have attempted to show that definitions of values and ethics lead directly into principles of practice and rules for good practice. Indeed, the basic values underlying social work have meaning only in so far as they are incorporated into practice.

Interprofessional practice is an essential element of good social work practice. It is often easier to commend in theory than to realize in practice. In order to promote it we have to have some understanding of different professional cultures and how they engender a distinctive professional identity. Differences between the professions in ways of knowing, doing and feeling have to be recognized, as it is the combination of these elements that provide professionals with a bounded and unambiguous identity (Edwards 1997). Equally we have to guard against taking a negative stance in relation to professions other than our own, defending ourselves by calling up stereotypes and closing ranks around what we conceive of as 'exclusive' values systems and rules of practice. To the extent that we do this, we risk overlooking the evidence for change and convergence in professional beliefs and behaviours, which both reflect what is going on in the wider world and help to shape it.

In the 2002 published statutory codes of ethical practice for nurses (NMC) and social workers (GSCC), there is a disappointing sense of a missed opportunity by the separate professional bodies to make explicit a shared values base for the health and social care professions as the bedrock of interprofessional practice. While such shared values may be implicit in the work of multi-disciplinary teams and services, more could be done to codify the values on which they base their practice, and pressure could be brought to bear accordingly on professional regulatory bodies.

In conclusion, we might visualize the movement towards the 'common ground' in health and social services in terms of a progression passing through the following stages:

- Stage 1: characterized by separation and segregation within our professional fortresses. To keep ourselves safe within the fortress walls we need not only to elaborate a distinctive scheme of values and the practice rules that flow from them, but to denigrate the values and practice rules of others.

- Stage 2: marked by a growing awareness of each other's 'ways of being' through working side by side. Contiguity gives us at least some insight into other professional perspectives.

- Stage 3: as the pressure for interprofessional co-operation builds up, we begin to see the value in incorporating various perspectives into practice within a multi-disciplinary framework and seeking genuine resolution of conflict involving different perspectives.

- Stage 4: signals the conscious adoption of a common values base as the shared ground on which to build common rules for practice. The importance of the shared ground is that it does not represent a 'lowest common denominator', but rather reflects a kind of 'multi-dimensional thinking' that makes possible a truly holistic approach to assessing and meeting the needs of people who use health and social services.

We might say that the progression from stage one to stage four in this schema represents a transition from 'professional led' to 'client led' practice. Or – expressed in organizational terms – that we move from working within our own professional boundaries to working as part of a team in which each member does their job, and finally towards working as members of a team combining different skills and areas of expertise but fundamentally interchangeable (in as much as each team member accepts and puts into practice a common values system and the rules governing practice that stem from it).

At the time of writing we are in a transitional phase in the management and delivery of health and social services which are coming together in primary care trusts employing both health and social work professionals. Professional education and training will have to reflect the changing picture in terms of the demands arising from the workplace, but they are also a potent factor in driving forward the agenda for change towards effective collaborative practice.

Acknowledgements

The authors gratefully acknowledge the contribution made to the development of this chapter by graduates of the BSc Nursing and Social Work Studies and the MA in Social Work, South Bank University.

References

Aymer, C. (2000) 'Teaching and Learning Anti-racist and Anti-discriminatory Practice.' In R. Pierce and J. Weinstein (eds) *Innovative Education and Training for Care Professionals.* London: Jessica Kingsley Publishers.

Banks, S. (1995) *Ethics and Values in Social Work.* Basingstoke: Macmillan.

British Association of Social Workers (1986) *The Code of Ethics for Social Work.* Birmingham: BASW.

British Association of Social Workers (1996) *The Code of Ethics for Social Work.* Birmingham: BASW.

British Association of Social Workers (2002) *The Code of Ethics for Social Work.* Birmingham: BASW.

CCETSW (1995) *Assuring Quality in the Diploma in Social Work – 1. Rules and Requirements for the DipSW.* London: CCETSW.

Clark, C.L. (2000) *Social Work Ethics.* London: Macmillan.

Davis, J., Rendell, P. and Sims, D. (1999) 'The Joint Practitioner: A New Concept in Professional Training.' *Journal of Interprofessional Care 4*, 13, 395–404.

Edwards, R. (1997) *Changing Places? Flexibility, Lifelong Learning and a Learning Society.* London: Routledge.

GSCC (2002) *The Draft Code of Conduct for Social Care Workers.* London: GSCC.

Laming, Lord (2003) *The Victoria Climbié Inquiry.* Norwich: HMSO.

Larson, M.S. (1977) *The Rise of Professionalism: A Sociological Analysis.* Los Angeles: University of California Press.

Macpherson, W. (1999) *The Stephen Lawrence Inquiry. Report of an Inquiry by Sir William Macpherson of Cluny.* Cm 4261. London: Stationery Office.

NMC (2002) *Code of Professional Conduct. Protecting the Public through Professional Standards.* London: Nursing and Midwifery Council.

Rokeach, M. (1973) *The Nature of Human Values.* New York: Free Press.

Thompson, N. (1998) *Promoting Equality. Challenging Discrimination and Oppression in the Human Services.* Basingstoke: Macmillan.

Thompson, N. (2001) *Anti-discriminatory Practice,* 3rd edn. Basingstoke: Palgrave.

UKCC (1992) *Code of Professional Conduct for Nurses, Midwives and Health Visitors.* London: United Kingdom Central Council for Nursing, Health Visiting and Midwifery.

UKCC (1999) *Fitness for Practice.* London: United Kingdom Central Council for Nursing, Health Visiting and Midwifery.

Wilmott, S. (1995) 'Professional Values and Inter-professional Dialogue.' *Journal of Interprofessional Care 9*, 3, 257–266.

Further reading

Dalley, G. (1993) 'Professional Ideology or Organisational Tribalism?' In J. Walmsley, J. Reynolds, P. Shakespeare and R. Woolfe (eds) *Health, Welfare and Practice. Reflecting on Roles and Relationships.* London: Sage/The Open University.

Irvine, R., Kerridge, I., McPhee, J. and Freeman, S. (2002) 'Interprofessionalism and Ethics: Consensus or Clash of Cultures.' *Journal of Interprofessional Care 16*, 3, 199–210.

Seedhouse, D. (2002) 'Commitment to Health: A Shared Ethical Bond between Professions.' *Journal of Interprofessional Care 16*, 3, 250–260.

PART II

Collaboration in Practice

Allies and Enemies: The Service User as Care Co-ordinator

Christine Barton

Introduction

> Effective partnerships are the only way of delivering a fully integrated
> and person-centred set of services. The best judges of partnership work-
> ing will be local people who receive a seamless service from health and
> social care. (DoH 2001)

'Seamless services' – a solution to many of the barriers faced by disabled service users, but more often I hear the words 'bureaucracy', 'fragmentation',
'isolation' and 'frustration'. For most of us reality falls a long way short of an
approach that is holistic, seamless and person-centred. I want to tell the stories of some disabled people who have been on the receiving end of service
provision and why they say things like:

> ...it is almost as if the disabled person is put in the role of detective. You
> have to go out and track things down. I have the time and resources to do
> this, but I am conscious that this is not true for everyone. (Service user in
> Atkins 2001, p.2)

> I tend to avoid them [social services] as much as possible. (Service user in
> Atkins 2001, p.2)

> They think that they are the professionals and you are not even a normal
> person. They believe that they have the authority to tell you how to run
> your life. (Service user in NISW 2001, p.2)

We need professionals to be our allies and advocates, not our enemies. In doing this they are part of the positive process of empowerment, enabling disabled people to take control of their own lives. (Service user in NISW 2001, p.4)

If society is to change to include and value all disabled people, we need to find ways of making our minority powerful enough to influence the future. (Campbell 1999)

...an exchange of jealously guarded trade secrets, the rules of the game and the coded language that attends it! (Campbell 1999)

This chapter uses direct accounts of disabled people's good and bad experiences of professionals to draw out clear guidelines for positive attitudes and good practice for collaboration with service users.

It is my own experience as a disabled woman, a service user and someone who has a commitment to improving service provision, that prompts me to try and strengthen the voice of people who are often not heard. I have a physical impairment and can only move my head. This means I cannot walk, stand, transfer from one chair to another, feed myself, drive my wheelchair or write my name. In other words I am completely physically dependent. Without support I would very quickly die.

With the help of personal assistance, technology, innovation and good design I have developed my own way of doing things. I live an ordinary life, I do the things that ordinary people do, I use the skills I have gained as both a disabled and a non-disabled person to benefit my community, but the everyday struggle is constant and overwhelming. The struggle is not against impairment; it is against the barriers that stand between me and an ordinary life. I am part of a society that has not been designed for me. Little attempt has been made to accept that people are different from each other and have different needs. I believe that we all have the same human rights, but for disabled people, achieving these rights depends largely on those non-disabled people who decide the face of social care.

My condition is progressive and I have found that my right to choice and control over my own life has diminished as my physical dependence has increased. Many service providers think they know what I need better than I do, or that what I need is too expensive. Others not involved in service provision believe that I should accept the minimal provision grudgingly made by a 'welfare state' and I should be grateful for what I'm given. I should not ask for more or fight for my rights. I should not expect a 'normal' life.

I can, and do, use my own financial, intellectual and social resources to overcome the barriers I face. However, while this makes my life possible, it makes no general improvements to the attitudes and values that are embedded deeply in our Western society. It means that in every new venture I have to overcome the same barriers time and time again. I am not alone in this fight: I have disabled colleagues and non-disabled allies. Words and phrases like 'one-stop shop', 'seamless service', 'empowerment', 'joined-up thinking' are indicators of a different way of working. However, they are meaningless unless accompanied by cultural change in society as a whole and the social care workforce in particular. Change is slow and traditional boundaries can be hard to cross, but progress depends on removing these boundaries and working together to identify and remove disabling barriers.

Disabled people have been fighting to overcome barriers and boundaries for many years. These fights and the reasons for them have been documented by those closely involved with the disability movement and disability studies (Barnes 1990; Morris 1991; Oliver and Campbell 1996). An increasing number of universities are now offering such courses. The British Council of Disabled People was established and more recently the National Centre for Independent Living and the Disability Rights Commission, organizations of disabled people working for disabled people. Although the Disability Discrimination Act 1995 is beginning to make some difference, the underlying causes of non-disabled people regarding disabled people as objects of pity, without the same rights as they take for granted, remain and underpin the work of many service providers.

I wanted to include the views of a wide variety of service users in this chapter by trying to find a number of people to contribute case studies, but this was difficult. I sought help through a disability mailbase and by advertisement to a local organization of disabled people. Unfortunately many of the people who responded did not have time to write in depth, or were very reluctant to share, even anonymously, personal experiences for fear of reprisals and loss of service. This last fact speaks volumes about how some workers in social care are perceived and about how hard care professionals must work to build trust and enable people to gain confidence to express their views.

To write the chapter, I have therefore used words from service users taken from publications and drawn on two case studies provided by people with different experiences of the social care system. One was provided through my request to the mailbase, the other in response to the local advertisement. The communication with me took place during 2001.[1]

Case study 1: Beth

Beth has been a service user for nine years. Formerly employed by the NHS as a district nurse, she is now dependent on disability benefits and the services provided by social services. She tells her story below.

> As part of my job I had many professional dealings with social workers and, although there were differences of professional opinion on some occasions, I had always found them helpful and co-operative.
>
> My life radically changed when I was diagnosed as having a debilitating, degenerative, chronic illness, and was medically retired from work. I found myself in a new position with implications that shocked and dismayed me. I became a client, and they were professionals. I had needs, and apparently they were the only people who could help me meet those needs, but only if they thought it necessary.
>
> My first shocking venture into this world of 'disabled person' meets 'gate keeper of services' was to be told that, although I had a doctor's referral for services, these requirements were 'wants' not 'needs'. I was assessed as 'wanting' some care at home, but as my husband was living with me it was not a 'need'; he could take care of me. This meant that he was trying to work, particularly important as I had been the higher wage earner, and getting home early if he could, to get an evening meal, plus doing a large share of the housework and caring for our daughter. He eventually gave up the struggle and left us, to start a new life with a colleague from work.
>
> I contacted social services as I was now without a carer, but was given the same response: 'my needs' were a social problem, not a social work problem! I had a teenage daughter at home who was there to care for me. I was informed that the Disability Living Allowance was there to purchase home care if my daughter found it a chore! I was also told that I was articulate enough to organize this for myself. This approach led to my daughter, although very caring at home, being 'picked up' by the police for heavy drinking.
>
> My doctor again referred the family for an assessment. The outcome of this was that I was granted three weeks' respite care but no home care. We were grateful for the respite care, but it came with problems attached. My social worker just booked me for a week away, without any

consultation on the suitability of dates. On one occasion it was arranged when my daughter was taking her GCSE exams. I refused to go as she was really upset about me going away at a time when she wanted my support. I was told that my case was being closed as I had rejected the services offered. I was stunned and devastated, as I had explained the issues surrounding my refusal to take that particular week.

I contacted my doctor who made an urgent referral and requested I was seen that day. I was allocated a new social worker. After discussion with the team manager for adult disability it was agreed that the new worker would not have access to any discussions, or actions, that had gone before, and I would try not to be hostile. By this point my personal views of social workers were at an all-time low.

My contact with social services then took a distinctly upward turn. This new social worker treated me as a person. The assessment took place during a series of meetings over six weeks. She did not come in and make an immediate decision based on one half-hour visit as had been done previously.

Together we assessed my needs, and home care was put into place: one hour each morning to facilitate a shower and dressing, any time over to go towards some meal preparation, and a quarter of an hour in the evening to put me to bed. My daughter's social life was her own again.

I was assessed as requiring respite care, to give my daughter a break, and allocated three weeks a year. I was also assessed as needing 'day care' once a week to alleviate my social isolation. My sight had deteriorated to the point that I had had to surrender my driving licence. This was eventually recorded as 'unmet need' as it was felt that the local day centre (which was the only service on offer) would not be an appropriate placement.

An occupational therapist came and did a comprehensive assessment of the adaptations and equipment that would enable me to be more independent in my home. This was referred to the local government offices for a direct finance grant and rapidly a stair-lift was installed, followed by a series of other adaptations throughout the house.

I had been asked to collect three estimates for the work that needed doing, and the council then contracted with the builder they felt to be the best one (not necessarily the cheapest). Although I had control over the choice of which builders I asked to quote it was a situation where some guidance could have been helpful, possibly an approved list to choose from. Once the builder started to work, the occupational therapist was in control, and she had to be contacted if there was the least problem. It was difficult to reach her, so the building work took far longer than it should have, as minor deviation from her original specifications invalidated the contract.

There were problems with the care, in that the agency that social services contracted to provide my care was not very 'caring'. Different carers turned up, and at random times, e.g. one turned up at 12.30 pm to get me up for the day and then returned at 3 pm to put me back to bed! Any complaints had to go through my social worker, and by the time one had been resolved there was probably another underway! My friends and family see me as an easy-going person, in some cases too easy-going, but the constant problems with the care agency put a lot of stress on me. My daughter and I ended up saying that we would be better off without the care after all.

Luckily at that point direct payments became an option and my social worker suggested that it might be the answer to the situation. It has been. I now purchase my own care. It has made such a difference as I deal direct with the agency and the carers and sort out any potential difficulties. I can let them know if there is a change in my requirements as soon as I know, i.e. a short stay in hospital, and when I will probably be discharged. My social worker now sees me to review the situation every three months and it is a 'working' meeting.

The respite care is now also up to me to arrange, and it feels more like 'taking a holiday from work' than an enforced stay away! I have been able to contract with respite centres away from my home area. The getting away has been even more beneficial for all of us, as there has been some real distance put between us!

The one need that still has not been met is my assessed need for 'day care'. My social worker and I had hoped that under direct payments we could use the local adult education facility as a better 'provider' of 'day care'. Sadly, as there are no new monies for direct payments, and it wasn't a need that had been previously met, there were no monies to fund that aspect of my life. Even so, this was easier to accept and understand as my social worker and I were both equally disappointed and that sharing made such a significant difference.

Beth clearly demonstrates in her story how the attitudes of some social care workers influence their practice. The excuse of insufficient resources disguises an attitude that makes the service user feel without value and without power. Different people interpret eligibility criteria in different ways and the service user has no feeling of being a partner in the process. Rather, she is made to feel that her requests are not reasonable, that she has no right to an ordinary lifestyle and that her family are expected to be unpaid carers.

Social care workers could demonstrate their commitment to the service user by:

- clearly explaining criteria during the full needs assessment
- putting the needs of the service user before those of the organization and the resources available
- recording unmet need
- listening to service users and respecting their views and opinions
- recognizing that service users should be treated as partners and be in control
- recognizing and valuing the experience and expertise of service users, particularly their understanding of their own requirements.

Case study 2: Simon

Simon has been disabled since birth, went to a special school and has been a service user for many years. He is actively involved in raising disability issues in his community. He talked to me about his experience of working with service providers and how he thinks things could be better.

Simon is a council house tenant, has home helps provided by the home care service and is able to use a day centre three days a week with some transport arranged for him. He has a key worker employed by social services in a day centre who negotiates the elements of Simon's care package with him.

Simon feels that he is in control of the services he receives, but he thinks that this is mainly because he has a lot of knowledge about disability and this helps him to decide what he needs and how to go about getting it. He works well with his key worker:

> He's more of a friend to me now than a professional. He's also very interested in what I do outside. He asks me what's going on if he hears anything…and what's happening.

Mostly Simon organizes his own transport using a local taxi service paid for through the mobility component of his Disability Living Allowance.

He says that things have changed a lot over the years. His first experience of social workers was when he was planning to marry a disabled woman in residential care. Before this he had lived with his parents. He and his wife insisted that they should have an assessment of what they would need to live independently.

> ...we fought to get a proper assessment. They actually wanted to send us to a secure unit when we talked about getting married. Instead we went to, I think it's the John Radcliffe hospital. This place has got a really good reputation and that's why we wanted to go and we had full assessment right throughout. Social services paid but we had a real fight to get them to fund it.

Once the local authority had agreed to the assessment they did provide the equipment and adaptations in a reasonable timescale.

Simon has frequently found social workers to be patronizing and 'to think they know best', ignoring his wishes or needing a lot of persuasion before they carry them out. While he does not personally feel threatened and says that he is well able to stick up for himself, he thinks that many other disabled people will have neither the knowledge nor the experience to do this. He has also found them to be invasive of his privacy: for example, when he and his wife decided that he should have a vasectomy, social workers insisted on being involved.

> They wanted to make sure that we were doing it for the right reasons. I'm sure that was patronising. So not only did I get a counselling session from the doctor, I had a sort of counselling session from the social worker as well.

Simon said that was not needed or requested and he could not understand why they thought they should be involved.

A few years later Simon's marriage broke down and he divorced. He found that social workers were discussing his situation with each other in a very negative way. He felt that they were reluctant to consider his needs again.

> It was a traumatic time. I had a real fight to get re-housed. She actually moved from the place where we were and then I had a real fight to get them to adapt another place...

In his experience services have been separate from each other and he has had to take the initiative to find what is there and then to have it provided. He thinks that different providers do not speak to each other often enough and may know little about each other's services. He feels that this is improving but there is still some way to go.

> I think there is more willingness to work together… It needs to be more structured…a lot of time is wasted. You have to have meetings with OTs (occupational therapists) and possibly their manager, and meetings with social workers.

He thinks it can be hard to find out what is available and how it can be accessed, particularly for people who do not have experience of how the systems work.

> Ordinary disabled, when I say ordinary I mean someone who isn't quite as active…social workers don't always give the information that you want. I think that's where people lose control. Social workers in my experience [think] 'we know which is best' [and] steer people down this route. I think it's got worse because of financial constraints…they only see what they might have to spend now rather than looking in the long term.

Simon does not think that getting the service you need is becoming easier. He says that now money is so restricted because budgets are continually cut, you have to wait a long time before anyone sees you.

> I think they are…endeavouring to work closer together…you have a harder job to get the social worker each year. Under the current situation you can't do a lot without one… You have to jump through so many hoops. When I started using services, if I needed a worker, I knew who to ring, when she might be where and how she could be contacted – a regular sort of contact.

He made suggestions about how he thought things should change.

> [They could]…look at streamlining the service, or services, try and make them work more effectively. Not piecemeal services. Make the gateways into the service a lot easier. Try and make it more structured really.
>
> I think they all need to publicize their services, to actually produce a pack that is clear to understand, to sort of write it down, stage by stage. If you require the service, this is what you need to do; this is who you may contact. In general how long it might take…break it down a bit, stage by stage, so people know exactly what they need to do rather than being… as it is now. You've got to have a social worker and say 'I need this.' If you have it my way, you would have received a pack. This is how you might go

about getting it. I'm not saying they will get it. I think they still need
some system of assessing when people need that service. But at least have
clear guidelines when you need that service rather than the social worker
being instrumental.

He argued that the service user should be able to make choices from a range
of options. They cannot do this if they do not know what is available and
whether they are entitled to it.

Simon is one of many people who have used services for a long time and
whose package of care was decided long before the community care legislation was passed. In his area, new procedures are now being put into place to
make sure that all existing users have a full needs assessment. Although it
could be years before this happens to him, he thinks that potentially it is a
threatening situation. People do not like change and as things are at the
moment the assessment is more likely to take services away than to offer
improvement.

Simon's and Beth's impairments and experiences are different but they
make similar points about services. Social care workers can demonstrate their
commitment to promoting the independence, rights and interests of the
people they work with by:

- making sure they recognize that service users are not a
  homogenous group and have as many differences between them
  as any other group of people

- using information as a tool for the service user, not as a means of
  maintaining control

- being prepared to co-operate more closely with colleagues in
  different services

- accepting that they have no right to intrude on the privacy of a
  service user

- challenging inappropriate behaviour and language used by
  colleagues

- recognizing the need to maintain confidentiality

- ensuring adequate contact arrangements are in place for the
  service user.

The issue of co-operation between colleagues and between services demands the accepting of responsibility for provision of support, within overall resource restraints, and not passing service users from one service to another in the hope that the cost will be met from an alternative source. This means making the most of the opportunities for pooled budgets offered through the Health Act 1999, ensuring effective multi-disciplinary working and clarifying the structure, communication and accountability processes for managers who lead teams drawn from different organizational structures. To meet these demands social care workers must ensure their own professional development equips them to gain the knowledge and skills required.

Relationships between social workers and service users

Service users make clear that the attitude of a social worker can make an immense difference to their situation. Over the last eight years my own experience has brought me into contact with social workers with different approaches and different values and beliefs. One of the first was a woman of vision who was prepared to listen and who was the prime mover in establishing a third-party direct payments scheme before the enabling legislation was passed. Her replacement was a very different kind of person. When I was filmed by a local news programme carrying out my role as a school governor, facilitated by my personal assistant, she was dismayed that viewers might see social services as paying for me to go out! She adopted the attitude that a personal assistant should meet only my care needs and not support me in my work with statutory services.

On another occasion when I was involved in a training session for social workers about direct payments, a participant suggested that intellectual and social independence was not possible if you were physically dependent. In other words, for these two people, I was supposed to stay in my house and relinquish control of my life to others.

Beth also made clear how important an individual's approach can be.

> I have had the experience of having no control at all in what is allocated, and the way in which it is implemented, and found it is a soul-destroying experience... My current social worker's approach to work is so different. I feel she sees me as a person, with my own unique situation, and that is the framework within which she is trying to provide my care, while keeping within the statutory (and financial) boundaries of her profession. She

is not a friend; she is a care professional who is working with me to enable me to get the best I can out of life. I dread her leaving.

Service users make unambiguous comments about how they would like to see relationships with social workers and other service providers change.

> There still is little, or really no, contact between the different agencies that care for me, especially between health and social services. I feel that, for people with complex problems, an annual review with all the professionals involved, and needless to say with the client and their family (with possibly an advocate for support if wanted) preferably at the client/patient's home, would be far more useful than the random meetings with all the different people over the year. We would all know where we were going and could all work together then. It could well turn out to be a more cost and time effective approach. (Beth)

Like Simon, Beth wanted social workers to play a more significant role in the provision of information and both recognized that their own experience could be a valuable source of support for others.

> Benefit information has never been volunteered, and I missed weeks of being able to claim certain benefits. Caring professionals do not seem to see information giving, of this nature, as part of their role. Finances are a significant area of concern to all of us, and disability can often equate to increased expenditure at a time of reduced income.
>
> I think that I now, probably, have more information on benefits and local amenities for disabled people than the professionals. I have gleaned this information from other disabled people, and of course use the Internet to keep that information as current as possible. I know that the professionals, especially those involved in my care, and their colleagues, now contact me for information for other patients/clients when the need arises. This in fact is beneficial for me too as it gives me a sense of still being useful. (Beth)

Jane Campbell MBE, Chair of the Social Care Institute for Excellence (SCIE), a disabled woman who has a long record of lobbying for disabled people's civil and human rights, makes plain the importance of a culture change that moves the balance of power from service providers to service users:

...professionals, experts and others who seek to help must be committed to promoting...control to disabled people...

In collaboration with civil servants, members of parliament, social service practitioners, the disabled people's movement were considered to be experts in our own situation. As a result we were given a central role in the planning of a social infrastructure... So, power changed hands. (Campbell 1999)

Suggestions from other service users include:

What is needed is a one-stop shop business...if they can't do it, they know who can. More like someone to co-ordinate the services for you. (Service user in Atkins 2001, p.4)

I think the codes [*Draft Codes of Conduct for Social Care Workers and Employers* (GSCC 2001)] might help stop the way services vary from area to area... You should be able to get the same support you are getting in one area if you go to another... (Service user in NISW 2001, p.2)

Improving relationships between care professionals and service users

Figure 5.1 summarizes the changes that service users think would enable them to live independent lives and take an active role in their communities.

Perhaps the voices of service users that have long been raised against discrimination on the grounds of impairment are beginning to make a difference. The appointment of disabled service users to non-departmental public bodies and other government organizations, although very much in a minority, is a real opportunity to make the changes that will enable disabled people to take their place in claiming their rights and living ordiary lives.

Figure 5.2 demonstrates a model whereby service users are at the heart of assessment and service provision.

A person-centred approach to service provision, a welcome development towards a social approach, would follow from an holistic assessment made by a generic social worker/care co-ordinator/key worker or, if needed, a joint assessment with a health-care professional, together with the disabled person. Financial constraints mean that this must be based on open, transparent criteria about eligibility written in plain English. These criteria should be developed and accepted by all service providers in collaboration with service users. Information would flow from specialist service providers

From		To
Service providers are in control.	⇨	Service users are in control
Services are fragmented and separated by rigid boundaries.	⇨	Services work together in a person-centred approach.
Health and local government service providers have separate budgets and provide separate services.	⇨	Health and local government service providers have pooled budgets and work together.
Separate services produce their own information. This is fragmented and difficult to find.	⇨	There is a single access point for information.
Information leaflets use jargon and complicated sentence constructions. They are produced in one format only.	⇨	Information is produced using plain English in appropriate formats.
Service providers determine support needs and solutions.	⇨	Service users determine support needs and solutions.
Teams work in a single discipline.	⇨	Teams are multi-disciplinary.
Workers have skills in one service.	⇨	Workers are multi-skilled and work across services.

Figure 5.1 The direction of change

Figure 5.2 A holistic approach to service provision[2]

to the care co-ordinator and service user and appropriate arrangements would be put in place. Information in appropriate formats concerning sources of supply of care and/or equipment would be readily available.

Good practice guidelines
Organizations and systems

- Service users welcome moves towards a social approach to service provision and government initiatives to modernize social services and the health service, but more work is needed if partnership and collaboration are to make any real difference to many of them.

- Social care workers and social care systems and organizations must ensure that their approach is not seen to be patronizing and driven by limited budgets, rather than by the requirements of service users.

- Organizations must work to ensure that service users do not have to fight disabling barriers created by fragmented and bureaucratic service delivery.

- Access to direct payments must be improved and should be seen as 'a right' and not something to be grateful for.

- Organizations must instil appropriate social work values because the individual beliefs of social care workers influence their practice and can either benefit or disadvantage service users.

- Information must be made accessible and easy to understand.

- Service users' self-esteem is raised through their involvement in policy decisions and recognition of their expertise in disability issues.

Inter-personal skills for social workers

- Maintain a friendly but professional manner that is neither patronizing nor threatening.

- Respect and trust individual service users.

- Maintain confidentiality.

- Listen to and act on service users' stated requirements.

- Provide information about other service provision.

- Explain criteria clearly and record unmet need.

- Be creative, open-minded and flexible within financial and procedural constraints.

- Keep appointments on time, return phone calls and make sure contact arrangements are clear.

- Work closely with other service providers and understand their procedures.

- Challenge budgets and organizational procedures that restrict partnership.

- Welcome service users as valued partners.

- Challenge inappropriate behaviour.

Role in relation to direct payments

- Understand the legislation and local arrangements for provision of community care through a direct payment.

- Offer a direct payment as an option available for every service user who is legally entitled to receive one.

- Regularly review the service user's requirements and the amount of the direct payment agreed.

- Understand and be able to explain clearly the benefits and constraints of a direct payment.

- Provide effective liaison between the service user and social services.

- Give support and appropriate advice to service users worried about being employers.

- Recognize that a direct payment is a right not a gift and behave accordingly.

Good social care places service users at the centre. Jane Campbell made this emphasis clear when, as Chair of the Social Care Institute of Excellence, she said:

> I hope my appointment will send out a clear message to everyone involved in social care that service users will not only be welcomed to

help shape service delivery but will be expected to participate at every level. (Campbell 2001)

Notes

1. Case studies 2001 – Beth and Simon (not their real names) are service users. Beth wrote her account, Simon was interviewed, both in 2001. Edited transcripts of the material were made available to both service users and amended by them.

2. Graphics for Figure 5.2 designed by Lindsay Yarrow (2001), Rotherham.

References

Atkins, M. (2001) 'Service Users.' In *Disabled People, Empowerment and Service Provision*. Sheffield University, unpublished research conducted in partial fulfilment of a PhD.

Barnes, C. (1990) *Cabbage Syndrome: The Social Construction of Dependence*. London: Falmer Press.

Campbell, J. (1999) Fabian Society Conference 'Working in Partnership with the Establishment – The Disability Agenda' (conference speech). London: Fabian Society.

Campbell, J. (2001) *SCIE Briefing*. London: Social Care Institute for Excellence.

Disability Discrimination Act (1995) London: Stationery Office.

DoH (2001) *Health and Social Care Awards 2001*. Leeds: Department of Health.

General Social Care Council (GSCC) (2001) *Draft Codes of Conduct for Social Care Workers and Employers*. London: GSCC.

Health Act (1999) London: Stationery Office.

Morris, J. (1991) *Pride Against Prejudice*. London: The Women's Press.

National Institute of Social Work (NISW) (2001) *Putting the Person First*. NISW Briefing No. 31. London: NISW.

Oliver, O. and Campbell, J. (1996) *Disability Politics*. London: Routledge.

Chapter 6

Collaboration or Confusion?
The Carers' Perspective
Sonia Douek

Introduction

Francis Bacon wrote in 1605 that 'knowledge is power', and for many informal carers this phrase sums up how they feel about the professionals involved with the person for whom they are caring. This knowledge should be used constructively to help all partners in care – client, professional and carer. Sharing knowledge creates better multi-disciplinary working and facilitates collaboration between involved parties and effective advocacy for client and carer.

There are obstacles to sharing. While carers sometimes have vital knowledge about the person they care for, they are often unwilling to share this with service providers because there is insufficient trust. On the other hand, in my experience of working with, for example, carers of people with mental health problems, service users' confidentiality can be given as the reason why professionals refuse to give carers vital knowledge about the service user's condition.

There is an assumption that carers will know who holds the knowledge they need. At an event held for carers to gain information, a social worker commented to me, 'I can't understand how these people don't know who does what.' My response was, 'Why should they?' Carers rarely have training in social services or health services, yet from the moment they become carers many of them are expected to become care managers, knowing where to go, who and what to ask, understanding complicated systems that others have studied for years, and negotiating jargon that changes on a daily basis (Holzhausen 1997).

A significant number of agencies and professionals will hold knowledge about a person receiving services. This could include:

- statutory social services – care managers, occupational therapists, home-care providers, day service providers, respite care providers

- health services – GP, medical consultant, district nurse, ward managers, pharmacists

- voluntary sector – day-care/home-care providers, carers' services, advocates etc.

- cared-for client

- carer

- other family members.

As service providers, we know how hard it is sometimes to get a clear picture of the other professionals or agencies that are involved with our clients and what their role is (see Chapter 3). Very often it is also difficult to get the information we need from these providers. They may become very parochial, and feel that we are stealing their client. Imagine then how carers feel when questioned about the care they provide – are they being judged? Similarly, when a professional or agency knows something about the person to whom the informal carer provides 24-hour care, imagine how it feels when the professionals will not share that knowledge with the carer.

Around 6.8 million adults in Britain are carers and around 3.8 million are the main support for the person they care for (Office for National Statistics 2002). They provide care on an unpaid basis to relatives, friends and neighbours who are sick, disabled, elderly or otherwise would not be able to manage and 1.7 million spend 20 hours or more per week on caring (Mooney, Statham and Simon 2002). Given the projected increase in the numbers of older people, it is estimated that 60 per cent more carers will be needed by 2037 (Carers UK 2001). Informal carers come in many guises, providing a huge variety of roles for a myriad of caring needs.

Jewish Care is a large voluntary organization providing health and care services to older people, people with mental health problems, people with physical disabilities and people with sensory impairment. The Jewish Care carers' service, which I have managed for the last five years, has grown incrementally as it has become increasingly clear that meeting the needs of carers is as important as meeting the needs of clients.

This chapter will focus on the benefits of shared information and knowledge when working with carers in the following areas of service: severe mental illness, dementia, physical disabilities and addiction. Key aspects of good practice for working with carers will be highlighted:

- effective and open communication

- multi-disciplinary working

- creative collaboration with voluntary and informal networks

- advocating between different professionals to assist with access to services.

My work as a carers' service manager in adult services means that the majority of contact is with adult carers. We do come into contact with young carers, but not as primary carers. Nevertheless, where care is the primary focus of a home life, this will inevitably affect the lives of any young person within the household. In this latter case, as we will see later in the chapter, a commitment by social service departments to work collaboratively and innovatively can make a significant difference and prevent one client becoming a family of clients.

In order to illustrate examples of good practice in working collaboratively with carers, I have chosen four case studies that best reflect the work we have done over the past five years with over 1000 carers. Although the service users and carers concerned all have very different problems and use different services, their stories demonstrate, in the words of one of our carers, 'what helps, and what hurts'.

Working with carers

The introduction of community care effectively meant a heavier shift than ever before onto families and friends to bear the brunt of community care. Jordan with Jordan (2000) point out that Section 2.22 in the White Paper *Modernising Social Services: Promoting Independence, Improving Protection, Raising Standards* (DoH 1998), about the needs of carers, 'largely restates propositions that have been piously repeated for many years ...' (Jordan with Jordan 2000, p.88). Although carers have clearly and consistently articulated their needs through the Carers' National Association (Rao 1996), it is not easy for formal public bodies to support informal personal and family networks and relationships. Research indicates that the improvements for users and carers that were supposed to follow from the implementation of the NHS and Community Care Act of 1990 did not materialize (DoH 1990b). On the contrary, they led to other problems (Hadley and Clough 1995). As Jordan and Jordan suggest:

> Caring is sustained by processes of communication (of identity and relationship, as well as shared history)… Into this maelstrom of mixed feelings, and often conflicting interests, a care manager arrives to assess resources and risks and to purchase a package of care. (Jordan with Jordan 2000, p.89)

This changing role of social workers to care managers has meant that very often the package of care will be arranged and the 'case closed', leaving no emotional support to the person with the disability, and the passing of the responsibility for monitoring and co-ordinating services back to the carer.

Health services too have changed over the years. District nurses will now only undertake 'nursing tasks' and bathing is left to the home carer. Carers tell me that in some local authorities, home carers are not allowed to offer bathing but only strip-washing. From the perspective of carers, the home-help who used to undertake cleaning and household chores for those unable to manage for themselves has been replaced to a large extent by the home carer who is only permitted to provide personal care (Mooney *et al.* 2002), causing additional pressure on carers who often have to undertake or manage these additional tasks.

The Labour government came to power with a promise to look at the needs of carers as a priority, and the government produced their *National Strategy for Carers* (HM Government 1999). The *National Strategy* requires service providers to see carers as partners in the provision of help to the person needing care. The way to make services more responsive, it advocates, is for the statutory services to work together, involving carers, carers' organizations and service users. The strategy also recommends the establishment of carers' centres and other sources of support, including training, practical support, respite and advocacy. In recognition of the enormous role that carers play in providing care to the population, the strategy estimated that replacement of this care would cost in the region of £57 billion per year.

To help facilitate these services, as part of the *National Strategy for Carers*, a carers' grant was introduced in 1999/2000 for a three-year period, now extended for a further two years (DoH 2002a), to provide ring-fenced money to local authorities to give carers access to more flexible breaks from their caring role. In addition, the Carers and Disabled Children's Act 2000 has extended the right of carers to an assessment from the original criteria contained in the Carers Recognition and Services Act 1995. The 2000 Act recognized that carers may need services of their own, and that there may be times when, even if the person being cared for refuses services, social services could help the carer financially or practically. It also empowered local authorities to provide direct payments to carers to assist them with purchasing the services they need.

This Act, together with the introduction of national service frameworks (NSFs) (DoH 1999, 2001), gives carers the right to more say and more knowledge about the person they care for than ever before. The NSFs recognize that conflicts may arise with service users and respect their continued rights to confidentiality. However, the NSF suggests that information about diagnosis, medication, prognosis, side effects and care arrangements should be shared with carers, unless users, who should be consulted, insist that this information is withheld.

In my experience of working with carers, some care providers are either unaware of these new rights or prefer to do as they have always done – protect themselves from conflict under the cloak of 'confidentiality'. This experience is reflected in the findings of a survey of 3800 carers undertaken by the Princess Royal Trust (Keely and Clark 2002). The survey found three out of ten carers had insufficient information about the services provided to the person they cared for. More than half said they had insufficient information about medication side effects and six out of ten did not have the necessary advice about the actual caring tasks they had to perform, such as lifting and moving their relative or applying medical procedures.

Nevertheless, perhaps the biggest change for carers from all this new legislation has come in the area of mental health, where the NSF standard 6 (DoH 1999) devotes a whole standard to the needs of carers – for many carers, progress and recognition at last. This standard acknowledges that the needs of carers of people with severe and enduring mental health problems have been neglected over many years. Special guidance has been made available by the Department of Health (2002b) to assist local mental health services to improve their services to the carers and families of people with mental health problems. It requires that these carers should be offered an assessment and that where needs are identified, a care plan should be put in place to meet them. It provides guidance to GPs and primary care groups on supporting carers and promotes the development of local support networks.

Sharing information – effective collaboration

Jewish Care provides social work, residential, day and community services to people with mental health problems. Regular feedback sessions with users and carers found that although most service users expressed satisfaction with services, the relatives of mental health clients felt quite marginalized. The carers' service has therefore been working with the mental health service to improve the services to carers and the case study below is an example of how this has been achieved.

Michael, who is now aged 50, was diagnosed with schizophrenia at the age of 18. His parents had come to this country as refugees and attributed his first episode to a bad experience on a school trip to the continent. Over the years, he had been abusive to his mother Ruth, and she in turn gets very angry with him and extremely angry with the system. Her complaints about the system are because she cannot understand why, as his mother, who cooks, cleans and launders for him, she is not consulted about his medication or about the care he receives.

Our service became involved with Ruth at the time that Michael was last compulsorily admitted to hospital when he had become very violent towards a member of staff at a day centre and had been refused the service. When Michael was due to be discharged, a carers' assessment was done and shared with all those services that we were aware were involved in Michael's care.

Until that time, Ruth had intermittently been involved with her own social worker as she is now quite elderly and has difficulty walking, dressing and cleaning her home. It became apparent that Ruth was probably in the early stages of dementia; her confusion and anxiety had led to her contacting anyone and everyone that she had ever had contact with, and not being clear who could provide what for her.

Michael was suffering from severe and enduring mental health problems so he was subject to the care programme approach (CPA) (DoH 1990a and see Chapters 3 and 8).

When Michael was discharged from hospital the CPA had to take note of standard 6 of the NSF explained above. A care package was set up for Michael and an advocate was appointed for Ruth to represent her at reviews.

Due to funding cuts, the advocate was removed a year later, and Ruth started calling everyone she had ever been in contact with all over again.

Ruth attended a carers' group and the facilitator of the group was very concerned that Ruth may be at risk from her son, and nothing was being done. An investigation into the services involved – voluntary and statutory – highlighted that there were 14 individuals or services involved in the one case:

- client – Michael

- carer – Ruth

- GP

- psychiatrist

- psychotherapist

- day-centre key worker

- drop-in centre manager

- care manager

- voluntary sector mental health manager (looking at permanent care)

- home carer

- carers' service manager

- facilitator of carers' group

- social worker for Ruth

- advocate for Ruth.

Most were unaware of the others. A multi-disciplinary meeting was set up, and two main contacts were established:

- Michael's care manager was the contact for Michael and a point of reference about his care for Ruth. The care manager also took responsibility of co-ordinating the home-care package for both Michael and Ruth.

- The carers' service advice worker acted as advocate for Ruth at CPA and other meetings, and continued to support and help her through the maze of services working with her son and herself.

A further carers' assessment was done and this formed the basis of the advocacy work to ensure that the package of care continued to reflect both Ruth and Michael's needs. The two main contacts met regularly and ensured that all information was communicated to everyone involved, with the permission of both Ruth and Michael.

Multi-disciplinary working

The *Carers' Compass for Primary Care* introduced by the King's Fund (2000), which now forms the basis of quality standards for all of those working with carers, puts a primary emphasis on information. This sharing of information can only work if all involved are treated as equal partners and recognize the contribution of each party.

This is especially important when working in the field of dementia. Carers hold the key to past knowledge of the client, but the strain of looking after a relative who no longer resembles the person of the past can be huge.

The Dementia Relief Trust and the Alzheimers' Society recognize these stresses and employ specialist workers called Admiral Nurses (Dementia Relief Trust 2002) to advise and advocate for carers. Social care workers and health providers must work closely with such specialist services to ensure that the carer is well supported. This can only benefit a confused person who will do better with continuity of care at home rather than an early entry into residential care.

The *National Strategy for Carers* (HM Government 1999) emphasizes the importance of providing appropriate respite care. The carers' survey (Keely and Clark 2002) found that two-thirds of carers wanted help with respite care. One-third of these wanted a sitting service. Yet in my experience there is little respite at home for clients with dementia, and many carers are reluctant to disturb their loved one's routine for fear of returning from a well-earned break to a more confused, more agitated relative.

In the case of Betty, the carer of her husband with quite advanced vascular dementia, the referral by her social worker to the local Admiral Nursing Service was the answer to her prayers. Betty had cared for her husband for many years and, while she knew he had memory problems, had not really gained enough information about his illness or prognosis to enable her to cope.

The social worker recognized that, without support, Betty was fast becoming a client in her own right, suffering from panic attacks and very tearful. The Admiral Nurse, a specialist in dementia care, visited Betty on a regular basis, explaining the illness and how to deal with her husband's challenging behaviour. She also provided Betty with one-to-one counselling and explored with her the sense of 'loss' of her husband after over 60 years together, and the fears of 'letting go' for either respite or full-time residential care.

At this stage, it was clear that Betty would not feel comfortable with her husband in residential care, not even for a short break. A local sitting service was called in twice a week to give Betty a day-time break to attend a carers' group, go out to the hairdresser, and do her shopping.

Gradually Betty's husband was encouraged to attend a special day-care centre and, long after his needs became greater than could normally be met by the centre, he continued to attend five days a week, to enable his wife to cope with him when he was at home.

At a stress management group run by the carers' service, Betty opened up that she no longer slept at night, as her husband woke her constantly. She is not alone. The carers' survey (Keely and Clark 2002) found that eight out of ten carers said that caring had had a negative impact on their own health. Almost nine out of ten reported stress, anxiety, depression or loss of sleep. The social worker, in discussion with the Admiral Nurse, arranged for a waking night service to attend to him twice a week so that Betty could sleep in another room.

As time went on Betty and her husband got used to changes in their routines, and he went for regular respite at a local residential home. Eventually, he went into care, but his wife continued to be supported and counselled by the Admiral Nurse, ensuring continuity of care for her once the social work task had been completed. This close relationship helped her through the very difficult transition period that many spouses experience when their partner has to move into care. Because Betty had been ensured an outlet for her feelings of loss and grief, her husband settled into the home more smoothly. Betty knew what to expect and also knew that she would always have someone who would answer her questions as well as listen to her concerns.

Throughout all this time the Admiral Nurse and social worker met regularly to discuss the package of care for Betty's husband that would best meet both of their needs. When appropriate, they included the home-care provider and the manager at his special day-care unit. Thus there was regular communication and effective collaboration between all the services and the carer. In this way Betty was able to care for her husband for as long as was humanly possible.

Collaborative working – creating flexible services

The *National Strategy for Carers* (HM Government 1999) recognizes that respite care provided in a manner that meets the needs of both carer and client will enable them to pursue as normal a lifestyle as the disability of the client will allow. However, the Princess Royal Trust for Carers, in their review of services (Warner and Wexler 1998, p.19), note that, 'as both social workers and GPs are client/patient focussed, the needs of older carers are… more likely to be addressed'.

This is best illustrated when client and carers cross age and service boundaries, and where there are still no mainstream services that will really meet the needs of the client and their carer and enable them to have some sort of normal relationship and lifestyle.

Sarah was referred to our carers' service out of desperation. Her health needs were evidently stress-related. Her husband had a rare neurological illness which meant that the degeneration in his physical movement was quite rapid. They had two children under five, and while there was respite available for him to enable her to take a break from caring, there appeared to be nothing available that would allow them to spend time alone without the children.

Because he was unable to work, the family savings were dwindling quickly and therefore Sarah was reluctant to engage a babysitter. Both sets of grandparents lived in other areas of the country, and the only break that they had shared together had entailed Sarah taking the children 300 miles to their grandparents before going back home to spend time with her husband.

What she was really looking for was one evening a week with her husband and without the children. However, services available were rigid and could not adapt to these particular needs because:

- the local sitting service could not oblige – they only provided sitting for children with disabilities to give the parents time off

- the local authority could not oblige

- children and family services could only provide money for sitting services if the children had disabilities or were 'at risk'

- adult disability services could only provide money for a sitting service for Sarah's husband so that she could have some time off.

The strength of the voluntary sector is that it reaches all parts of the voluntary and community services, and has contacts with local welfare groups that are part of synagogue, church, mosque, temple or other specialist communities. In this case, a telephone call to Sarah's local synagogue welfare group helped us engage a group of teenagers who are obliged to do community service as part of their sixth-form work. A rota of babysitters was set up so Sarah and her husband were able to have their night off together.

Sarah also meets regularly with a support worker from the carers' service to explore all the issues of being a young mother and wife who carries the burden of so many caring roles but few of the pleasures. This service is open to her on an ongoing basis, whereas statutory health services could only provide her with four to six sessions which, for someone in an ever-changing role, can often be more frustrating than helpful.

Service providers need to look more creatively at crossing boundaries. Despite Sarah having had a local authority carers' assessment, her needs were not met in the statutory sector because of boundaries created by budgets. The carers' grant was supposed to break down these boundaries but the mindset of local service providers found this a difficult concept. From the experience of our carers' service the single assessment process (DoH 2002c) should produce outcomes that create packages of care that are holistic and inventive – combining the resources of health, social services and the voluntary sector. However, the carers' survey (Keely and Clark 2002) found that many carers are still not even receiving assessments of their needs and, of those that are offered assessments, only half said that the assessment led to improvements in the services provided. The researchers calculated that only 14 per cent of carers receive an assessment that actually makes a difference to the services they receive.

In the case study described above, a joint health and social services assessment of all the family – children and parents – would have shown a need for the family to do what other families do, and should have funds to enable the sitting to happen. When the sixth formers move on a new set of helpers will need to be identified. If funds could be allocated out of social service budgets directly to Sarah she could use the money effectively to give her the breaks she and her family need from one another.

This case study shows how rigidity in service provision runs the risk of four clients being created in this family as the strains of looking after husband and children take their toll. It must be more cost-effective to pay for a babysitter. In the words of the Princess Royal Trust for Carers (Warner and

Wexler 1998) it is 'more effective and cheaper to identify carers' needs and provide support...rather than to implement emergency measures' later (p.19).

Advocating and negotiating – accessing services for carers

By 2001, an identified need to support those who were caring for someone with an addiction was slowly emerging within our service. Since that time other carers' centres have identified a similar need as drug and alcohol problems escalate throughout the country. The needs of carers in such a situation are extremely complex.

Those with the addiction are very often not service users. They may not accept that they are in need of help, and the nature of the addiction will not allow them to acknowledge the role that family or friends are playing in their care. It was intended that this service would work in groups, breaking down barriers of shame and stigma, and for many carers this was the first step in admitting that there may even be a problem.

The development of the service has been to provide one-to-one support to carers that will encourage them to set realistic boundaries between themselves and the person they care for, especially with respect to finance. In addition, by helping families open lines of communication between carer and addict, and carer and other family members, there has, in some cases, been an opportunity for carers to discuss their fears with the addict and the options for rehabilitation.

The service has made links with statutory and voluntary sector organizations that work in the addiction field, and is able to advise carers about the system, but also advocate on their behalf with regard to funding and placement. In situations like this, where carers are excluded from making contact with a service provider, their isolation becomes exacerbated. This, in turn, does not help the client with an addiction as there is no-one close to them that can advise or help them through that first step of making the decision to seek help.

The emotional and financial toll on carers in this sphere is unimaginable. I met John after he had seen some publicity about the introduction of the new service. His wife died suddenly when their daughter was 14, leaving him as her sole carer.

Prior to his wife's death the parents had been contacted by their daughter's school about truanting and behavioural problems. Eventually the school expelled her and with three further expulsions she left school without any qualifications. She did hold down a job for a year but walked out one day when she was asked to make a cup of tea for a client. At this point, John, who has two other children from a previous marriage, believed that her behaviour was 'teenage hormones' and later put it down to the loss of her mother. In his words, what does a man of his generation know about drugs?

With failing health, exacerbated by the stresses of caring for his daughter single-handedly, he asked for rehousing when a further heart operation left him with a leg amputation. His daughter chose to stay in the house and at the age of 20 turned what had once been the family home into a 'crack house'.

John has never closed his door to his daughter. Since her home was last raided she has effectively moved in with him, but often goes missing for three or four days, returning agitated or high when her money has run out.

The service offered to John allows him to offload all his concerns for his daughter and her behaviour. He is well aware of how she funds her habit, and often voices concerns about her safety as well as his own. Having somewhere to talk these things through allows John an opportunity to reflect, which in turn allows him to speak more calmly to his daughter about his concerns, rather than enter into an argument.

For our part we have managed to highlight these concerns to John's GP and have asked him to liaise with his daughter's GP so that, should she wish to access rehabilitation services, these could be more readily available. The GP has, reluctantly, been persuaded to do this, but needs constant reminders that his client's health needs are related to the situation at home. The GP, nevertheless, does not discuss the situation with John, and therefore the two of them enter into a game, ignoring the main source of his failing health.

We have also advocated on the family's behalf when John's daughter was looking for emergency detoxification. Once we had provided as much information to John about services that were available in his area, and how the system worked, he was able to convince his daughter to give it a try. The rehabilitation centre, while unreceptive to accepting calls from John on the grounds of confidentiality, provided a place almost immediately when we explained our fears for his safety.

Only by directly observing the chaos that an addict can create in a family home can anyone truly understand how vital it is to listen to the addict's family members. The emotional, psychological and in turn physical harm that an addict's behaviour creates cannot be emphasized enough. Because of the anti-social nature of the addict's behaviour, there is a danger of social exclusion for both the addict and the family unless advocacy, negotiation and support are offered to enable access to relevant services.

Conclusion – lifting the confusion

The work with families such as John and his daughter has highlighted to our carers' service that person-centred care can only work within the context of that person and those who are close to him/her.

I began this chapter stressing the need for information for carers. The other side of this coin is that carers hold the information that is vital for services to provide the best possible care for an individual. Care-planning documentation can be very task-focused, and will not tell the whole story. Busy care professionals need to be sure that they do not look at their clients in a vacuum. It is absolutely vital that carers are encouraged to contribute to the care plan both at the stage of providing history and background and then on a regular basis at reviews. Those who provide the majority of care are normally families and friends, and therefore cannot be ignored. After all, we are now told (Carers UK 2001) that one in two of us will, at some stage, be a carer ourselves.

Guidance on good practice

Strategic recommendations

- Agencies should collaborate to develop a carers' information strategy.

- More training in awareness of carers' needs should be provided to staff in relevant agencies.

- There should be a publicity campaign to promote carer assessments together with ring-fenced funds to provide the services identified by the assessment.

- A joint strategy should be developed in each local area between all relevant agencies to provide flexible respite and breaks for carers.

Good practice recommendations for social workers

- While respecting the service user's views on confidentiality, encourage the carer to tell you as much as possible about the client and his/her needs.

- Ensure that the information provided by carers is included in the care plan and that carers regularly contribute to and endorse the care plan and review documentation.

- While respecting the service user's views on confidentiality, share as much information about the client as you can with the carer.

- Make sure you have the details of all the different services and individuals involved with the service user.

- Make sure that everyone involved is brought together with the service user and carer to agree a system for information sharing.

- Don't exclude the carer from the interprofessional team.

- Ensure that carers are offered their own multi-disciplinary assessment and needs-led care plan.

- Be creative – don't get stuck with mainstream services if they do not meet identified needs; use the voluntary sector and informal networks to meet individual needs.

- When assessing a person who is part of a family, ensure the care plan takes into account family relationships and lifestyle.

- Sometimes you will have to advocate or negotiate on behalf of service users and carers to ensure that other agencies become involved where necessary. (This is particularly true of service users who are vulnerable to social exclusion because of their condition or behaviour.)

References

Carers and Disabled Children's Act (2000) London: Stationery Office.

Carers Recognition and Services Act (1995) London: Stationery Office.

Carers UK (2001) *It Could Be You*. Available from Carers UK, 20–25 Glass House Yard, London EC1A 4JT.

Dementia Relief Trust (2002) *What is an Admiral Nurse?* (6 December 2002) Dementia Relief Trust website: http://www.dementiarelief.org.uk/admiralnurse.htm.

DoH (1990a) *The Care Programme Approach for People with a Mental Illness Referred to the Specialist Psychiatric Services*. HC 23 LASSL. London: Department of Health.

DoH (1990b) *The National Health Service and Community Care Act.* Cm 19. London: HMSO.

DoH (1998) *Modernising Social Services: Promoting Independence, Improving Protection, Raising Standards.* London: Department of Health.

DoH (1999) *National Service Framework for Mental Health.* London: Department of Health.

DoH (2001) *The National Service Framework for Older People.* London: Department of Health.

DoH (2002a) *Carers Grant 2002/3.* DoH website (6 December 2002): www.doh.gov.uk/carers/grantguidance.0203.pdf.

DoH (2002b) *Developing Services for Carers and Families of People with Mental Illness.* DoH website (6 December 2002): www.doh.gov.uk/mental health/devservcarers.htm.

DoH (2002c) *The Single Assessment Process: Guidance for Local Implementation.* London: Department of Health.

Hadley, R. and Clough, R. (1995) *Care in Chaos: Frustration and Challenge in Community Care.* London: Cassell.

HM Government (1999) *Caring About Carers, A National Strategy for Carers.* London: Stationery Office.

Holzhausen, E. (1997) *Still Battling? The Carers' Act One Year On.* London: Carers' National Association.

Jordan, B. with Jordan, C. (2000) *Social Work and the Third Way.* London: Sage.

Keely, B. and Clark, M. (2002) *Barclays Carers Speak Out Project.* London: Princess Royal Trust for Carers.

King's Fund Carers' Impact Team (2000) *The Carers' Compass for Primary Care.* London: King's Fund.

Mooney, A., Statham, J. and Simon, A. (2002) *The Pivot Generation: Informal Care and Work After 50.* London: Policy Press.

Office for National Statistics (2002) *Carers 2000, General Household Survey.* London: Stationery Office.

Rao, N. (1996) *Towards Welfare Pluralism.* Dartmouth: Dartmouth Publishing Company.

Warner, L. and Wexler, S. (1998) *Eight Hours a Day and Taken for Granted.* London: Princess Royal Trust for Carers.

Chapter 7

Working Together to Improve Children's Life Chances: The Challenge of Inter-agency Collaboration

Ruth Gardner

Introduction

This chapter presents an overview of evidence drawn from recent research and practice on collaboration, with particular relevance to services for children and families. First of all I discuss levels and models of joint work, differentiating between strategic and operational collaboration with a particular focus on the involvement of service users. I then move on to consider the policy context for collaboration, and how this has been implemented through a range of specialist projects, programmes, infrastructure developments, and an important emphasis on empowering families. I conclude with an analysis of a number of research studies in terms of the costs and benefits of 'joining services up' for children and families. These provide pointers to some key issues for further research and practice development. The chapter draws on literature from the USA and the UK as well as from original research that I have undertaken.

Levels and models of joint working

Collaboration – literally 'working together' – takes a number of forms, from planned communication, through co-operation between agencies, to joint planning, financing and service delivery. The terms are often used interchangeably, and some examples are given here in order to clarify their use in this chapter. An example of planned communication might be the production of resource manuals, to inform the public and other agencies of new services and their referral processes. (Consultation with users reveals such information to be inadequately provided in many areas.) An example of co-operation might be joint production of inter-agency guidelines or a case review, requiring separate agencies to appoint officers to work together and provide data to an agreed format. Collaboration in public services implies much more, the ability of diverse individuals to agree, plan, resource and accomplish a medium- or long-term goal on behalf of their agencies and service users – no mean feat.

Graphic representations of 'ladders' indicating the strength of key relationships are reproduced in Figures 7.1 and 7.2. They offer definitions of the various possible levels or degrees of both joint working and involvement of service users, as explained below:

- **Communication**, the planning relationship at the top of the diagram, is confined to agencies telling one another what they intend to do.

- **Consultation**, the planning relationship represented by a solid joining line, involves activities where an agency asks another for opinion, information or advice before finalizing a plan.

- **Collaboration** in this representation involves a degree of joint working on plans, mutual adjustment and agreement on the extent and limits of each other's activities, but operationally the agencies provide services independently.

- **Bilateral planning** implies an overlap in service provision so that although each agency will retain its own plan, there will be operational interaction arising out of common planning.

- **Joint planning** is a seamless integrated process.

(Extracted and adapted from *Children's Services Plans* [SSI 1996])

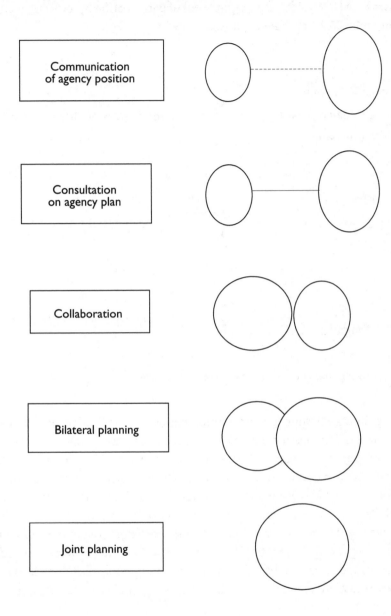

Figure 7.1 Levels of co-operation in planning (adapted from SSI 1996, p.24)

Arnstein (1969) identified eight levels of participation by 'citizens' recreated in Figure 7.2 (reproduced in Kahan 1989, p.215).

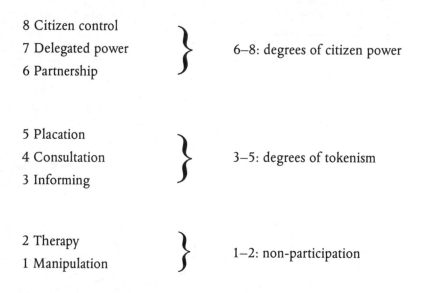

8 Citizen control
7 Delegated power   }   6–8: degrees of citizen power
6 Partnership

5 Placation
4 Consultation   }   3–5: degrees of tokenism
3 Informing

2 Therapy   }   1–2: non-participation
1 Manipulation

Figure 7.2 Ladder of citizen involvement in service provision

We should question any assumption implicit in the 'ladder' that degrees of collaboration form a hierarchy, or that any one type or form of joint working – for example, locating different providers together – is necessarily better or more highly developed than another. The evidence suggests that different forms of collaboration apply to different situations and that there are key skills in joint work, whatever the model (Barr 1998). These include the capacity to negotiate 'win-win' outcomes; to maintain a focus on joint rather than separate goals; to 'translate' across organizational cultures and vocabularies; and to ensure that, in a child-care setting, tools such as referral forms, assessment frameworks and child protection policies are functional and compatible.

The literature and research presented in this chapter propose that, in spite of acknowledged problems, joint working does have the potential to provide positive outcomes in services for children and families. Among the suggested benefits are:

WORKING TOGETHER TO IMPROVE CHILDREN'S LIFE CHANCES: ...   141

- a more integrated, timely and coherent response to complex human problems

- fewer unnecessary contacts and processes for service users to cope with

- more efficient transfer of information

- cost efficiency

- some reduction of unnecessary risk.

However, the costs and difficulties inherent in joint working also need to be better acknowledged and understood. For instance, injunctions to work collaboratively, without clear understanding of and commitment to the benefits of so doing, may be counterproductive. Guides and procedures on joint working, if imposed, may undermine the relationships on which collaboration is based and may thus increase perceived or actual risk (see discussion about child protection in Chapter 3 of this collection and in Lupton *et al.* 1999).

Distinguishing between strategic and operational collaboration

Descriptions of strategic arrangements needed for the joint provision of services are found more in the literature from the USA than from the UK. Walter and Petr (2000) offer a 'continuum of service integration' similar to the Social Services Inspectorate (SSI 1996) 'ladder' reproduced above. Co-operation is seen as a voluntary exercise, whereas co-ordination involves more formal exchanges. Collaboration means even greater shared accountability, structures and resources as integration breaks down boundaries.

Anderson (2000) describes the creation of jointly funded services to support children with emotional and behavioural disabilities and their families in Indiana, USA. He distinguishes between the strategic and the operational alliances. At a *strategic* level the necessary steps include:

- agreement about the philosophy of care

- using regional (meta) systems to provide vision

- needs assessment

- multiple evaluation. (Anderson 2000, p.486)

Anderson describes the formation of a strategic consortium between representatives of those services dealing with children with challenging

behaviour – including mental health, special education, children and families, and juvenile courts. The consortium hired a co-ordinator and decided
on a mission statement, set of values and eligibility criteria. A service
co-ordinator was allocated to each family accepted for a service and brought
together a service team including family members and informal as well as
formal supporters. Necessary *operational* stages in such a development were:

- resolving issues in advance and recording designated agency
  responsibilities, the location, timing and content of programmes,
  and financial responsibility

- identifying a target population

- co-ordinating a network of services. (Anderson 2000, p.491)

In a rare analysis of the benefits and costs of strategic collaboration in public
services in Britain, Huxham (1993, p.22) proposes the idea of 'collaborative
advantage'. This she describes as the achievement of:

> something unusually creative…perhaps…an objective…that no organi-
> sation could have produced on its own; [and] each organisation, through
> the collaboration, is able to achieve its own objectives better than it could
> alone. (Huxham 1993, p.22)

Huxham argues that public services have always collaborated on some scale
to achieve their ends: '…the distinctive task of management in any public
organisation is getting things done through other organisations' (p.22).
Huxham explains that each organization weighs the 'pitfalls of individual-
ism' – which may include repetition (or duplication) of services, omission,
divergence and counterproduction of actions – against the 'pitfalls of collaboration', including loss of control, flexibility, (undivided) glory and some
direct costs (p.22). This thesis acknowledges the psychological costs of
working across the more easily understood and supportive boundaries of
team and organization. While agencies continue to have large numbers of
discrete goals and targets, they want at least to see their efforts and expenditure on joint ventures achieve some of these aims. Where joint ventures are
not obviously successful in these terms, agencies tend to be deterred from
further experiment.

Collaboration with service users

Consultation with service users suggests, as one might expect, that for them the degree or nature of joint working matters less than the end result; they want to receive well-informed, responsive but not over-intrusive assistance when and where needed (Braye 2000; see also Chapters 3 and 4). Collaboration offers the possibility of an improved *process* for children and families. This could mean faster access to services, reaching more families and reducing the stigma of seeking or receiving support through more efficient and less intrusive referral procedures.

It is unclear what degree of joint working is necessary to achieve these process improvements; they could be achieved without necessarily co-working or co-locating services. 'One-stop shops' – offices where a number of services have co-located their reception points to ease access – are an example that has not yet been fully evaluated. We do not have evidence of improved *outcomes* for families over time as a result of such developments.

The inter-dependence of the two activities – *consultation* as a basis for the greater involvement of service users and *joint work* between agencies – is insufficiently recognized. Sound consultation relies on synthesizing data from a number of sources (for instance, needs analysis and opinion surveys), while collaboration (at both policy and practice levels) builds on a keen awareness of service users' (including children's) views as one means of establishing joint priorities. Later in this chapter we look at examples of the two practices and argue that each reinforces the other.

Walter and Petr suggest that family-centred values are the glue that holds a service integration effort together, such values being central to all other dimensions of collaboration such as shared aims, tasks and evaluation (and presumably shared outputs or outcomes). They identify the family as the key child-care resource, focusing on family strengths and ensuring maximum involvement, choice and cultural sensitivity. This, they say, avoids 'a common pitfall promoting inter-agency collaboration...that the professional agency network is placed at the centre of the helping system' (Walter and Petr 2000, p.497). When the needs of the family, the main purpose for collaboration, are not kept centre stage, this can lead to an emphasis on the inter-organizational process rather than outcomes for the family. Walter and Petr identify the following agency tendencies as counterproductive:

- a tendency to collude in seeing families as 'toxic' and to rely on interventionist approaches

- a tendency to reduce choice to meet providers' interests rather than services users' interests. (Walter and Petr 2000, p.498)

We can add:

- a tendency not to share their understanding of their duties and responsibilities with families which impedes essential communication.

Walter and Petr acknowledge that a family-centred approach is not without controversy and risk, in that such an approach may tend to 'reverse a common historical trend across service systems that focus on the individual child, rather than the child's family, as the primary unit of attention' (Walter and Petr 2000, p.498). There is a potential problem here in those cases where a child, or indeed any individual family member, suffers from abuse of power within the family. If responsibility for challenging such abuse is not clearly acknowledged and located, service providers may, by omission, collude. Where a constructive partnership is not possible between the professionals and the parents, the need to protect a child must be of paramount concern for the professionals.

Clear guidelines providing an inter-agency framework for addressing such risks within an agreed set of principles are not enough. It is essential for community providers not only to have agreed guidelines, but to be committed to their use and to regular joint training and informal discussion (Charles and Hendry 2000). The more accessible and informal services are, the more likely they are to have to deal with crises and emergencies where all the circumstances are not known and where decisions may have to be taken on imperfect data. (For more on child protection, see Chapter 3.)

The policy context of collaboration

The present UK government sees collaboration as essential to policy success in almost every sphere from local to international, and certainly in welfare services. The Children Act 1989 laid the foundations for joint working which led to a range of locally commissioned services for children, from family centres to therapeutic services.

The powers set out in Section 27 to call on the co-operation of education, health and housing authorities were qualified and less effective (SSI

1999). However, the recent Health Act 1999, by permitting funds to be pooled, seems to have given more specific and workable guidance for different agencies to collaborate effectively (see Chapter 1 and evaluation cited below). Guidance on producing children's plans (DoH 2002b) proposed an even more integrated approach whereby a single plan will meet the Part 3 requirements of the Children Act 1989, the expectation of inter-agency work for Quality Protects and the joint investment plans for health and social care.

Following the 1997 election, the then Minister of Health proposed that a 'joined up' strategy would deliver benefits such as a more unified service, cost-effectiveness and a faster response for preventing family breakdown. In his words:

> ...one major thrust of this government is to recognise that early interventions are not only the most effective in terms of enhancing people's lives and opportunities, but also the most cost-effective... There is, therefore, to be much closer liaison between the various departmental responsibilities – health, social services, education, employment, juvenile justice and social security – in order to develop a coherent set of children's policies. (Boateng 1997, p.15)

These aims were to be achieved through new cross-cutting policy initiatives such as the Social Exclusion Unit (Social Exclusion Website 2002), the Children's Task Force (DoH 2002a) and the Children's Fund (Children and Young Person's Unit (CYPU) 2003). However, there seems to have been greater success in setting up specific programmes aimed at supporting children and families than in creating a shared understanding of what they are to achieve. A recent report of the Public Accounts Committee (2002) comments that, five years on, individual government departments still prefer to launch discrete initiatives whose funding they can control than to work cross-departmentally. The report concludes that civil servants need more skills in designing joint programmes, particularly joint financial arrangements. The possible prize for better joint working is seen as a wider spread of services and better value for money.

The assumptions here are that central government will have hands-on involvement in designing service programmes across agencies, and that 'wider impact' equates to 'greater effectiveness', and that programmes can reach whole 'groups in society' (rather than carefully selected sub-groups as at present).

Morgan (1995) argues from the American experience of federal and state programmes that different types of collaboration are effective in different circumstances. She describes four models: home and neighbourhood based; community-based 'one stop shops'; school-based delivery; and school-based comprehensive services. I give examples of the development of some of these programme types in the UK elsewhere in the chapter. Morgan (1995, p.1332) argues that such models may 'bring some needed order to a fragmented service system', but may equally 'overlap one another and add to, rather than solve the problem [of fragmentation]'.

She draws a helpful distinction between *policy* for collaboration and *programmes* for collaboration, and quotes criticisms that the programme approach prevents the development of true policy (Esterline 1976). This perspective can 'create gaps and overlaps…and is in part responsible for the large number of…funding sources, the turf battles, and the fragmentation among funded programmes' (Morgan 1995, p.1332).

While large-scale government funding (in the UK as in the USA) of collaborative programmes might suggest that *all* services to *all* families would be better provided in this way, the programmes (hitherto) have been confined to poor communities where the mainstream services are underfunded. The inference might be that providing targeted programmes to achieve selected high profile indicators in disadvantaged communities is seen as more cost-effective than attempting to bring mainstream services up to the same high standards.

Morgan argues that the best of mainstream (usually statutory in the UK) and small-scale (usually voluntary) provision could be brought together if an infrastructure agency independent of all funders and providers existed for every community. This would integrate consumer information and advice about all available services, as well as offering training, capacity building, community planning, evaluation and research, policy reports and assistance to employers. In her view, such agencies would act as mediating structures and make collaboration possible.

The next section discusses the effectiveness of some of the collaborative projects, many involving service users, that have been established with the aim of improving outcomes for vulnerable children and their families.

Examples of joint operational service provision

Early years projects

Describing ten popular and well-run multi-agency early years centres, Makins (1997, p.160) called for long-term evaluation of the 'costs and benefits' (including long-term savings on 'welfare benefits, child protection and the like') of 'combined centres that offer a range of linked services, including education for children under three, social services family support, community health services, therapy for children with special needs, and adult education and training'. Makins' review of the ten centres suggested that they could, among other things:

- meet young children's needs as a whole (including those of young children with a disability)

- give families support as and when they need it, minimizing labelling and stigma

- improve assessment of need

- promote quality educational opportunities for children from a very early age, involving parents. (Makins 1997, p.151)

Some centres had managed to combine specialist services for children who were particularly vulnerable, and Makins (1997, p.149) concludes that 'the comparatively low numbers of child protection cases and of children with extensive behaviour and learning difficulties in areas with well-established under fives centres, are suggestive [of the effectiveness of preventive projects]'. This work holds out hope of less intrusive work achieving positive outcomes for children potentially or actually at risk.

Sure Start, a major government initiative to provide family support in disadvantaged areas, is centrally funded and monitored in over 260 projects across England. Sure Start project managers work for local 'lead agencies', usually voluntary organizations, and are accountable to trustee boards composed of service-user and local agency representatives. Where local needs have been accurately appraised, the partnership should reflect them; but many other considerations influence the form of local arrangements. Over a dozen different area-based initiatives, grant regimes, local and national voluntary organizations may operate in one Sure Start location (DfES 2002, pp.24–5). Taking into account the relevant statutory agencies (local health trusts, schools, social services) this is potentially a massively complex co-ordination exercise in terms of public relations alone, even without joint planning and provision being agreed. The evaluation of Sure Start initiatives (Sure Start 2002) will, it is hoped, provide evidence of its effectiveness.

Sure Start is one of the few central initiatives that emphasizes family involvement, with most Sure Start schemes having parents helping to run them. Evaluation of other projects (Gardner 2002) indicates that if each agency maintains a focus on the family, co-ordination improves.

Education-based projects

Another model of collaboration is the establishment of inter-agency teams dealing with specific issues (for example, school absenteeism) that involve more than one agency. This kind of scheme provides a social worker to several schools, offering counselling, solution-focused work, advocacy and liaison between services to children on fixed-term exclusions. Benefits include clear criteria and measurement of outcomes, reduction in school exclusions, improved classroom behaviour and better inter-agency communication.

Another example of school-based preventive programmes are behaviour and education support teams (BESTs). These are multi-agency teams being piloted in a number of areas that work closely with defined groups of schools to support teachers and provide early intervention. They provide supportive services to pupils who have emotional and behavioural problems and involve and support their families. The overall aims are to improve attendance, achievement and social inclusion by offering direct services, appropriate referrals and whole school support on behaviour management. The development will require co-operation, collaboration and partnership between local education authorities (LEAs), social services departments, primary care trusts, youth offending agencies and voluntary sector providers. In the light of our discussion about the importance of the location of infrastructure it is of interest that LEAs are designated 'to implement an effective day to day management process for each team [including] clear methods of co-ordination and information-sharing' (Teachernet 2002, p.1).

Involving children and families in inter-agency projects

A recent national research study on family support provided by a UK voluntary organization found that collaboration at operational level and the involvement of families in the provision of child care can successfully challenge severe forms of isolation and social exclusion (Gardner 2002).

Family support projects whose neighbouring agencies rated their collaboration highly were those where service users, including children, also felt that they collaborated with the providers. This finding reinforces the need to include families in partnerships and indicates the following principles for best practice:

- clear and practised routes for formal and informal communication between families and workers and between agencies – including reflection on complaints or mistakes

- an emphasis on developing family members' proficiency, using skills training, education, volunteering, and strong advocacy for resources

- transparency and enforcement of codes of conduct for both staff and families while using the service

- support from within the agency and a level of trust in staff to engage in collaborative activity.

Examples of good joint working were the provision of support for children who have been abused – including links to school and therapy; working with police, housing and social services in cases of domestic abuse; and joint advocacy for better health and mental health services. Interviews with children and their parents undertaken as part of the research (Gardner 2002) identified that service users appreciated this connective work.

The lead organization here emphasized the child's centrality to its work in all these areas. Most children who were interviewed were aware of why and how they could make a complaint and how and when they could talk in confidence to project staff. Like their parents, they could choose a number of ways of being involved – for example, attending children's activities, helping with family events or group sessions, or receiving one-to-one counselling. The great majority of parents who were interviewed thought that this approach neither exploited nor undermined them, but was consistent with an emphasis on mutual respect and support, values that were also applied to inter-agency relationships.

An evaluation of the project undertaken as part of the research study (Gardner 2002) found evidence of apparent resolution of many children's behavioural problems and some parents' past victimization; children gaining confidence and self-esteem; and parents actively acquiring and applying parenting, practical and educational skills, often by co-working with staff and moving on to paid employment. Of particular relevance were findings that:

- informal support (from friends and family) appears to be associated with fewer problems and better outcomes

- family support can extend, or even temporarily replace, such networks

- skills and support are transmitted in both directions through the various levels of a partnership network.

For instance, professionals gain a better awareness of local needs and services and make earlier, more appropriate referrals, and service users provide peer support to parents through volunteer schemes. The study also found that collaboration initiated through a voluntary organization was effective on the whole except that one area, the health (including mental health) needs of parents, required more joint work. The study (Gardner 2002) found that parents' health and stress worsened over six months and that strong advocacy was needed to obtain any preventive health services in some areas. It is hoped that the proposed NSF for Children's Services to be published in 2003 will address this crucial issue (DoH 2002a).

Family group conferences and collaborative decisions

Another process that involves children and families as part of the interprofessional team is the family group conference (FGC). Family group conferences achieve inter-agency collaboration in child welfare, including child protection, through a clear child- and family-focused philosophy and an emphasis on competency rather than pathology. They differ in style from mainstream child protection conferences which are far more prescribed and procedural (Lupton *et al.* 1999).

FGCs are:

> meetings of extended family and relevant professionals, to consider the welfare of a child and to decide if possible on a suitable course of action. They are conducted in such a way that the family can engage in quite detailed negotiation both with professionals and among its own members. There is a new job of co-ordinator required to make sure that the Conference is conducted well. Preparation of all parties beforehand is

very important and the meeting itself comprises three main stages; the giving of information by professionals and family members, private family discussion and finally the development if possible of a plan agreed by all parties. (Marsh and Crow 1998, p.14)

In their evaluation, Marsh and Crow found that agencies other than social services (for example, education and health) are more frequently involved in FGC plans than in other planning forums. Where there had been an FGC, the great majority – between 60 and 80 per cent – of plans relating to child protection and children accommodated away from home were carried out – or, if the situation changed, the family found a satisfactory solution. In two-thirds of cases, social workers interviewed as part of the study thought that FGCs protected children better than other plans, and in the remaining third, equally well. This is an example of inter-agency work based firmly on partnership, and an expanding area of investment. Some local authorities now run hundreds of conferences with families each year, including children at risk of harm, young offenders and children excluded from school.

Examples of infrastructure developments

Funding

Work has started to ensure that funding for various inter-agency projects is co-ordinated. For example, within local planning areas, requests for services above a given cost or for joint funding have to be approved by joint service panels. This involves senior officers in education, child and adolescent mental health services and social services who will consider an assessment of local needs and a plan for service provision. The benefits of this approach are more consistent decision-making, a better understanding across agencies of inter-agency involvement, reduced duplication and more complete assessments.

Joint assessment

Consistent frameworks for child protection (see Chapter 3) and assessment of need have made inter-agency assessment teams a possibility in child care generally. (At the moment they are available for children with disabilities and children with mental health problems in some areas.) There is also the possibility of using computer packages to introduce integrated assessment tools that could be accessed by a number of relevant agencies as long as issues of data protection are addressed. Work on a computerized 'integrated children's system' is intended to improve the infrastructure for 'joined-up' working by providing:

- a framework for assessment, planning, intervention and review
- core data requirements for social services, which will set out the information essential for effective multi-agency practice
- exemplars which will demonstrate how information can be structured and used to generate particular reports (DoH 2002c).

Infrastructure support

The Integrated Care Network (ICN) is an English initiative set up by national and local government umbrella organizations. These include the Health and Social Care Change Agent Team and the National Primary Care Trust Development Programme (DoH 2002d). The aim is to provide 'an infrastructure of support to those wishing to progress integrated working between local authorities and the NHS' (Integrated Care Network 2002, p.1). Its services include meetings and learning sets, consultation, evaluation and a website, and it has the great advantage of being free. It remains to be seen whether its offer of voluntary membership will limit its coverage and it will not be able to substitute for adequately funded local infrastructures built on local knowledge.

Communication

Inter-agency collaboration can use a number of different structures to ensure good communications and family members' involvement. Swan and Morgan (1993), for instance, describe an inter-agency council guiding joint working in a number of different ways. This example comes from the USA where collaboration between services is mandatory. The council undertakes the tasks of the consortium in Anderson's (2000) model, but goes further, engaging in quality control. Examples are given of joint communications and information sharing, analysis of need and services, case management methods and inter-agency collaboration. The council can review cases and publicize learning, hold services accountable to their stated values and purposes and potentially survey or accredit agencies using a check-list of indicators. The inter-agency council, including service users, can also set priorities, hire staff and allocate funding. It is able to promote family-friendly employment and training practices that ensure front-line staff as well as service users are supported.

Findings from evaluations and research
Factors that assist joint working

As part of a project to improve joint working in an area of the UK, Huxham (1993) rated the collaborative capacity of the organizations involved. She concluded that the following elements assisted joint working:

- a joint, agreed 'meta-strategy' to provide a framework and address some of the identified pitfalls – a strategy that is in some respects superordinate to the strategies of the individual organizations

- allowing for differences between organizations in planning collaboration – the meta-strategy should be a broad statement of mission and high-level objectives, if possible capturing the existing objectives of organizations

- the process of dissemination within participating organizations must be attended to or those responsible for implementation will be unaware of the meta-strategy

- finally, the learning capacity of the contributing organizations – 'The more complex the issue...the greater the need of self reflection... Potential collaborators need to acknowledge their ignorance of what is involved'. (Huxham 1993, p.25)

Huxham (1993) found from her consultation work that the collaborative capacity of organizations is made up of dimensions such as:

- the existing culture of internal collaboration and trust

- permission to form creative alliances

- degree of organizational autonomy

- degree of individual autonomy

- cohesiveness of organizational structure

- development of strategic processes

- degree of elaboration of strategy statement
- degree to which collaboration is an issue.

She concluded that a clear organizational identity and staff confidence in the *internal* working practices of individual organizations assist work across boundaries. In other words, organizations need to do work on getting their own communications in order before they launch into more complex initiatives; but if joint work is a genuine aim, it can speed up internal learning.

Managers' expectations of collaboration

I used Huxham's findings as a framework for a survey of senior managers' expectations in a local authority area where an inter-agency family support service was to be set up. Managers in the health trust, education and social services and a voluntary organization were interviewed (Gardner 1995). The majority of them had real aspirations for 'collaborative advantage', citing their motives as their values, improved identification of need, quality of outputs and avoiding duplication rather than legal, political or financial motivation. All the managers interviewed thought that full service integration was achievable.

However, when asked to identify possible hurdles, they spoke of precipitate change, of needing more commitment from budget holders, of possible resentment, and of risk. Financial arrangements and skills in joint working are two key areas to resolve. Other key issues are a joint framework to address possible risk, and the need for consultancy and support for individuals to tackle the psychological barriers to collaboration. As we have noted, injunctions to work together, however authoritative, are just not enough.

After the survey, a local multi-disciplinary team was set up and, despite having to tackle many problems, it created innovative joint practice that has lasted as part of both local and more recent central government initiatives.

How systems and climates within organizations affect outcomes for children

All this evidence needs to be considered in the light of research which reinforces the earlier argument that systems and 'climates' *within* organizations affect outcomes for children at least as much as co-ordination *between* organizations. Co-ordinating systems have been found to affect outcomes adversely in some situations.

For example, Glisson and Hemmelgarn (1998) evaluated a pilot programme in the USA, along the lines of that described by Anderson (2000). The programme created new case management teams to co-ordinate services for children entering care and custody and 12 pilot counties were compared with 12 matched 'control' counties. The study attempted to describe the organizational aspects of effectiveness, both within and between agencies.

Their findings challenged the thesis, which they believe is founded on aspiration rather than hard evidence, that inter-organizational services co-ordination can improve effectiveness.

> This argument is based on the belief that the relatively low cost of improving service co-ordination...will ensure that each child receives the most appropriate service, regardless of which system has first contact with the child. It is assumed that more appropriate services will result in better outcomes. (Glisson and Hemmelgarn 1998, p.402)

Key findings were that improvements in children's psycho-social functioning (separately and independently rated) were significantly greater in offices with more positive working climates – *irrespective of the presence or absence of service co-ordination*:

> The success that case workers have in improving children's psycho-social functioning depends heavily on their consideration of each child's unique needs, the case worker's response to unexpected problems and their tenacity in navigating bureaucratic and judicial hurdles to achieve the best placement and the most needed services for each child... These findings suggest that agencies with higher levels of job satisfaction, fairness, role clarity, co-operation and personalization, and lower levels of role overload, conflict and emotional exhaustion are more likely to support case workers' efforts... Children who were served by agencies with more positive climates were more likely to experience improved psychosocial functioning... They also received more comprehensive services, there was more continuity...and their case workers were more responsive and available. (Glisson and Hemmelgarn 1998, p. 417)

In this study, increased service co-ordination appeared to lower effectiveness, by removing key aspects of case management from those responsible for individual outcomes:

> The objective of service co-ordination is to eliminate parallel, redundant competing service systems by centralising service decisions. This centralisation ironically can diffuse rather than focus responsibility for casework activities...by transferring key decisions to those who do not work directly with a child, personal responsibility for the child is reduced for those who do... While this may be effective in controlling services and costs as intended in managed care, it cannot be expected to improve service quality or outcomes. (Glisson and Hemmelgarn 1998, p. 417)

This study suggests that accountability is a key issue in new collaborative ventures. A recent evaluation of Section 31 of the Health Act 1999 suggests that the 'flexibilities' it has introduced may have helped with some of these thornier issues (Hudson *et al.* 2002, p.31). The legislation allows the NHS and local authorities to pool budgets, delegate commissioning and employ their staff in new organizations. Many of the challenges we have described have had to be addressed:

> legal agreements...had to be drawn up between the partner organizations setting out arrangements for governance, accountability, financial probity and risk management...[and] negotiated in a way that underpinned rather than displaced, the trust and commitment of the partners. (Hudson *et al.* 2002, p.31)

Where this was achieved there were some real benefits: a shift from a blame culture to a whole-system approach underpinned by shared visions and objectives; improvements in efficiency through cutting out duplication in commissioning; and improved funding leverage and staff morale through integrating services.

Conclusions

While the vision and rationale for joint work between specialist groups are powerful, there is as yet insufficient evidence to argue that greater collaboration between services will necessarily produce better outcomes for all children and families. This is particularly true since such collaboration is largely confined to specific operations or programmes of service delivery and not fully integrated as mainstream. While acknowledging that more rigorously evaluated service development is needed, I draw out below some key points indicated by the findings described in this chapter.

Current challenges for collaboration

- More evidence is needed of the outcomes of joint and single agency programmes with specific groups and larger populations.

- Collaboration is only as strong as the confidence, capacity and skills of the workforce to undertake it. Plans for inter-agency working are frequently undertaken when the agencies are in flux, and their workers unable to represent a coherent set of systems or policies to one another.

- Where collaboration is perceived as rushed, imposed or both, it can paradoxically become a barrier to trust and good communication. Collaboration is a medium- to long-term venture, not a 'quick fix'.

- Strategic collaboration, providing leadership and vision as well as the infrastructure that will sustain joint programmes and the capacity for learning, is the engine for joint service delivery; it requires earlier and more thorough consideration than has hitherto been the case.

- While special collaborative projects and programmes can be effective, they continue to marginalize deprived children and families rather than integrate them into mainstream provision.

Critical success factors for collaboration

- Commitment and leadership in each organization.

- Good communication *within* as well as between collaborating agencies.

- Consultation, training, planning and reflection time.

- An infrastructure to deliver these key elements of support.

Working collaboratively with children and families

- Preventive work with children and families, linking housing, education and health-care services, can lead to improved outcomes for children.

- Empowering families and helping to improve parenting skills is critical to the achievement of improved outcomes for children.

- Special programmes are more effective if children and families are consulted and involved in planning and service delivery.

- Developing trusting relationships with families assists providers in supporting children. However, the welfare and safety of the child is paramount and this may conflict at times with the interests of families.

- It is important to ensure that inter-agency policies and procedures support (and do not undermine) the individual relationship between the social worker and the family.

Findings such as those discussed in this chapter need wider dissemination. Critical debate and research on strategic and operational collaboration should be undertaken more widely and consistently in the UK. While there is some evidence to show that collaboration with children and families and between professionals can improve outcomes for children, the findings to date show consistency and indicate that inter-agency collaboration is not necessarily either labour or cost saving.

References

Anderson, J. (2000) 'The Need for Interagency Collaboration for Children with Emotional and Behavioural Disabilities and their Families.' *Families in Society: The Journal of Contemporary Human Services 81*, 5, 484–493.

Arnstein, S. (1969) 'A Ladder of Citizen Participation.' *Journal of the American Institute of Planners 35*, July, 4, 216–224.

Barr, H. (1998) 'Competent to Collaborate: Towards a Competency Based Model for Interprofessional Education.' *Journal of Interprofessional Care 12*, 2, 181–188.

Boateng, P. (1997) Ministerial speech reported in *Community Care*, September 1997, p.15.

Braye, S. (2000) 'Participation and Involvement in Social Care: An Overview.' In H. Kemshall and R. Littlechild (eds) *User Involvement and Participation in Social Care*. London: Jessica Kingsley Publishers.

Charles, M. and Hendry, E. (2000) *Training Together to Safeguard Children: Guidance on Inter-Agency Training*. London: NSPCC.

Children Act (1989) London: HMSO.

Children and Young Person's Unit (2003) The Children's Fund (consulted 16 January 2003): www.cypu.gov.uk/children'sfund/index/cfm.

DfES (2002) *Sure Start National Evaluation: Early Experiences of Implementing Sure Start.* London: Stationery Office.

DoH (2002a) Children's Services NSF. See information on proposed Children's Services NSF (consulted 16 January 2003) at www.doh.gov.uk/nsf/children.

DoH (2002b) Consultation on New Guidance on Children's Services Planning prepared in 2000 (consulted DoH website 16 January 2003) at www.doh.gov.uk/pdfs/cspconsultations.pdf.

DoH (2002c) Integrated children's systems (consulted DoH website 16 January 2003) at www.doh.gov.uk/integratedchildrenssystem.

DoH (2002d) National Primary Care Trust Development Programme: information can be found on DoH website (consulted 16 January 2003) at www.doh.gov.uk/pricare/teachingpcts/1.

Esterline, B. (1976) 'Coordination: A Conceptual Model and Practical Consideration.' Unpublished paper presented to the Education Commission, Boston, Mass.

Gardner, R. (1995) *Plan for Creating Multi-disciplinary Family Support Teams.* Unpublished dissertation for Chartered Institute of Public Finance and Accountancy.

Gardner, R. (2002) *Supporting Families: Child Protection in the Community.* Chichester: Wiley.

Glisson, C. and Hemmelgarn, A. (1998) 'The Effects of Organisational Climate and Inter Organisational Co-ordination on the Quality and Outcomes of Children's Services Systems.' *Child Abuse and Neglect 22,* 5, 402–421.

Health Act (1999) London: Stationery Office.

Hudson, B., Glendinning, C., Hardy, B. and Young, R. (2002) *National Evaluation of Notifications for Use of the Section 31 Flexibilities in the Health Act 1999.* Final Project Report. Manchester: University of Manchester and Nuffield Institute.

Huxham, C. (1993) 'Collaborative Capability: An Inter-organisational Perspective on Collaborative Advantage.' *Public Money and Management,* Autumn, 21–27.

Integrated Care Network (2002) *ICN Launch Programme.* London: Department of Health.

Kahan, B. (ed) (1989) *Child Care Research, Policy and Practice.* London: Hodder and Stoughton.

Lupton, C., Khan, P., North, N. and Lacey, D. (1999) *The Role of Health Professionals in the Child Protection Process.* Portsmouth Social Services Research and Information Unit, Report No. 41. Portsmouth: University of Portsmouth.

Makins, V. (1997) *Not Just a Nursery... Multi-agency Early Years Centres in Action.* London: National Children's Bureau.

Marsh, P. and Crow, G. (1998) *Family Group Conferences in Child Welfare.* Oxford: Blackwell Science.

Morgan, G. (1995) 'Collaborative Models of Service Integration.' *Child Welfare 74,* 1329–1341.

Public Accounts Committee (2002) *Twenty-eighth Report: Better Public Services Through Joint Working.* HC 471. London: Stationery Office.

Social Exclusion Unit (2002) Social Exclusion website (consulted 16 January 2003): www.socialexclusionunit.gov.uk.

SSI (1996) *Children's Services Plans.* London: Social Services Inspectorate.

SSI (1999) *Planning to Deliver.* London: Social Services Inspectorate.

Sure Start (2002) National Evaluation of Sure Start website (consulted 16 January 2003): www.ness.bbk.ac.uk.

Swan, W. and Morgan, J. (1993) *Collaborating for Comprehensive Services for Young Children and Their Families.* Baltimore, USA: Paul Brookes Publishing.

Teachernet (2002) Behaviour, Education and Support Teams (consulted 16 January 2003): www.teachernet.gov.uk.

Walter, U.M. and Petr, C.G. (2000) 'A Template for Family-centred Interagency Collaboration.' *Families in Society 81,* 5, 494–503.

Chapter 8

Mental Health Policies and Interprofessional Working

Tony Leiba

Introduction

Partnerships, collaboration, interprofessional, multi-professional and inter-agency are the words used in mental health documents emanating from the Conservative governments of 1979–1997 and the Labour governments since 1997. These words have become the keystone of current policies to modernize health and social services. Their meanings are aimed at the achievement of interprofessional working between health and social care professionals and the removal of boundaries between primary health care, secondary health care and social care, in order to provide a community-centred and user-led seamless service (DoH 1990a, 1997, 1998).

The concerns here will be to focus on aspects of the following policy documents: the National Health Service and Community Care Act (DoH 1990a); the *National Service Framework for Mental Health* (DoH 1999b); and the *NHS Plan* (DoH 2000a) in terms of the structure they provide for collaboration in mental health services. These documents and, in particular, the care programme approach (CPA) (DoH 1990b) will be scrutinized to ascertain what their suggestions are for interprofessional working between health and social care professionals, users and carers and how these are working in practice.

I will then move on to review some of the research about barriers to effective interprofessional collaboration from the perspectives of organizational and professional cultures, interaction between different mental health professionals, the experiences of service users and the problems that arise between agencies. This will be followed by a critical appraisal of proposed new mental health legislation, which, I will argue, is unpopular with both professionals and service users because its approach to collaboration is flawed. The chapter will conclude by recommending interprofessional education and training for mental health professionals as a crucial way forward for improving collaboration. In particular, diversity and conflict issues within the team will be addressed as examples of how practice could be improved.

A framework for collaboration in mental health

The *NHS Plan* (DoH 2000a) states that if users are to receive quality care, the old divisions between health and social care need to be overcome. The NHS Plan proposes: a new single assessment, not separate assessments by health and social service; improved local co-ordination between health and social services; the local pooling of health and social services' budgets; and the establishment of care trusts to bring together health and social services. The NHS Plan also requires that the relationship between health and social services is kept under review, because service users have the right to expect that local services are working as one care system not two. There are, however, demarcation disputes and problems which arise in part from fundamental differences of structure and culture between the organizations and professions involved.

The Health Act (1999) provides greater flexibility for health and local authorities to co-operate with each other and jointly plan care, make payments to each other and to create pooled budgets where this will improve services. In mental health, health and social services have responsibilities for aftercare duties under the Mental Health Act (1983), and the care programme approach requires collaboration between health, social care, users and carers (DoH 1990b).

The *National Service Framework (NSF) for Mental Health* (DoH 1999b) sets out seven national standards for working-age adults. The NSF asks for specialist services to work in partnership with the independent sector and agencies which provide housing, training and employment. The specialist services themselves, which include health and social care, should work together to ensure effective and timely interventions for individuals whose mental health needs cannot be met in primary care alone.

The guiding principles of the NSF expect that services will involve service users and carers in the planning and delivery of care and will be well co-ordinated between all staff and agencies. Standard 4 of the NSF states that all mental health service users must be cared for by the care programme approach. To achieve standard 4 therefore requires health and social care agencies to develop integrated systems for assessment, care planning, care delivery and review and to work in collaboration with users and carers.

Standard 6 states that all individuals who provide regular and substantial care for a person under the care programme approach should have an assessment of their caring activities, physical and mental health needs, and have their own care plan. Standard 7 states that local health and social care agencies should work together to prevent suicides by delivering accessible high quality local primary mental health care. The NSF offers opportunities to modernize the National Health Service and the social services, requiring these services to work in partnership to provide integrated services to users and carers.

Community care and the care programme approach

The concept of service-user involvement in the planning, delivery and evaluation of health and social care has been an essential part of health and social care service delivery since the NHS and Community Care Act (DoH 1990a) and *The Care Programme Approach for People with a Mental Illness Referred to the Specialist Psychiatric Services* (DoH 1990b).

The introduction of the care programme approach coincided with the NHS and Community Care Act (DoH 1990a) and a series of reports following inquiries which concentrated political attention on the failings of the mental health services (Blom-Cooper, Hally and Murphy 1995). As a result of concerns over failing policy and practice, health care and social care workers were challenged to develop new ways of working intra-professionally and interprofessionally with colleagues, users and carers.

The care programme approach proposes an integrated service delivery between health and social care, to minimize the distress and confusion sometimes experienced by people referred to the mental health system and their carers. It is an integrated approach to care co-ordination which provides for: a single point of referral; a key worker; a unified health and social care assessment process; co-ordination of respective roles and responsibilities of each agency in the mental health services; assessment through a single process and full participation and involvement of users and carers in the decisions about care and treatment (DoH 1999a).

Furthermore, mental health service users, particularly those with the most complex and enduring needs, may require help with other aspects of their lives – for example, housing, finance, employment, education and physical health needs. Mental illness places demands on services that no one profession or agency can meet alone. Therefore, a system of effective care co-ordination is necessary if all services are to work in harmony to benefit the service user.

These principles are relevant to the care and treatment of younger and older people with mental health problems. For example, the move from child and adolescent services to adult services must be managed sensitively and effectively; services should have protocols for meeting the needs of younger and older people moving from one service to another.

Structural difficulties in achieving the interprofessional promise of the CPA

Norman and Peck (1999) suggested that there are some key reasons why interprofessional working to deliver the care programme approach might prove difficult. These include attachment to uni-professional cultures through separate education, different entry qualifications, status and financial rewards (Vanclay 1997). Maintaining uni-professional cultures might be a way of staving off the possible threat of one professional assuming the roles of another. If this threat is felt, one response might be defensive activities to establish inflexible role demarcation. This may lead to working practices which are muddled, with unclear boundaries, resulting in unclear lines of accountability. For example, professional autonomy is strongest among psychiatrists and clinical psychologists, because they are more concerned than other professionals about being drawn into interprofessional teams as they see this as entailing a loss of professional status and power (Onyett and Ford 1996).

Onyett and Ford (1996) suggested that the absence of a shared ideology and philosophy about mental health, mental illness and community care points to disagreements between health and social care workers which cause tensions in joint working within community mental health teams. Tensions such as communication difficulties, conflict about leadership, team management and accountability function as inhibitors to effective care programme approach development (King's Fund 1997).

Mistrust of managerial solutions is fostered by the lack of managerial skills of some team managers. Most community mental health team managers are themselves former health or social care professionals or professional health and social care managers, and relatively few have had relevant interprofessional training (Norman and Peck 1999).

Managerial solutions are seen by managers as value free; of course they are not. Managers working in interprofessional settings must be able to balance managerial values with clinical values in decision-making. To achieve this balance in interprofessional working, there must be the practice of democratic principles in the relations between professionals, users and carers. In practice this means examining roles, responsibilities, accountability, power and ideology, in order to free up teams to develop more effective arrangements for working together (Peck 1991).

Some views on collaboration expressed by different health and social care professionals

Many social care practitioners remain sceptical about the possibility of successful collaboration with other professions and agencies. Peck and Norman (1999) researched interprofessional working to make the care programme approach a reality, through a series of facilitated group meetings which established interprofessional dialogue between the health and social care professionals in a community mental health team. The different professionals reported their perceptions of their own profession and of the other professions. Peck and Norman (1999) report that the information collected offers insights which help to explain why health and social care professionals working in interprofessional teams often experience problems in establishing and sustaining interprofessional collaboration.

They found that clinical psychologists perceived themselves as high status and free floating with considerable individual autonomy and they preferred to work in the spaces between other professionals. The other professions envied their relative autonomy and status but desired a greater commitment from the psychologists to teamwork.

Social workers felt there was a threat to social work culture and values, because the community mental health team was dominated by health workers. They also felt that professional support and supervision were crucial to ensuring a distinct social work contribution to the team. For example, the expectation of democratic decision-making within social work enables issues to be discussed rather than avoided. Furthermore, social services are a part of local government and social workers are accountable not just to their line manager but also to politicians, service users and carers. The other professionals appreciated that the social workers strive for the democratic values in social work to facilitate creative discussion to benefit services to users and carers. They shared the social workers' discomfort with the medical model and valued their critical perspective on mental health. While social workers were becoming interprofessional team players they argue that teams must be sensitive to the culture and objectives of social work, social services and local government.

The nurses saw themselves as close to the users and carers and taking the emotional strain associated with managing people's vulnerability, befriending and establishing therapeutic relationships with them. They felt they were highly valued by the public, but undervalued within the mental health context. The other professions felt that nurses have general and specialist skills, but that they do not emphasize these enough.

The psychiatrists saw themselves as performing a major containment function within the team. They did not feel able to exercise their power and authority in current mental health services and felt that they did not have enough influence over resources to take up the strong leadership role expected of them. Many psychiatrists did not accept that team membership means equality of status among members and democratic decision-making. The other professions felt that the psychiatrist should share power and not feel the need to carry everyone's emotional burden. They would also value the psychiatrist having a greater appreciation of the skills of other mental health professions and a greater awareness of wider mental health issues – for example, discrimination, poverty and social class.

The occupational therapists reported that they felt misunderstood and undervalued. They were positive about teamworking but were concerned that it could result in a distortion of their priorities and the best use of their skills. The other professions valued them as good team players and their contribution to user employment. However, colleagues from other professions suggested that they should let the team know more about their specialist role and be more assertive.

Peck and Norman (1999), by trying to reveal and clarify interprofessional roles through the engagement of the community mental health team, demonstrate that interprofessional working cannot be achieved solely through government and professional directives. The professionals themselves must work out how they see themselves and how the other professions see them and use this understanding to achieve closer working.

Service users' views on failures in collaboration

Wolfe *et al.* (1997) investigated the implementation of the care programme approach in an inner city London service. This research was done in 1997 and only one service was evaluated. The findings cannot be generalized and since 1997 many changes in services have taken place. Nevertheless there are some insights which can be gained. The study shows that although many users and carers were involved in care planning there appeared to be considerable difficulty in ensuring that adequate explanations are given to them. Users reported that approximately half of them were only aware of their key worker on the day of discharge. This is surely not indicative of effective care planning and discharge planning.

McDermott (1998) explored the views of one group of users about their experiences of the care programme approach in an outer London borough. The findings show that users did not understand what the care programme was about nor why they were placed on it. Although the majority of users said that they had received the relevant documentation, they reported that they did not understand the information contained in the documents. A third of the users said they did not know why they were prescribed their medicines and they did not know about the side effects. The majority of users said that they wanted their care programme meetings to take place outside of the hospital. Since the care programme approach was designed to enable user and carer involvement and participation, this study points to some of the areas which must be addressed to achieve effective collaboration between users, carers and health and social care professionals.

On a more positive note Carpenter and Sbaraini's (1997) evaluation found that users with a care programme felt more involved in the planning of their own care, and that the carers who were involved had a more positive view of the services.

Nevertheless, while health and social care professionals aim to work better together, and might believe they do, service-user feedback is variable and much of it still points to damaging boundary disputes and failures of communication (see Chapter 5). Causes of disputes can be: the decision-making processes in social services bureaucracies which differ from those in health; opposing models of understanding, leading to disagreement about the focus of interventions and decisions about priorities; and the conflict which can arise when there is ambiguity as to which profession provides what.

Inter-agency problems with collaboration

Secker and Hill (2001) investigated the partnership relationships between health, social services, the police, housing and education and concluded that there is a need to work for this wider partnership, but in doing so attention must be given to relevant inhibitors to partnerships.

For example, social services staff working with children and families reported problems with health and education services around confidentiality. Mental health voluntary organizations reported that statutory mental health agencies would not provide them with information about risk. In the voluntary organizations' view this was due to the statutory services seeing them as unprofessional. Workers in the criminal justice system also reported problems in obtaining information both about users' mental health status and about risk. Police officers described situations where mental health services had refused to accept people with drug and/or alcohol problems. Housing staff also reported problems in obtaining adequate information from health and social care services, and that community mental health teams would refuse to accept referrals on the grounds that the tenant had a personality disorder rather than a mental illness. Housing staff also felt that mental health staff had unrealistic expectations of the extent to which housing workers could support people with mental health problems.

Such poor inter-agency working raises serious health and safety issues in that staff could find themselves dealing with unanticipated behaviour and responses without adequate support systems. Factors such as these cause difficulties in establishing a sense of shared purpose and agreed priorities.

A critical appraisal of proposed new mental health legislation

The Draft Mental Health Bill (DoH 2002) presents for consultation the government working party's proposals for new mental health legislation to replace the Mental Health Act 1983. The review of the Mental Health Act presents the government's strategy for the modernization of mental health services by providing an up-to-date legal framework which purports to promote patients' rights as well as safety for users and the public. Furthermore, the government is making it clear that patients, carers and other citizens must be properly involved in the consultation process, to ensure that the care and treatment for mental disorder provided on a compulsory basis is in the best interests of both patients and the public.

There have been responses to the consultation from, among others, the Royal College of Psychiatrists, MIND, survivor groups, the Law Society and the Mental Health Alliance. Many of the criticisms in the responses centre on the controversial proposals to compulsorily detain and treat people with a personality disorder who are deemed to present a significant risk of harm to others, and to extend compulsory treatment to people within the community.

Few people involved in service-user and survivor organizations welcome the Bill, as they consider that more control is not the answer. Campbell (2002) argues that since the introduction of the Mental Health Act 1983 there have been attempts to extend compulsion in community settings. A mental health survivor, Campbell opposed these developments, arguing that mental health workers have more than enough powers over the mentally ill, and what is really needed is more understanding of the survivor experience. The Bill does not address the issue of why service users should be compulsorily detained if they are not a danger to others, when this is not proposed for people with other illnesses. The argument is that to impose compulsory treatment in this way is discriminatory.

Although the Royal College of Psychiatrists, along with users and carer organizations, has been calling for a review of the Mental Health Act 1983 that reflects modern practice, its members (Royal College of Psychiatrists 2002), with the Law Society, have argued against the proposals. The proposed criteria for compulsory treatment have been so widened that large numbers of users would find themselves inappropriately placed under sections of the Mental Health Act. The increased numbers of users would overwhelm already overstretched acute wards and community teams. User care would suffer and the level of risk would be increased rather than reduced. These measures, the Royal College of Psychiatrists emphasizes, may be incompatible with the terms of the European Convention on Human Rights. The Bill is an example of how responding to isolated high-profile incidents tends to make poor law. Mike Shooter (2002), president of the Royal College of Psychiatrists, argues that the legislation would be one of the most racially discriminatory laws ever seen in the UK because Afro-Caribbean men face a disproportionate risk of mistaken diagnosis and imprisonment, and that there is an element of institutional racism in psychiatry which would be magnified.

Some of the other proposals expected to find their way into the new Mental Health Act are: sections to support multi-disciplinary and inter-agency working in line with the NSF for Mental Health; the proposal to include a suitably trained mental health professional among those professionals able to decide an order under a section of the Mental Health Act, so removing the sole right of the approved social worker; a new right to independent advocacy; safeguards for people with long-term mental illnesses, including a new Commission for Mental Health; the right to have a care and treatment plan; a new duty covering the disclosure of information about patients between health, social care and other agencies; and the use of new mental health tribunals and other mechanisms to safeguard the rights of children and young people.

The proposal to develop a new role of 'mental health professional' who might be a nurse, a psychologist or a social worker is a clear example of the way in which interprofessional working can be said to be leading towards the blurring of boundaries between different professionals. The proposed demise of the approved social worker role gives rise to concern because the role is distinct and unique, requiring skills to facilitate the provision of an independent voice, and to be able to say no to the powerful medical profession.

The Mental Health Act proposal overlooks the function of social work as having a particular contribution through the special role of the approved social worker. The approved social worker brings a separate professional perspective and model to mental disorder, providing for the principle of independent judgement which must underpin a compulsory order. The value base of independence and democracy which the approved social worker brings to the multi-disciplinary process is vital. The approved social worker is trained to assess the social factors relevant to individuals and communities and ensures both that the practical tasks of the admission processes are carried out and the provisions of other relevant legislation are adhered to. Although there is a shortage of approved social workers, there is already a dedicated group continuing to work in mental health. It is hoped that an outcome of the new legislation will be to build on this already accumulated expertise and ensure that any new mental health professionals receive a similarly rigorous training to that provided for approved social workers.

Interprofessional education and training context

Over the years the professional bodies for social work, and the professions allied to medicine, nursing and midwifery have increasingly sought to encourage joint training and interprofessional programmes at both pre-registration and post-registration levels (Freeman, Miller and Ross 2000). This has contributed towards interprofessional collaboration and teamwork becoming the preferred model of practice promoted for mental health care.

If health and social care professionals are to be able to deliver an integrated mental health service, they must be given opportunities to learn how to work interprofessionally in a team and how to collaborate and work in partnership with users and carers.

Shared learning, joint learning, shared teaching and common learning are used to indicate teaching and learning experiences where students from health and social care courses are taught a range of subjects and topics together. Although these students learn together, they may never have a conversation with a student from another profession about what they do in practice.

What is needed, in addition to shared, joint and common learning, is interprofessional learning. Interprofessional learning engages the students interactively in dialogue and constructive criticism of the meanings of interprofessional working, partnership and collaboration with colleagues and users and carers, providing a better preparation for inter-agency working and teamwork.

Furthermore, the wider interprofessional team must be addressed – for example, administrators, managers and receptionists. They must be included in the training activities, so that they can give firsthand information on their functions, roles and professional codes of practice, which define how they work together and how they work with health and social care professionals, users and carers. Workers in the voluntary sector, housing, education and the police must also be included because they function within the interprofessional team as and when their expertise is required.

Areas to be addressed in the interprofessional learning enterprise include power, status, ideological differences, working with diversity within teams, and conflict and its management. The suggestions here are but a starting point; the list is in no way final. Two essential topic areas which lend themselves well to interprofessional teaching and learning – working with diversity within teams, and conflict and its management – are discussed below.

Diversity issues

The diversity issues to be addressed relate to class, religion, age, sexuality, gender, race, ethnicity, ability and mental illness. Because of the powerful position which white people hold within Western society and in health and social care institutions, they are not a racially oppressed group. However, many health and social care professionals are other than white and they will bring different views to the work interface, which may oppress white users and carers. It is relevant here to remind ourselves that white women have been discriminated against and oppressed by men, both black and white, within the mental health system.

When diversity is examined interprofessionally, the essential elements of working together that require partnership and collaboration with colleagues, users and carers can be addressed. The related diversity issues must not be taken for granted but analysed to ascertain what is happening and what is expected. It must be remembered that oppression, discrimination and stigma find very fertile ground in mental health services (Littlewood and Lipsedge 1989).

Diversity issues must be addressed in relation both to the health and social care team and the user and carer populations if difference is to be adequately recognized. All of us are users or carers at some time and we could all fit into any one or a combination of diversity categories. Edwards (2000) argues that the key point of an oppressive system is that it does not listen to the oppressed and that health and social care staff vehemently deny this. Furthermore, Edwards argues that the views of users must be listened to, particularly if they feel they are vulnerable and frightened. In a democracy, publicly supported services are accountable to the citizen and the way to achieve accountability is through participation. If health and social care professionals remember and act upon this point, it may help to reduce the feelings of alienation their service users often experience and express and help to reduce the us and them relationships and resentments that are often present (Sheilds 1985).

An investigation into the appropriateness of statutory psychiatric services for black people which defined users as Black British, Black English, Welsh, Scots, Irish, African and African Caribbean offers an example of diversity issues that requires attention by all mental health professionals. Pierre (2000) interviewed black service users from the groups described above and found: inconsistencies among professionals in relation to diagnosis which supported black users' claims of misdiagnosis; black people were overrepresented in the schizophrenic diagnostic category; lack of support for service users from staff who were seen by users as custodians; and the staff's readiness to dismiss as invalid any views black service users volunteered about their illness. It was also apparent from the data that users' rights were forfeited in hospital. Their length of stay, treatment, dietary needs, Mental Health Act legislation affecting their right to freedom and consent, and the right to have their complaints heard were considered by staff to be marginal to their treatment.

The study also points out the lack of knowledge among professionals about the cultural backgrounds of the people they treat and the persistent and pervasive institutional racism. While it must be remembered that this investigation researched a small group of black service users and carers in Liverpool, it tells us what might be happening elsewhere. This cannot offer a licence to extrapolate without further research, but it gives us pointers about action that is needed to begin to transform and deliver health and social care services to black people.

Conflict

Conflict between professionals

For this discussion, conflict – according to Skjorshammer (2001) – occurs when an individual or group feels negatively affected by another individual or group. Although conflict is usually perceived as negative, if well managed it can make groups more innovative and enhance the development of open and non-threatening forums for discussions and decision-making (Tjosvold 1998).

Bringing health and social care professionals together into a unified team may be problematic when differing professional knowledge converges. Indeed, social service staff often regard their own analysis of need as more complex, in terms of searching for underlying social problems, than that of health-care workers, whose approach they perceive to be based on a more concrete biomedical model (Higgins, Oldman and Hunter 1994). The view that particular professions' roles are more complicated, more diverse and demand a higher level of knowledge, before entry and during training, is commonly held among health and social care professionals. The status relationship where different professional group members in their behaviour indicate that they are more important, better educated and superior to other professionals can result in resentments (Higgins *et al.* 1994).

Unfortunately, such interprofessional behaviours occur with service users and their carers too (Higgins *et al.* 1994). Furthermore, conflict may be fuelled when staff find themselves doing work when other professionals are not available, but receive no recognition for doing so.

Skjorshammer's (2001) analysis of how health professionals manage conflicts related to co-operation at work suggested that the three most prevalent approaches were avoidance, forcing and negotiation, and usually in that order. Avoidance means not talking about an issue publicly or not bringing it up later with the other party. This might be expressed as silent withdrawal after a confrontation, keeping the issues and feelings to oneself or actively talking to one's peers or reference group. By behaving in this way neither oneself nor the other party is confronted or made responsible for whatever caused the conflict. Professionals according to Skjorshammer opt for avoidance usually because they are unsure as to the consequence of confronting the problem, and whether they will be blamed.

Forcing is the use of informal and formal power, where conflict is not addressed until it is close to explosion. Forcing is not usually done in formal meetings but behind closed doors and it is done hastily without consulting other involved parties or bothering about hurt feelings. The result of forcing is usually communicated as a warning with notes on group rules, regulations and procedures. Participants with high professional status or a high formal position in the hierarchy most often determine whose viewpoints will prevail. With forcing, a solution may have been found, but the conflict remains unresolved or repressed. It may also create winners and losers, who will continue to play out the conflict in ways which will affect interprofessional relationships for the worst.

Negotiation, Skjorshammer (2001) suggests, enabled staff to confer with a view to compromise or agreement. The benefit of negotiation is to come to a compromise of a satisfying nature with which all parties can live, pointing out how mistakes arose, the work done well and the changes which must be made. Negotiations are usually worked at when senior leadership staff, personnel and unions are required to find a solution to the conflict. Usually there are more actors, interests, legal and procedural aspects to take into account in negotiations. Negotiation may also occur informally on a daily basis between staff with satisfactory results.

Conflict with service users

Within this area of conflict and its management in the workplace must also be the inclusion of aggression and/or violence from users against workers in the course of their work. Health and social care professionals in all specialities have reported their experiences of aggression and/or violence from users and carers. This situation has prompted a range of publications (DoH 2000b, 2001; Royal College of Psychiatrists 1998; UKCC 2002).

If violence in the workplace is to be addressed, health and social care staff and their employers must work together to develop policy guidelines, monitoring systems, risk assessment, risk management systems and support for staff. Service users and their carers must also be involved in collaboration with professional staff. The Department of Health (DoH 2001) offers the following steps to prevent violence occurring: working with users and carers to provide individualized care planning and intervention; the provision of a service that treats people with respect and meets their needs and wishes; and providing a service which listens to users and carers. Furthermore, it is vital to ensure the working together of all the members of the team, including administrators, receptionists and managers, with users and their carers.

Value of interprofessional education

The nature of conflict and its management in interprofessional teams in health and social care present challenges to managers and clinical leaders when it comes to advancing interprofessional co-operation. Interprofessional education and training around the issues of diversity and conflict provide two examples of where learning together could be must useful. If the team is not working together around these issues then users, carers and staff will be involved in a continuous uphill struggle.

According to Reeves (2001) the evidence relating to the effects of interprofessional education involving staff who care for adults with mental health problems is patchy. From his study of 19 evaluations he concluded that there was inadequate information about the methods employed, little or no account of the impact on user care and limited applicability to practice. To address this situation there is a pressing need to produce sound evidence through research designs which include quantitative, qualitative, multi-method and longitudinal research to address the impact of interprofessional education over the longer term and its effects on user and carer care.

Conclusion and learning points

- Collaboration between different professional groups, agencies, users and carers is an essential element in the provision of high quality care for people with complex mental health and social care needs.

- Collaboration should always be underpinned by sound recognition that an individual's health and social care needs are often closely related and therefore need to be met by a seamless service.

- So far the legislative guidance framework for collaborative working in mental health is insufficient to overcome the structural professional barriers, the interprofessional clashes and the inter-agency tensions. More work is required to address the process and communication aspects of interprofessional working.

- Where the care programme approach is effective and collaboration implemented, service users and their carers will feel involved and empowered.

- The proposed new mental health legislation with its extension of compulsory treatment to the community, and the demise of the approved social worker, could lead to increased tensions between professionals and service users and their carers.

- An effective way of addressing the barriers to interprofessional working is to promote interprofessional education whereby trainees would prepare for team and inter-agency working by learning about each other's roles and addressing together the challenges of working in mental health. There needs to be a wide curriculum for interprofessional education but, in particular, it should help professionals to recognize and challenge racism and discrimination and deal more effectively with conflict and challenging behaviour.

References

Blom-Cooper, L., Hally, H. and Murphy, E. (1995) *The Falling Shadow, One Patient's Mental Health Care.* London: HMSO.

Campbell, P. (2002) 'More Control is Not the Answer.' *Community Care,* 12 September, 23. www.community-care.co.uk.

Carpenter, J. and Sbaraini, S. (1997) *Choice Information and Dignity: Involving Users and Carers in the Care Programme Approach in Mental Health.* Bristol: Policy Press.

DoH (1990a) NHS and Community Care Act. London: HMSO.

DoH (1990b) *The Care Programme Approach for People with a Mental Illness Referred to the Specialist Psychiatric Services.* HC 23 LASSL. London: Department of Health.

DoH (1997) *The New NHS: Modern, Dependable.* London: Stationery Office.

DoH (1998) *Modernising Social Services: Promoting Independence, Improving Protection, Raising Standards.* London: Department of Health.

DoH (1999a) *Effective Care Co-ordination in Mental Health Services: Modernising the Care Programme Approach: A Policy Booklet.* London: Department of Health.

DoH (1999b) *The National Service Framework for Mental Health.* London: Department of Health.

DoH (2000a) *The NHS Plan.* London: Department of Health.

DoH (2000b) *Zero Tolerance.* London: Department of Health.

DoH (2001) *National Taskforce on Violence Against Social Care Staff.* London: Depatment of Health.

DoH (2002) *Mental Health Bill: Consultation Document.* Cm 5538–11. London: Department of Health.

Edwards, K. (2000) 'Service Users and Mental Health Nursing.' *Journal of Psychiatric and Mental Health Nursing 7,* 555–565.

Freeman, M., Miller, C. and Ross, N. (2000) 'The Impact of Individual Philosophies of Teamwork on Multi-professional Practice and the Implications for Education.' *Journal of Interprofessional Care 14,* 3, 237–247.

Health Act (1999) Section 22 (1) (2). London: Stationery Office.

Higgins, R., Oldman, C. and Hunter, D.J. (1994) 'Working Together: Lessons for Collaboration Between Health and Social Services.' *Health Society and Care in the Community 2,* 5, 269–277.

King's Fund (1997) *Transforming Health in London.* London: King's Fund.

Littlewood and Lipsedge (1989) *Aliens and Alienists, Ethnic Minorities and Psychiatry,* 2nd edn. London: Unwin Hyman.

McDermott, G. (1998) 'The Care Programme Approach: A Patient Perspective.' *Mentally Ill in the Community 3*, 1, 47–63.

Mental Health Act (1983) London: Stationery Office.

Norman, I.J. and Peck, E. (1999) 'Working Together in Adult Community Mental Health Services: An Inter-professional Dialogue.' *Journal of Mental Health 8*, 3, 217–230.

Onyett, S. and Ford, R. (1996) 'Multi-disciplinary Community Teams: Where is the Wreckage?' *Journal of Mental Health 5*, 47–55.

Peck, E. (1991) 'Power in the NHS – A Case Study of a Unit Considering NHS Trust Status.' *Health Services Management Research 4*, 120–131.

Peck, E. and Norman, I.J. (1999) 'Working Together in Adult Community Mental Health Services: Exploring Inter-professional Role Relations.' *Journal of Mental Health 8*, 3, 231–242.

Pierre, S.A. (2000) 'Psychiatry and Citizenship: The Liverpool Black Mental Health Service Users' Perspective.' *Journal of Psychiatric and Mental Health Nursing 7*, 240–257.

Reeves, S. (2001) 'A Systematic Review of the Effects of Interprofessional Education on Staff Involved in the Care of Adults with Mental Health Problems.' *Journal of Psychiatric and Mental Health Nursing 8*, 6, 533–542.

Royal College of Psychiatrists (1998) *Management of Imminent Violence.* London: Royal College of Psychiatrists.

Royal College of Psychiatrists (2002) *Reform of the Mental Health Act 1983: Joint Statement by the Royal College of Psychiatrists and the Law Society.* London: Royal College of Psychiatrists.

Secker, J. and Hill, K. (2001) 'Broadening the Partnerships: Experiences of Working Across Community Agencies.' *Journal of Interprofessional Care 15*, 4, 342–350.

Sheilds, P. (1985) 'The Consumer View of Psychiatry.' *Hospital and Health Services Review,* May, 117–119.

Shooter, M. (2002) *Reform of the Mental Health Act 1983: Joint Statement by the Royal College of Psychiatrists and the Law Society.* London: Royal College of Psychiatrists.

Skjorshammer, M. (2001) 'Co-operation and Conflict in a Hospital: Interprofessional Differences in Perception and Management of Conflicts.' *Journal of Interprofessional Care 15*, 1, 7–18.

Tjosvold, D. (1998) 'Conflict with Interdependence: Its Value for Productive Individuality.' In C. De Dreu and E. De Vilert (eds) *Using Conflict in Organisations.* London: Sage Publishers.

UKCC (2002) *The Recognition, Prevention and Therapeutic Management of Violence in Mental Health Care: A Summary.* London: United Kingdom Council for Nursing Health Visiting and Midwifery.

Vanclay, L. (1997) *Exploring Inter-professional Education: The Advantages and Barriers. Discussion Paper for the UKCC Multi-professional Working Group of the Joint Education Committee.* London: CAIPE.

Wolfe, J., Gournay, K., Norman, S. and Ramnoruth, D. (1997) 'Care Programme Approach: Evaluation of its Implementation in an Inner London Service.' *Clinical Effectiveness in Nursing 1*, 85–91.

Chapter 9

Learning Disabilities: Effective Partnership and Teamwork to Overcome Barriers in Service Provision

Tony Thompson

Introduction

For many of us the delivery of an effective learning disability service has been haunted by the constraints of insufficient resources to implement the numerous required local and national changes to our services (Heddell 2003). However, just as we encourage clients to enjoy a quality of life despite their disabilities, so might we be able to promote collaboration and teamwork in spite of and maybe with the help of the political culture.

This chapter will consider the special needs of people with learning disabilities, paying particular attention to the gap that still exists between policy aims and practice outcomes. A consideration of partnership and collaboration in the context of the historical landmarks of service development will be offered as a background to a discussion of the proposals set out in the document *Valuing People* (DoH 2001). Finally, it will be argued that, while progress has been slow towards ensuring genuine choice along with full social inclusion for people with learning disabilities, services can be improved through a strong emphasis on shared learning, inter-agency collaboration, and the integration of different professionals into a single effective team.

Synopsis of developments in learning disability services

The Royal Commission on the law relating to mental illness and deficiency (the Percy Report) established in 1957 started the community care movement. It created a growth in interest which in subsequent years developed to embrace other groups including children and older people. For people with a learning disability community care policy gained particular expression in the White Paper *Better Services for the Mentally Handicapped* (DHSS 1971). Other significant influences on the development of care in the community included the report of the Jay Committee (DHSS 1979). This report introduced a model of care based on meeting the needs of people and their families throughout their life span (Nally and Steele 1992).

Throughout the 1980s and 1990s, community care, as developed following the Griffiths Report 1988 and the NHS and Community Care Act 1990, has been defined differently by statutory, voluntary, professional and pressure groups, usually in accordance with the motives they had in mind when they applied the term. Government, in spite of its rhetoric about person-centred services, was seen by many to be motivated by cost-cutting (Leathard 2000), while service users, represented in the learning disability movement by organizations such as People First, were looking for dignity, independence and, above all, choice (Stevens 1998). For many parents and carers, the notion of 'community care' for their learning disabled children was a myth; their reality was that they were expected to care for their children well into adulthood, with minimum support (DoH 2003; Vagg 1998).

The impetus for change continued in the late 1990s and was highlighted in examples of central initiatives such as *The New NHS: Modern, Dependable* (DoH 1997). This proposed that a statutory duty should be placed on those commissioning and those providing health and social care in local authority services to work in partnership to meet the needs of service users (see Chapter 1).

The majority of initiatives by both central and local government described above aimed at achieving successful teamworking and collaboration. This presented key organizational, professional and interpersonal challenges that needed to be addressed if the hoped-for outcomes were to be achieved (Barr 1997).

The difficulties presented by these challenges were illustrated in the 1999 DoH report entitled *Facing the Facts*. This confirmed that, in spite of good will and some progress, the desired results had not yet been achieved. There was disenchantment with the provision of interprofessional learning disability services and this was emphasized when the government became quite explicit in its message to those who manage services. This echoed previous concerns that the public and service users had lost a degree of confidence in the ability of the contributing agencies to deliver effective community-based provision (DoH 1998b). Some of the failures identified were:

- inadequate care, poor management of resources and underfunding

- the proper range of services not always being available to provide the care and support people need

- patients and service users preferring not to remain in contact with services

- families who have willingly played a part in care have been overburdened

- problems in recruiting and retaining staff.

(DoH 1998b, Executive Summary)

The government saw a number of these failings as resulting from the failure of co-ordination between different agencies and committed itself, yet again, to providing integrated care focusing on the needs of the service users and their carers (DoH 1999). They therefore introduced a radical and focused initiative entitled *Valuing People* (DoH 2001), as a further attempt to address the problems. Before discussing this critical initiative, it is useful to consider in more detail some of the service development problems that led to its introduction.

Key issues in services for people with learning disabilities

People with a learning disability need timely and effective help if they are not to become handicapped by their condition. Issues of personal security and safety are of real importance if people with learning disabilities are to remain positive contributors to their communities.

In recent years some aspects of the services provided have been strong on professional rhetoric but weak on practicalities. For example, an examination of services in 24 authorities undertaken in 1999 by the Department of Health found that in spite of a commitment by professionals to local 'domestic- style' living arrangements, two-thirds of service users still lived either away from their own locality or in institutional settings including NHS hospitals (DoH 1999). Day care for the majority of service users was still provided in old style 'adult training centres' and few service users were in 'normal' employment. Other deficiencies identified in the study included poor access to primary health care and other mainstream services and vulnerability to stigma, abuse or other forms of exploitation (DoH 1999). In January 2003, 500 people were still living in 21 long-stay hospitals (*Community Care* 2003a).

In order to address these issues a combined and cohesive effort across agencies, professions and disciplines is required. People with learning disabilities may require direct help in order to have a more complete life – to initiate and sustain friendships, to obtain and retain some form of worthwhile employment, to network with others, to develop new skills and to receive or continue training and education. Individuals with a learning disability who have experienced the effects of institutions will require practical assistance to rehabilitate, to re-orientate, and to develop a variety of skills and interests that will help in the reconstruction of their lives in the community. Furthermore, people with specific needs benefit from receiving culturally appropriate assistance (Baxter 1998) which is in accordance with their wishes and takes place in appropriate settings.

When there is inadequate collaboration between agencies and professionals, people with learning disabilities are precluded from building, retaining or returning to an ordinary life. This was evidenced in the DoH report (1999) which found that the commissioning of appropriate person-centred services was undermined by lack of communication and confusion about roles and responsibilities between different agencies.

Since the Griffiths Report (1983) the policies introduced to achieve social inclusion for people with learning disabilities have required social services to work closely with health, housing, employment, benefits, education and voluntary agencies. While there has been considerable inter-agency progress, specific problems continue to persist within the services, many of which are associated to some degree with breakdowns in partnership, collaboration and teamworking. For example, research and monitoring of services have identified that there are inconsistencies of services for different groups of people with learning disabilities (DoH 1999; Walker and Ryan 1995); that there continues to be inadequate support for carers (DoH 1999, 2003; Walker and Walker 1998); that people with learning difficulties still have problems with accessing basic health care (DoH 1999, 2003; Flynn

1999); and that there are often problems for service users and carers at the transition between children's and adults' services (DoH 2003; Hopkins 2002).

The study undertaken by the Department of Health (DoH 1999) found significant inconsistencies between services for people with learning disabilities living in different areas. These were linked to different service models, different stages of collaboration and different agreements between agencies about funding policy. The report shows that the situation had not changed significantly since Walker and Ryan reported in 1995. For example, they found that people with learning disabilities who lived with their carers were likely to attend a day centre but had few links with other services and no key worker. People with learning disabilities living independently in the community were more likely to have a key worker who provided access to a broader range of disability services. Those living in hospitals and hostels scheduled for closure received priority consideration for community placements whereas people being cared for at home were only offered a community placement if there was a family crisis or illness or death of the carer. Both studies suggest that differences in funding, service policies and ways of working together mean that people do not always receive fair and equitable services (DoH 1999; Walker and Ryan 1995).

These failures to deliver appropriate and required services as identified by users and carers are further illustrated by an inspection of learning disabilities services by the Social Services Inspectorate (DoH 1998b). This found that care plans put too much emphasis on services to be received rather than identifying the individual needs, choices and hoped-for outcomes for the service user. Service users and carers want a single point of access, flexible services tailored to their individual needs and better inter-agency working (DoH 1999; Walker and Walker 1998).

Concerning joint working between health and social care, the inspectors also found that it was hard to combine formal top-level commitment with effective joint working at ground level. Even where health and social care staff had moved into the same building, few inspected agencies addressed effectively the combined issues of inter-agency and multi-disciplinary assessment. The report concluded that moving in together without adequate team development did not make for successful joint working (DoH 1998b).

A common area for the breakdown of teamwork in services for people with a learning disability is in the transition between children's and adult services (*Community Care* 2003b; Hopkins 2002). Children's services are now, in the main, effective and well co-ordinated. Once young people reach their nineteenth birthday, they are transferred to adult services. Co-ordination between the two is notoriously poor and a transition from the caring school environment to an adult day centre can be extremely traumatic. Respite care arrangements may change for the worse and this can be a stressful time for the family. They and their learning disabled relative need support services which must be holistic, flexible and simple to access (Poxton, Greig and Giraud Saunders 2000).

To address the ongoing difficulties described above, a new initiative, *Valuing People* (DoH 2001), was introduced. Described as 'a world-leading mile-stone' and a 'revolutionary concept' to achieving independence, choice and inclusion for people with learning disabilities (Heddell 2003, p.38), its progress is reviewed in the next section.

Valuing People: new service – new understanding for the team

Following the publication of *Facing the Facts* (DoH 1999) which, as explained above, highlighted the failure of previous attempts to bring about real changes to the lives of people with learning disabilities and their families, a new approach was devised by the government. The strategy outlined in the government White Paper *Valuing People* (DoH 2001) is structured around four key principles – rights, independence, choice and inclusion – and will have a direct influence upon how learning disability teams function.

The resulting new national objectives for services for people with learning disabilities are supported by new targets and performance indicators as well as an injection of funds. These have been designed to provide a clear direction for local agencies. Furthermore, *Valuing People* describes how the government intends to provide new opportunities for children and adults with learning disabilities and, indeed, their families to enjoy a full and more independent life as part of their local communities.

The policy intends to improve services for people with a learning disability by addressing interprofessional and inter-agency partnerships and collaboration. The proposals build on existing inter-agency planning structures to establish learning disability partnership boards in all local authority areas, which are responsible for services for adults. There continue to be separate planning structures for children but these must ensure improved links with adult services. The partnership boards operate within the overall framework of local strategic partnerships (LSPs).

The development of LSPs offers a framework for local partnership working, bringing together public, independent, community and voluntary sectors in order to provide effective co-ordination. These arrangements aim to simplify and expand the scope of partnerships concerned with community well-being. It is intended that these closer links will foster a common direction and help to address wider issues such as access to other local services, including health and transport.

While partnership boards are not statutory, the arrangements for how they function should ensure they meet their responsibilities in the following areas:

- developing and implementing the joint investment plan for delivering the government's objectives

- overseeing the inter-agency planning and commissioning of comprehensive, integrated and inclusive services that provide a genuine choice of service options to people in their local community

- ensuring that people are not denied their rights to a local service because of a lack of competence or capacity among service providers

- the use of Health Act (1999) flexibilities (this enables local authorities to work more closely with health authorities to provide improved services)

- ensuring arrangements are in place to achieve a smooth transition to adult life for learning disabled young people.

It is emphasized within the above initiatives that partnership boards will particularly ensure that:

- people with learning disabilities and carers are able to make a real contribution to the work of such boards

- the cultural diversity of the local community is reflected in its membership

- local independent providers and the voluntary sector are fully engaged.

The government was determined to promote collaborative working in learning disabilities services. It made the local council responsible for putting the partnership board in place with appropriate membership. This has to include senior representatives from social services, health bodies, education, housing, community development, leisure, independent providers and the employment service. Representatives of people with learning disabilities and carers must be able to take part as full members. Minority ethnic representation is also reinforced in the White Paper.

The *First Annual Report of the Learning Disability Task Force* (DoH 2003), presented two years after the publication of *Valuing People*, found that although some progress had been made, there was still significant work to be done. Ageing parents of people with learning disabilities were still not receiving adequate support, and housing continued to be a serious problem. Access to health care and dentistry remained problematic for people with learning disabilities and services for people with severe learning disabilities continued to be institutional in nature. From the structural perspective, the development of partnership boards was still patchy and the genuine involvement of people with learning disabilities, especially those from minority ethnic groups, had not yet been achieved.

In my experience of over 30 years of working in the field of learning disabilities, the teams who deliver the service face increasing demands while funding problems inhibit their work. The delivery of effective services continues to be undermined by ongoing confusion about funding and commissioning responsibilities between different agencies (Heddell 2003). Although agencies and learning disability teams now subscribe to the principles of social inclusion, citizenship and local community living for their service users, improvements in practice have been very slow (DoH 2003). In the following sections I will argue that in order to achieve faster progress, two key and linked aspects – shared learning and inter-disciplinary team building – need to be addressed.

The development of joint training/shared learning

Multi-disciplinary work, although involving co-operation, reinforces time-honoured divisions in the forms of precious knowledge held by service contributors. It is significant that policy makers in the learning disability field were pioneers of ideas and projects to promote shared learning and joint qualifications which, when they emerged 30 years ago, were extremely radical.

The *Report of the Committee on Nursing* (DHSS 1972) emphasized the difficulties that nurses would be likely to experience when working in teams in the community, delivering services for learning disabled people. The report recognized that nurses were providing a community service while their entire training had been undertaken in the old institutions. In its revision of nurse training, the Committee looked towards preparation in the social work field as being the most appropriate and, ahead of its time, argued for a separate caring profession to emerge for work with learning disabilities.

The Jay Committee (DHSS 1979) recommended that the Certificate of Social Service should replace the qualification of specialist learning disability nurse (then Registered Nurse Mental Handicap [RNMH]). This proposal was rejected and antipathy and competition to be the 'experts' in learning disability services continued between nursing and social work.

Nevertheless, in the latter part of 1986, new moves and pressures emerged for improved collaboration in education and training, from the professional bodies for nursing, social work and occupational therapy. This resulted in the publication of a report recommending shared learning (English National Board for Nursing, Health Visiting and Midwifery (ENB)/Central Council for Education and Training in Social Work (CCETSW) 1986). Two pilot schemes were established at qualifying level resulting in a joint Certificate of Social Service (CSS)/Registered Nurse Mental Handicap (RNMH) qualification (Brown 1994) which helped to lay the foundation for the later joint Diploma in Social Work (DipSW)/Registered General Nurse (RGN) programmes. (See Chapter 4 of this book.)

Since then, the training rules have changed again, new statutory bodies have been introduced and they continue to reform (see Chapter 1). New requirements expect programmes to involve academics and planners to work together with service providers, clients and families. They also require the students to understand the collaborative context and to learn teamworking and collaborative skills.

Nevertheless, in the view and experience of this author, the move towards ensuring that health and care professionals experience a common foundation in their qualifying training has not been fast enough to keep pace with changing disability service models. Undertaking consultancy work in a range of settings, at the time of writing in 2002 the author still hears concerns expressed, particularly by carers and managers, about the relevance of current training and the fitness to practise of newly qualified staff. Practitioners in learning disability services often appear unclear and uncertain about their roles within a team in a multi-disciplinary setting. It remains doubtful whether all academic and teaching staff have been able to keep pace with the changes in the disability services.

One way of rectifying these problems would be to ensure that a fundamental core of the education for learning disability professionals, which should be undertaken as shared learning, must be the theory and practice of inter-agency collaboration and effective teamworking outlined in the following sections.

Foundations of sound collaborative working

Most practitioners in the social care field will recognize the considerable amount of inter-disciplinary teamwork that has to take place in order to provide effective services, yet there are factors that get in the way. Although some workers feel most comfortable in a closely defined team with clear boundaries and uncomplicated relationships, some people working in the learning disabilities field, as in other areas of social care, may encounter individuals who avoid teamworking because they prefer to work in an autonomous way or who will only feel comfortable in a team with members of their own profession.

Social workers are expected to understand the nature and forms of teamwork and Brill drew specific attention to the similar characteristics displayed by teams (Brill 1976). He offered the following definition:

> A group of people, each of whom possesses particular expertise; each of whom is responsible for making individual decisions; who hold together a common purpose; who meet together to communicate, collaborate and consolidate knowledge from which plans are made, actions determined and future decisions influenced. (Brill 1976, p.11)

The above definition is well suited to modern service delivery if it embraces the contribution of the client himself or herself. Indeed such inclusion is necessary to meet contemporary expectations for person-centred care planning which must be needs-led and ensure involvement of service users and carers as well as collaboration between professionals (DoH 1998a,1998b). If user involvement is to be effective, there must be a clear understanding of why it is necessary (Hattersly 1995). The main criterion to judge the efficiency of a multi-disciplinary team is evidence that as a consequence of their joint working, the members bring about improvement in mutually agreed client outcomes (West and Slater 1996). These outcomes depend on attending to the following:

- effective team and inter-agency working

- effective communication

- effective recording of relevant information

- appropriate exchange of full and detailed information

- focus on how the agencies involved in learning disabilities care relate to each other

- focus on issues relating to support, stress, risk and safety in the work situation

- methods of establishing, maintaining and reviewing the effectiveness of the team's working relationships.

A competent inter-disciplinary team should have two broad goals in their support of people with learning disabilities: first, to ensure that mainstream community services meet the social and health care needs of users and carers and, second, to identify and design new specialist services when they are needed. I shall return to aspects of teams later but wish first to identify features that increase the prospect of successful collaborative working. They include:

- real commitment to collaboration to be reflected at all levels in the agency or service

- a focus on the client or user of the learning disability service and their full involvement in the partnership

- sensitivity to specific individual needs, particularly with regard to people from minority ethnic groups

- commitment to client and carer inclusion in the planning and implementation of care

- agreed and understood standards and procedures for accessing the learning disability service

- appropriate arrangements for accurate inter-agency information exchange

- commitment to joint staff training and development
- systematic approaches to quality assurance and performance management within and across agencies (DoH 1999)
- continuous review of collaborative arrangements.

Fault lines in collaborative working

While good communication, co-operation and mutuality are widely supported in principle, disability services (in common with services for other disadvantaged groups) have a long tradition of rivalry and non-co-operation within and between agencies (Richardson 1997). Shaw (1993) highlighted two fundamental problems for any professional organization when collaboration becomes a strategic aim. First, it inhibits a profession's freedom to act independently when it would prefer to retain full control. Second, scarce resources have to be invested in maintaining and developing relationships, when the returns from that investment may be uncertain. Consequently professions, like other organizations, may prefer not to collaborate unless compelled to do so. Appeals to collaborate for the sake of client well-being may not, in themselves, be enough.

There are other professional and organizational barriers which weaken both collaboration and social inclusion and which all involved must challenge and work to overcome:

- lack of agreement about values and service objectives
- inability or unwillingness to agree financial arrangements
- low priority being given to joint working within organizations
- barriers between residential and community-based services
- stereotypical views of professions and agencies, reinforced by narrow socialization and uni-professional education and registration
- organizations and professions being 'sidetracked' with regard to theories of disability rather than working together to provide proper services based on the consequences of a disability
- lack of involvement and resultant disempowering of the client
- mistrust of motives between departments and agencies

- passing people with learning disabilities between organizations and professions, because of insufficient clarity about where responsibility rests for ensuring effective service provision (DoH 1999)

- barriers created by ignorance, stigma and fear.

Inter-disciplinary teams were developed to enhance the delivery of specialized, co-ordinated care but there are doubts about the degree of success achieved (Braye and Preston-Shoot 1995; Brown 1992). Part of the difficulty arises from the complexity of the work involved and the lack of measures of performance quality applicable across professional groups (Sines and Barr 1998). While solutions are awaited, work can be done on leadership and team development, which are discussed in the next section.

A role for team management

Social workers and other professional colleagues may be familiar with working in a team and the management of individual relationships, but it is important to recognize that the team is a group with its own processes. Understanding this can help in the process of managing the development of the way in which people work together as a team. Tuckman (1965) described four phases in the development of a team: forming, storming, norming and performing. The phases do not necessarily occur in this order and the approach is only one of a number of perspectives on team processes. Nevertheless, it offers a useful framework for understanding processes both in newly established teams and those that have been restructured. (Some other aspects of teams are discussed in Chapter 2.)

Forming phase

When the team first comes together, members may be nervous, tentative and polite as they begin to explore and test out boundaries. They are defining tasks, exploring appropriate forms of group behaviour, deciding the form and content of information and identifying problems.

Storming phase

As people come to know each other better, differences become more evident and individuals begin to struggle to protect or establish their own views or territory. This may be particularly pronounced when the team consists of people from different professional groups. If well managed, this is a potentially 'healthy' phase of group development because resolution of the conflicts can lead to better performance and mutual understanding. The alternative may mean the suppression of differences that are spoken about in twos and threes in corridors but never openly addressed. However, this can be a challenging phase to manage because it may involve defensiveness, argument, establishing a 'pecking order', and sometimes anger, jealousy, hurt and tension.

Where the issues are not resolved, the team may remain a fragmented and negative in-fighting group of individuals or sub-groups. The real challenge is to enable the team members to manage and resolve their conflicts while keeping the team focused on their common task.

Norming phase

At this point team members start to establish ground rules to which they can all sign up. Team responses include: constructive management of conflict, communication, problem sharing, and a growing sense of team identity. During this phase, management can facilitate discussions as differences are worked out.

Performing phase

This is a highly constructive phase with healthy relationships and clear expectations. The team performs in a functional way, problem resolution takes place and changes are implemented. Typical responses include: constructive exchange of viewpoints; an atmosphere of relaxed humour; task-focused behaviour; and the acceptance of individual and team responsibility. At this level of teamwork development, a manager can delegate more to the team members and they can support and cover for each other. The introduction of co-operative joint planning and critical performance review can also be introduced. A 'performing' inter-disciplinary team is likely to provide an excellent service to users.

If the government's objectives for improved partnership are to be achieved in services to people with learning disabilities and their families, the development and consolidation of effective inter-disciplinary teams will be essential.

Conclusion

Good intentions about providing person-centred services for people with learning disabilities have been part of public policy since 1973. However, the reality at the beginning of the twenty-first century is that quality services are patchy and the majority of people with learning disabilities are still cared for in 'congregate forms of care' (DoH 1999) with limited access to mainstream services. The government's policy set out in *Valuing People* (DoH 2001) is yet another attempt to turn this around. As with previous proposals outlined in this chapter, the new approach relies heavily on inter-agency collaboration and interprofessional working. However, unless the lessons of previous failures of teamwork and collaboration are learnt, and unless funding is targeted appropriately and joint training is integrated into the mainstream, the vision of full social inclusion for people with learning disabilities may continue to remain a pipe-dream.

Key learning points for practice
The development of collaborative working

- The changing nature of learning disability services over the past 20 years has led to progressive collaboration between agencies and service providers.

- Key organizational, professional and inter-personal challenges need to be addressed in order to enhance teamwork.

- Policy expectations for the development of partnership working pose organizational, personal and professional challenges for individuals and teams.

- Collaborative working has been consistently advocated as the most desirable method of structuring the delivery of care.

- Inter-disciplinary teamwork demands high levels of communication.

- Teamwork in learning disability services requires the setting of mutual goals which are client-focused and dependent upon collaborative planning.

- There is a potential for positive effects or job satisfaction and morale from working within a supportive collaborative team.

Impact on service

- The promise of progressive policies to deliver an effective, socially inclusive learning disability service has been beset by constraints of insufficient resources and by professional and organizational obstacles.

- Many service users and their carers have lost confidence in the ability of agencies to deliver effective community-based provision.

Proposed improvements to service delivery systems

- Although resources remain a problem, services can be improved through a stronger emphasis on the *needs of service users and carers, shared learning, inter-agency collaboration,* and the *integration of different professionals into a single, effective team.*

- The provision of timely and effective services means listening to service users and their families, acting upon research findings and structuring services around four key principles: rights, independence, choice and inclusion.

- Effective user involvement relies on there being a clear understanding of what involvement is to achieve, expressed as mutually agreed client outcomes.

- Care plans must put less emphasis on services to be received and more on responding directly to the individual and ethnically influenced needs, choices and desired outcomes of the service user.

- Structurally, service users and carers want a single point of access, flexible services tailored to their individual needs, and better inter-agency working.

- Effective inter-agency partnerships and collaboration must include service users in strategic and individual decision-making processes and must keep collaborative arrangements under review.

- Good inter-agency communication and clarity about roles and responsibilities will facilitate effective, person-centred commissioning.

- Pioneering proposals made decades ago for shared learning among professionals in learning disability services have had limited implementation and need to expand widely to equip staff for effective inter-agency and inter-disciplinary team practice.

- The staff of inter-disciplinary teams themselves need development to achieve successful joint working.

- Team development can be facilitated by managers and team members using their understanding of the kinds of processes that teams may undergo as they establish themselves and do their work.

- The measures described, together with appropriately targeted funding, are vital to achieving the vision of full social inclusion for people with learning disabilities.

Good practice guidance for collaborative working

- Acknowledge differences in value systems.

- Don't become defensive in order to overcome any shortcomings in the management of the service.

- Don't form cliques or professional minority interest groups.

- Avoid closed language structure such as professional shorthand.

- Overcome the urge to reinforce a professional distance.

- Share your professional skills.

References

Barr, O. (1997) 'Clinical Management: Inter-disciplinary Teamwork: Consideration of the Challenges.' *British Journal of Nursing 6*, 17, 1005–1110.

Baxter, C. (1998) 'Competency in Diversity: Providing Care in a Multi-cultural Society.' In T. Thompson and P. Mathias (eds) *Standards and Learning Disability*, 2nd edn. London: Baillière Tindall.

Braye, S. and Preston-Shoot, M. (1995) *Empowering Practice in Social Care.* Buckingham: Open University Press.

Brill, N.I. (1976) *Teamwork: Working Together in the Human Services.* Philadelphia: Lippincott.

Brown, J. (1992) 'Professional Teams.' In T. Thompson and P. Mathias (eds) *Standards and Mental Handicap: Keys to Competence.* London: Baillière Tindall.

Brown, J. (1994) *The Hybrid Worker – Lessons Based Upon a Study of Employers Involved with Two Pioneer Joint Qualifying Training Courses.* York: University of York.

Community Care (2003a) 'Learning Difficulties: Verdict on Valuing People Delivered.' News, 16–22 January, 6.

Community Care (2003b) 'Task Force Calls for Greater Effort to Implement Valuing People Strategy.' News Analysis, 16–22 January, 18–19.

DHSS (1971) *Better Services for the Mentally Handicapped.* London: HMSO.

DHSS (1972) *Report on the Committee on Nursing (Briggs Report).* Cm 5115. London: HMSO.

DHSS (1979) *Report of the Committee of Enquiry into Mental Handicap Nursing and Care.* Cm 7468 (Report of the Committee Chaired by Mrs Peggy Jay). London: HMSO.

DoH (1997) *The New NHS: Modern, Dependable.* Cm 3807. Department of Health, London: Stationery Office.

DoH (1998a) *Modernising Mental Health Services, Safe, Sound and Supportive.* London: Department of Health.

DoH (1998b) *Moving into the Mainstream: The Report of a National Inspection of Services for People with Learning Disabilities.* London: Stationery Office.

DoH (1999) *Facing the Facts: Services for People with Learning Disabilities: Policy Impact Study of Social Care and Health Services.* London: Department of Health.

DoH (2001) *Valuing People: A New Strategy for Learning Disability for the 21st Century.* Cm 5086. London: Department of Health.

DoH (2003) *Making Things Better: First Annual Report of the Learning Disability Task Force.* (Consulted 30 January 2003.) www.doh.gov.uk/learningdisabilities.

English National Board for Nursing, Health Visiting and Midwifery (ENB)/Central Council for Education and Training in Social Work (CCETSW) (1986) *Report of the Joint Working Group: Cooperation in Qualifying and Post Qualifying Training in Mental Handicap.* London: ENB.

Flynn, M. (1999) 'Involving Users at All Levels.' In K. Billingham, M. Flynn and J. Weinstein (eds) *Making a World of Difference.* London: Royal College of General Practitioners.

Griffiths, Sir Roy (1983) *Report of the NHS Management Inquiry.* London: DHSS.

Griffiths, Sir Roy (1988) *Community Care: Agenda for Action, a Report to the Secretary of State for Social Services.* London: HMSO.

Hattersly, J. (1995) 'The Survival of Collaboration and Co-operation.' In N. Malin (ed) *Services for People with Learning Disabilities.* London: Routledge.

Health Act (1999) London: Stationery Office.

Heddell, F. (2003) 'Small Step Forward.' *Community Care,* 16–22 January, 38–39.

Hopkins, G. (2002) 'Falling through the Gap.' *Community Care,* 19–25 September, 46–47.

Leathard, A. (2000) *Health Care Provision: Past, Present and Into the 21st Century,* 2nd edn. Cheltenham: Stanley Thornes.

Nally, B. and Steele, J. (1992) 'Organisation and Practice in the Provision of Community Services for People with an Intellectual Disability.' In T. Thompson and P. Matthias (eds) *Standards and Mental Handicap: Keys to Competence.* London: Baillière Tindall.

National Health Service and Community Care Act (1990) London: HMSO.

Poxton, R., Greig, R. and Giraud Saunders, A. (2000) *Best Value Reviews for Learning Disability Services for Adults: A Framework for Applying Person-centred Principles.* London: Department of Health.

Richardson, M. (1997) 'Addressing Barriers: Disabled Rights and the Implications for Nursing of the Social Construct of Disability.' *Journal of Advanced Nursing 25,* 1271–1274.

Royal Commission on the Law Relating to Mental Illness and Mental Deficiency (The Percy Report) (1957) London: HMSO.

Schön, D. (1983) *The Reflective Practitioner. How Practitioners Think in Action.* New York: HarperCollins.

Shaw, I. (1993) 'The Politics of Interprofessional Training – Lessons for Learning Disability.' *Journal of Interprofessional Care 7,* 3, 255–262.

Sines, D. and Barr, O. (1998) 'Professions in Teams.' In T. Thompson and P. Mathias (eds) *Standards and Learning Disability,* 2nd edn. London: Baillière Tindall.

Stevens, A. (1998) 'Active Contributors: Service Users, Advocates and Support Networks.' In T. Thompson and P. Mathias (eds) *Standards and Learning Disability,* 2nd edn. London: Baillière Tindall.

Tuckman, B.W. (1965) 'Developmental Sequence in Small Groups.' *Psychological Bulletin 63,* 6, 384–399.

Vagg, J. (1998) 'A Lifetime of Caring.' In T. Thompson and P. Mathias (eds) *Standards and Learning Disability*, 2nd edn. London: Baillière Tindall.

Walker, T. and Ryan, T. (1995) *Fair Shares for All.* Brighton: Pavilion Publishing.

Walker, C. and Walker, A. (1998) *People with Learning Difficulties and their Ageing Family Carers.* Brighton: Pavilion Publishing.

West, M.A. and Slater, J. (1996) *Teamworking in Primary Health Care: A Review of its Effectiveness.* London: Health Education Authority.

Chapter 10

Social Work and Multi-disciplinary Collaboration in Primary Health Care

Kirstein Rummery

Introduction

This chapter will give a brief introduction to some of the fundamental changes that primary care organizations and practitioners have undergone in recent years, to provide the context for some of the issues facing social workers and social work managers when they attempt to work collaboratively with primary care. It will then look at some of the barriers to successful collaboration, and discuss examples from research evidence that show that these barriers are not necessarily insurmountable.

However, the overall tone of this chapter is deliberately cautious rather than optimistic, particularly about the *costs* and *benefits* of working in partnership with primary care, not only for social workers, managers and health professionals, but also for users and carers. The chapter will conclude with a critical discussion about what working in 'partnership' with primary care might mean for social workers, and whether true 'partnership' is possible or desirable, ending with a list of lessons for social workers working in collaboration with primary care. It will focus on research evidence that primarily concerns older people's services but the lessons – particularly those about inter-organizational and interprofessional collaboration – are salient for other groups of service users.

Primary care and partnership in The New NHS

There is a long inglorious history of the NHS and social services departments failing to work effectively together, which has often served to
highlight how inter-dependent the NHS and social services are, particularly
in providing services for older people. Even before the current emphasis on
primary care in the NHS, organizational divides between health and social
care have acted as barriers to joint working. These have not necessarily been
helped by the substantial upheaval that has taken place on both sides of the
divide, but particularly since 1997 in the NHS. New Labour's abolition of
GP-fundholding and reorganization of the NHS has shifted the focus on the
commissioning of health services, and thus also the responsibility for working jointly with social services, from health authorities to primary care
groups (PCGs) (DoH 1997). This has become even more apparent since the
demise of health authorities in 2002 and the signalling of two new developments in the NHS Plan that are key to joint and integrated working between
primary health and social care (DoH 2000). By 2004 all English PCGs will
have to become primary care trusts (PCTs) and take over the responsibility
for commissioning health services, while some will go further and both
commission and provide primary and community health services. The NHS
Plan also signalled the proposed development of the integration of primary
health and social care services within one organization, called a care trust.
The NHS Plan states that: 'Care Trusts will usually be established where
there is a joint agreement at local level that this model offers the best way to
deliver better care services' (DoH 2000, paragraph 7.10).

There is some evidence that suggests that creating 'joint' organizations
does not, in itself, overcome interprofessional barriers to joint working
(Forsgarde, Westman and Nygren 2000; Withington and Giler 2001). However, the advent of care trusts has been cautiously welcomed, with
commentators feeling that they will overcome some of the barriers to joint
working that besiege services for older people (Bowman 2000; Hughes
2001; Jones 2000; Lewis 2000).

Efforts to facilitate joint working between social services and health care
have tended to focus on strategic collaboration between health and local
authorities – for example, around joint commissioning of services for older
people (Hudson 1999; Poxton 1999; Rummery 1999) – which has not
involved front-line social workers or primary care practitioners. There is a
history of operational level collaboration between front-line practitioners
(for example, by outposting social workers in GP surgeries) which continues,

despite the evidence that these are difficult to extend and sustain over a wider area than individual surgeries (Lymbery 1998; McIntosh and Bennett-Emslie 1992; Ross and Tissier 1997). In the following sections I will discuss the opportunities and barriers to joint working at the operational level and look at the evidence at the strategic level from the case of the new primary care groups and trusts ('primary care organizations').

Working in collaboration with primary care professionals at the front line

Although a plethora of schemes have been piloted that have attempted to improve collaboration between social workers and primary care practitioners (primarily GPs and community nurses), four 'models' have endured and become popular. The first is to locate social workers in primary care settings, sometimes creating truly integrated 'teams' (usually where the GP practice employs the social worker), but more often by 'outposting' statutory social workers either full or part time to cover one or more GP surgeries. Statutory social workers working in such posts do run the risk of professional isolation and have to be skilled networkers and communicators to assimilate themselves into a team with an overwhelmingly 'medical' focus, but such schemes are popular with doctors, and with users and carers, who find accessing social care easier when done through the auspices of a primary care setting rather than a remote social services office (Ross and Tissier 1997).

The second is to train community nurses to carry out assessment and care management for older people, an option that was put forward under the 1990 NHS and Community Care Act and is growing in popularity as the new primary care organizations get greater powers to employ their own staff. Again, this improves access to services for users and carers, removes the need for duplicate health and social care assessments, and can give community nurses much appreciated additional skills and perspectives. However, community nursing is an often overstretched service, and some nurses are unhappy with implementing some elements of care management (such as the need to undertake financial assessments to calculate service charges, and the rights of people who appear to nurses' eyes to be at risk to refuse services). Social workers working with community nurses in such teams have also voiced the concern that some nurses may miss some of the wider social needs a social worker would pick up on (such as carers' needs) and that nurses' overwhelming concern with health-related issues may leave out other issues (such as anti-poverty or anti-discrimination work) that social workers consider important.

The third is for the local authority (sometimes jointly with the health authority or primary care organization) to employ 'liaison' workers, whose duties are specifically around fostering interprofessional networks and supporting workers on both sides to make appropriate referrals. These are popular among primary care workers because they can navigate what can appear to be a very complex system of statutory and voluntary sector services, thus saving a lot of time and frustration. However, unless their remit is to work specifically with users and carers, it is unlikely that users and carers themselves will experience the benefits of such workers. They may benefit indirectly from improved referral pathways which lead to reduced waiting times for access to services.

The fourth is to place voluntary sector workers (social workers, welfare rights workers and similar professionals) in GP surgeries. In many respects this has all the advantages of the first model with none of the disadvantages, because non-statutory workers will have a great deal more freedom to design their own 'job specification' than statutory workers, and thus be able to refine the service they offer to meet the needs of both primary care professionals and users and carers. They can be more responsive to local needs (for example, offering services specifically designed for minority ethnic carers) than mainstream services. However, because they are often funded through charities, their status can be insecure, and there are legions of examples of innovative practice that made a temporary difference to users and carers only to disappear through lack of systematic funding or support.

There has been little systematic work done comparing these models so it cannot be said with any confidence that one is better than another at fostering and sustaining interprofessional collaboration. Some analysts have found that no one model is substantially superior to another, but that they all offer improvements on the standard pattern of service organization (Tucker and Brown 1997). However, there are certain barriers and benefits that appear to be universal, regardless of which model is adopted, and the remainder of this section will be used to discuss them.

Barriers and benefits for health and social care managers

The biggest barrier to getting front-line collaborative projects off the ground and sustaining them from the perspective of managers is the failure to 1. plan them properly and 2. ensure that all the stakeholders are committed to and involved in the project. Planning needs to take into account that the NHS and local authorities have different planning cycles, priorities, management structures and accountability arrangements. For example, social services departments are accountable to locally elected councillors in a way which their NHS counterparts are not, and priorities for spending on services may not be the same on both sides. These differences need to be made explicit and understood by all stakeholders at the outset of planning projects, as they can derail successful projects later on. Social services departments and the new primary care organizations are rarely co-terminous, which can make planning any new service development difficult.

However, if these organizational barriers are acknowledged and over-come there can be significant benefits to front-line collaborative projects for both health and social care managers. There is evidence that such projects may result in lower use of hospital beds and residential or nursing home care, because it has proved possible to target preventive interventions more appro-priately – usually due to improved communication and information sharing between professionals (Rummery and Glendinning 2000). Such schemes therefore offer a more effective way of accessing services without there nec-essarily being a significant increase in the level or cost of services used.

Nevertheless, there is some evidence that the cost of running such pro-jects falls disproportionately on social services, who tend to make the most changes in their working practices and bear most of the unforeseen or hid-den management costs; and that the corresponding benefits (most often reduced frustration, reduced service costs, better interprofessional communi-cation and collaboration) are greater for NHS managers and practitioners (Rummery and Glendinning 2000).

Barriers and benefits for GPs and community nurses

GPs in the NHS are usually independent contractors who traditionally work as small businesses, although the advent of the new primary care organiza-tions and practice-based contracts has changed the culture of primary care slightly. Nevertheless, they remain a professional group whose history and experiences do not predispose them to working collaboratively (Callaghan *et al.* 2000). Relationships with other primary care professionals such as com-munity nurses are not necessarily good or consistent – much depends on the nature and priorities of individual GPs. Even where relationships are good with key GP partners in a surgery it does not necessarily follow that these relationships will extend to include other GPs within the same surgery.

This lack of a real 'team' in primary care can affect relationships between that team and external collaborators such as social workers. In projects attaching social workers to GP surgeries, social workers often found that they had negotiated good relationships with one key GP, only to find that other GPs or, perhaps more crucially, community nurses were not committed to the project because of a lack of involvement in the planning stage (Rummery and Glendinning 2000). As such projects tend to involve a lot of time and effort to overcome interprofessional mistrust resulting from a low level of understanding about each other's roles and responsibilities, having to redo the work with each new GP or practice can be time-consuming and disheartening for social workers.

Relationships with community nurses can be more consistent, particularly around older people's services where nurses and social workers will often find themselves working with the same users and carers. In many respects, community nurses can be more important collaborators for social workers than GPs, and I would argue that investing in improving collaboration in this area can be more effective than focusing on GP–social worker relationships.

Research has consistently shown that the primary care partners in collaborative projects, regardless of the nature of the project, experience considerable benefits as a result of being involved (Rummery and Glendinning 2000). These largely result from the improved interprofessional relationships with social workers, which in turn lead to improved communications. This can result in a reduction in delays in referrals and frustration and better feedback, which leads to more appropriate and timely referrals, a reduction in inappropriate GP consultations by users and carers and a more holistic approach to working with patients.

Barriers and benefits for social workers

Working in collaborative projects such as GP surgery attachments can be a headache and a liberation for social workers. In order to be successful, social workers do need to be effective networkers, have excellent communication skills and be very flexible and adaptable in their working practices. Working in such projects can be very isolating and adequate arrangements for professional supervision, support and backup have to be in place. Social workers in primary care settings often have to undertake a lot of work educating primary care practitioners about their role and responsibilities, and may find themselves in the position of having to make considerable changes in their practice without similar accommodations being made by GPs and community nurses. It is highly likely that social workers in such settings will find themselves with appreciably bigger workloads than their colleagues in traditional teams (Rummery and Glendinning 2000).

However, there is no evidence that social workers in these situations are opening up a 'floodgate' of unmanageable demand. What appears to happen is that workload rises because of two factors. First, users and carers find a practice-based social worker easier to access (in part because it is less stigmatizing and in part because primary care practitioners make more appropriate referrals). Second, social workers (particularly if they are working for a voluntary rather than statutory agency) in primary care settings often find themselves unable to limit their work to the core 'assessment and care management' tasks that their colleagues in traditional teams often find themselves having to do. Primary care-based social workers, in contrast, usually find themselves working more holistically with families, and acting as advocates and liaison workers with other agencies. The result of this is that while users and carers do not necessarily end up using more social care services, they do end up accessing a range of services more appropriately and often in a more preventative way than users who access services through traditional social work teams.

Therefore, while social workers in primary care settings do need adequate managerial support to ensure that they are not overwhelmed with work, and can become isolated without that support, they can experience considerable professional satisfaction from being able to work in new, flexible ways which often meet the needs of users and carers more effectively than work in traditional social work teams is able to do. Many social workers in such settings have voiced the view that their work is more like 'real' social work, more in line with their professional training and values, than the risk-based assessment and care management tasks their colleagues have to undertake.

Barriers and benefits for users and carers

There has been very little systematic research that has explored what the benefits of these projects are for users and carers. Some benefits can be surmised from the benefits experienced by the workers involved. For example, it is likely that users and carers benefit from easier access to social workers when they are based in primary care settings, and that such access is considered less stigmatizing than access to social workers working in traditional teams. It is also likely that users and carers will experience the benefits of a reduction in duplication of assessments and better targeting of services that results from improved communication between social workers, GPs and community nurses.

However, it is very rare for users and carers to be systematically involved in the designing or running of these projects. Collaborative projects tend to reflect the aims and priorities of the key stakeholders *only* if those stakeholders are involved from the planning stage onwards. This means that while such projects often address the needs of the professionals involved they do not necessarily meet the needs of users and carers. The few projects that did involve users and carers strategically from the outset often found that they had priorities that did not necessarily accord with the priorities of either the organizations or professionals involved in the project – for example, one project wanted GP receptionists to be trained in mental health awareness, and another wanted bathing services to be freely available to all users, which were not considered priorities by project funders (Rummery and Glendinning 2000).

While users and carers may benefit from the improved *processes* that often result from these collaborative projects, there is no evidence that they experience the kind of improved *outcomes* (such as increased independence, ability to stay in their own homes, control over the timing, delivery and cost of services) that older people value (Qureshi and Henwood 2000).

Working strategically with the new primary care organizations

New Labour's reorganization of the NHS, particularly the formation of the new primary care organizations, has opened up new challenges but also new opportunities for multi-disciplinary collaboration between primary care and social services. The original guidelines for the make-up of primary care group boards recommended that the social services representative be someone with 'operational' level responsibility (DoH 2000). However, most social services departments ignored this advice and in the first year of their existence, 90 per cent of social services representatives had some kind of strategic responsibility within social services (Rummery, Coleman and Jacobs 2001).

The level of seniority of the social services representative can be important in many respects. The boards of the new primary care organizations (PCOs) are specifically designed to allow front-line primary care practitioners, particularly GPs and community nurses, to play a significant part in deciding and putting into practice the aims and priorities of the organization. Initially, primary care groups were constituted as sub-committees of the health authority, although this will change as they all move towards primary care trust status. Initially, social services representatives on PCG/T boards were found to be able to exert much less influence than GPs, health authorities and community nurses – in the first year of a study looking at relationships between the new PCOs and social services, 27 per cent of social services representatives on PCG/T boards felt that the interests of social services were poorly represented on the boards in comparison to other stakeholders such as GPs, nurses and health authority members (Rummery 2002a). In order to counteract this lack of influence, it was important that social services representatives could bring some 'power' to the table in the form of being able to affect service commissioning decisions within social services.

An ongoing study of how the new primary care organizations are working with social services departments (details of the methods of this study can be found in Rummery and Coleman 2003) has found that the role of the social services representative on the board of the PCG/Ts is a crucial and difficult one (Glendinning, Coleman and Rummery 2002; Rummery et al. 2001). Initially, many social services representatives found it difficult to become integrated into the working of the board. This was due to several reasons. First, many social services departments underestimated the commitment, particularly in terms of time and management support, that was needed for social services representatives to fulfil their role on top of their 'day job' in social services, as this social services representative pointed out:

> I find the total agenda difficult to manage within a thirty-seven hour week. The agreement was...that it equates to half a day a week. I think in terms of my Board commitments that is probably a good reflection of the time...but when you start adding in some of the commissioning work, particularly around the health development group for older people and around the carers...that isn't included in the half day. (Social services representative, PCG board, site C, year 1)

Second, there was an initial lack of understanding of each other's roles and responsibilities, as explained by these two interviewees:

> I was starting from a very low knowledge base of GPs and how they worked and what drove them. It took me a while to actually understand

> them and understand what drove them in terms of how they function. (Social services representative, PCG board, site A, year 1)

> I can't get my head around the thing you find with social services is their bureaucracy and they way in which they have to go through their committee structure and elected members to almost do anything. It's really quite frustrating. (Nursing manager, community trust, site C, year 1)

Third, many social services representatives found that their influence was limited by the lack of experience that other board members, particularly GPs, had in working strategically around health and service commissioning issues, let alone thinking about working collaboratively with social workers or other organizations, as these interviewees explain:

> There's still quite a lot of development to be done, especially around GPs who are learning new ways of working. GPs are independent contractors with the health authority and have been used to developing their own practices and I think to take on the role of strategic thinkers is really quite a hard job. (Social services representative, PCG board, site A, year 1)

> I would say that [my influence] is not so extensive and that is related to the capacity of the Board and the people on it to be able to think more widely than their health care interests. (Social services representative, PCG board, site B, year 1)

Fourth, the organizational development needs of the new PCG/Ts and the early priorities of the boards made them very inward-focused and militated against the social services representative being able to exert much influence:

> Out of necessity a lot of work in PCGs up until now has been fairly inward-looking as you've got the transition from fundholding to PCGs at the start. There's a lot of work having to be done in terms of sorting out contractual arrangements, prescribing, etc., and no sooner had that settled down than there was the actual pressure involved to consider becoming a PCT. (Social services representative, PCG board, site D, year 1)

This inward focus was not helped by the rapid policy changes that PCGs had to accommodate in the early years, with the pressure to become PCTs and the disappearance of health authorities in 2002 placing them under enormous pressure to develop rapidly as organizations.

Nevertheless, by year two of the study there were some encouraging signs that interprofessional relationships between social services representatives and other members of the PCG/T boards had improved and were able to weather some of the organizational and other upheaval experienced by both sides:

> When we costed what would have been our gold standard for our older peoples services then we didn't have enough to do everything we wanted and we had to prioritize. But in return for that, you know our local Social Services department has been very heavily squeezed recently because, you know education is top of the list, and children's services in this local authority in common with many others. So it did look for a while as if Social Services funding was going to become a major issue and that they weren't going to have enough money... I think the relationships are good enough, you know we all recognize at the end of the day we have to meet our waiting list targets, if you all know one another you know that Social Services aren't – they're being squeezed from externally, you know that they would do it if they could. (Chief officer, PCT board, site D, year 2)

There was also some evidence that investment in interprofessional work throughout primary care and social services organizations was paying off and professionals were welcoming the chance to learn from each other:

> Where we work jointly with people that's really good because both start to, you know practices that we've been working with for over a year, the information about community resources and community options and choices is better now than it was a year ago because we take in our community knowledge and I think that is an issue that we can, if we work jointly, can influence, the rights to say no and the rights to die, things that, you know, our Health colleagues can't quite get their heads round. (Social work front-line manager, site A, year 2)

As the new PCOs matured as organizations they were able to benefit from the experience of their social services colleagues and from social services departments' more developed information systems:

> I do think there's been a general shift towards looking at the broader determinants of health, looking at less focus on the medical model. (Chief officer, PCT board, site D, year 2)

Social care have got far more well-developed information systems, particularly because they've been dealing with the population at that level for
far greater length of time, and they have things like systems panels, systems juries, local assemblies, they have data on deprivation, they can
match it to crime statistics, they can identify pockets of problems in terms
of crime and disorder, social isolation, to some extent social inequalities,
you know, far more. (Chief officer, PCG board, site A, year 2)

Social services representatives and front-line social work managers reported
improvements in their understandings of how primary care professionals,
particularly GPs and community nurses, worked. They felt that this
improved interprofessional understanding had led to positive outcomes such
as quicker referral pathways and improved multi-disciplinary assessments.

However, by year two of the study very little progress had been made in
respect of the new PCOs actually commissioning joint services with social
services departments. When interviewees in both the health and social services organizations were asked to identify tangible benefits for users and
carers as a result of their multi-disciplinary working, the common refrain was
'it's early days'. While the benefits to the professionals involved of improved
multi-disciplinary work at both the operational and strategic level were clear,
there was less compelling evidence that these were being translated into
improved services for users and carers.

Partnership with primary care: Holy Grail or dangerous liaison?

It is to be hoped that the cautious note about the barriers to and benefits of
partnership working with primary care have not sounded too disappointing.
'Partnership' after all has such overwhelmingly positive connotations that
who could possibly object to working in partnership with another organization or group of professionals (Clarke and Glendinning 2002)? When you
add to that the centrality that 'partnership' takes in the current policy climate, with both the NHS and local authorities being under specific statutory
duties to work 'in partnership' with each other, then it is perhaps unsurpris-
ing that social workers may find themselves in several situations where
working in 'partnership' with GPs, community nurses and PCG/T managers
is assumed to be the 'Holy Grail'.

However, it is worth remembering that 'partnership for partnership's
sake' can be a fruitless enterprise. The Audit Commission recommends that
organizations only engage in partnership working with outside organiza-

tions where the organizations have significantly overlapping aims and where working in partnership can enable the organizations to meet their own aims more effectively (Audit Commission 1998) and it is worth applying this salient lesson to multi-disciplinary partnerships involving social work and primary care as well. Partnership working is distinguished from other forms of working by the presence of inter-dependence and trust between the partners (Rummery 2002b) and there need to be significant benefits for *both* sides to make it worthwhile.

Working in partnership is not a cost-neutral activity. Social workers and social work managers are professionals whose time is a resource in short supply (and the same may be said for GPs, community nurses and other primary care professionals). Working in partnership with another profession or organization diverts attention and resources away from the core business of professionals and organizations (time spent in 'partnership board' meetings is time spent away from working directly with users and carers, for example) and it cannot be assumed that investment in partnership working will result in better services for users and carers simply because it makes life easier for professionals. Indeed, in some cases working in partnership with outside agencies or professionals can result in net *losses* for the participants concerned, particularly if one side is significantly less powerful than the other (Craig and Taylor 2002).

However, because joint working between primary health and social care is in many cases compulsory in the present policy climate it can be argued that the government has created the inter-dependence that is a necessary prerequisite for partnership working. Both the NHS and local authorities have to show evidence of collaboration around certain key areas – for example, the areas, such as joint assessment and rehabilitation services, highlighted under the *National Service Framework for Older People* (DoH 2001) – in order to meet their own objectives. It is also worth remembering an argument I have made elsewhere in analysing the state of partnership working in the current policy climate:

> Partnership working New Labour-style benefits powerful partners. Such partnerships reinforce power inequalities that are already in existence, placing central government in a relatively powerful position vis-à-vis local government, the private sector in a relatively powerful position vis-à-vis the public sector and the public sector in a relatively powerful position vis-à-vis the voluntary and community sector. They divert resources away from the core business of welfare service delivery and

they do relatively little to empower users or local communities. (Rummery 2002b, p.243)

In the present policy climate, with the NHS benefiting from additional resources and power, and social services departments looking relatively impoverished in comparison, social workers and social work managers may do well to be wary when working with primary care. To prevent such partnerships becoming dangerous liaisons, they should satisfy themselves that their status and values are not going to be compromised or overwhelmed by their relatively powerful primary care colleagues, that the benefits of multi-disciplinary working will be felt by themselves as well as by GPs and community nurses and, perhaps most importantly, that users and carers are not excluded from either the process or the outcome of joint working.

Nevertheless, it is important not to lose sight of the indisputable evidence that multi-disciplinary working between primary health and social care colleagues can result in significant benefits for the professionals involved. As one interviewee in the above study explained:

> I think there's been an enhancement of understanding and mutual respect, and I do think that's quite genuine. I think…you know, one of the biggest complaints you get from GPs and I know there are […] you can never, you know, never get to see a social worker, never get hold of anyone and people are quite elusive, and I think the face to face contact breaks that barrier down, and they see these people and they can see that they're very professional and able, and I think that makes a big difference. (Health authority manager, site C, year 2)

The challenge for social workers, social work managers and their primary care partners is to translate these gains in interprofessional understanding into real benefits for service users and carers.

Lessons in partnership for social workers
In order to maximize the social work contribution in joint working and to protect social workers' professional identity and status in work with potentially more powerful primary care partners, the following lessons are suggested for social workers:

- Work at developing relationships with GPs, but be prepared for the possibility that their professional culture may not give them the same sense of teamworking as your own and may affect their collaboration with you.

- Work at collaborating with community nurses – it is more likely to be reciprocated, and to show benefits for your users and carers, than concentrating on GPs, and good interprofessional relations here can spill over into the wider primary care team.

- Practise and develop your communication and networking skills, and be prepared to be flexible even when it seems others are not.

- Seek and use support and supervision to reduce and manage isolation.

- Take the opportunity to benefit from the increased professional rewards that the opportunity to do 'real social work' will inevitably present.

- Make an effort to understand the organizational, strategic and funding issues that affect everyday work in primary care and social work settings (such as the implications of becoming a primary care trust, and what best value means for users and carers) and be prepared to communicate these to fellow professionals who may be unfamiliar with them.

- Be encouraged by the prospect that collaborative working with primary care may enhance the service to users and carers and make use of any opportunities you have to contribute to the evidence base in this area.

References

Audit Commission (1998) *A Fruitful Partnership: Effective Partnership Working.* London: Audit Commission.

Bowman, A. (2000) 'Gin and Tonic, or Oil and Water?' *Professional Social Work,* September, 6–7.

Callaghan, G.M., Exworthy, M.M., Hudson, B. and Peckham, S. (2000) 'Prospects for Collaboration in Primary Care: Relationships Between Social Services and the New PCGs.' *Journal of Interprofessional Care 14,* 1, 19–26.

Clarke, J. and Glendinning, C. (2002) 'Partnership and the Remaking of Welfare Governance.' In C. Glendinning, M. Powell and K. Rummery (eds) *Partnerships, New Labour and the Governance of Welfare.* Bristol: Policy Press.

Craig, G. and Taylor, M. (2002) 'Dangerous Liaisons: Local Government and the Voluntary and Community Sectors.' In C. Glendinning, M. Powell and K. Rummery (eds) *Partnerships, New Labour and the Governance of Welfare*. Bristol: Policy Press.

DoH (1997) *The New NHS: Modern, Dependable*. Cm 3807. London: Stationery Office.

DoH (2000) *The NHS Plan: A Plan for Investment, a Plan for Reform*. Cm 47818–1. London: Stationery Office.

DoH (2001) *National Service Framework for Older People*. London: Department of Health.

Forsgarde, M., Westman, B. and Nygren, L. (2000) 'Ethical Discussion Groups as an Intervention to Improve the Climate in Interprofessional Work with the Elderly and Disabled.' *Journal of Interprofessional Care 14*, 4, 351–361.

Glendinning, C., Coleman, A. and Rummery, K. (2002) 'Partnerships, Performance and Primary Care: Developing Integrated Services for Older People in England.' *Ageing and Society 22*, 2, 185–208.

Hudson, B. (1999) 'Joint Commissioning Across the Primary Health–Social Care Boundary: Can It Work?' *Health and Social Care in the Community 7*, 5, 358–366.

Hughes, L. (2001) 'Bloodless Revolution.' *Community Care*, 8 February, 20–21.

Jones, R. (2000) 'A Question of Trust.' *Health Service Journal*, 19 October, 28–29.

Lewis, C. (2000) 'Friend or Foe?' *Community Care*, 14 December, 26–27.

Lymbery, M. (1998) 'Social Work in General Practice: Dilemmas and Solutions.' *Journal of Interprofessional Care 12*, 2, 199–208.

McIntosh, J. and Bennett-Emslie, G. (1992) 'The Health Centre as a Location for Care Management.' *Health and Social Care in the Community 1*, 91–97.

NHS and Community Care Act (1990) London: Stationery Office.

Poxton, R. (1999) *Partnerships in Primary and Social Care: Integrating Services for Vulnerable People*. London: King's Fund.

Qureshi, H. and Henwood, M. (2000) *Older People's Definitions of Quality Services*. York: York Publishing Services.

Ross, F. and Tissier, J. (1997) 'The Care Management Interface with General Practice: A Case Study.' *Health and Social Care in the Community 5*, 3, 153–161.

Rummery, K. (1999) 'The Way Forward for Joint Working? Involving Primary Care in the Commissioning of Social Care Services.' *Journal of Interprofessional Care 13*, 3, 207–218.

Rummery, K. (2002a) 'Progress Towards Partnership? The Development of Relations Between Primary Care Organisations and Social Services Concerning Older People's Services in the UK.' Presented at Annual Social Policy Association Conference, Teeside University, July.

Rummery, K. (2002b) 'Towards a Theory of Welfare Partnerships.' In C. Glendinning, M. Powell and K. Rummery (eds) *Partnerships, New Labour and the Governance of Welfare.* Bristol: Policy Press.

Rummery, K. and Coleman, A. (2003) 'Primary Health and Social Care Services in the UK: Progress Towards Partnership?' *Social Science and Medicine 56,* 8, 1773–82

Rummery, K., Coleman, A. and Jacobs, S. (2001) 'Uneasy Bedfellows? The Development of Partnerships Between Primary Care Groups and Local Authorities Concerning Services for Older People.' In D. Taylor (ed) *Breaking Down Barriers: Reviewing Partnership Practice.* Brighton: Health and Social Policy Research Centre, University of Brighton.

Rummery, K. and Glendinning, C. (2000) *Primary Care and Social Services: Developing New Partnerships for Older People.* Abingdon: Radcliffe Medical Press.

Tucker, C. and Brown, L. (1997) *Evaluating Different Models for Jointly Commissioning Community Care.* Bath: Wiltshire Social Services and University of Bath Development Partnership Report 4.

Withington, S. and Giler, H. (2001) 'Multidisciplinary Working and the New NHS: More Messages from Northern Ireland.' *Managing Community Care 8,* 6, 24–29.

Chapter 11

Collaborating for the Social and Health Care of Older People

Mark Lymbery

Introduction

These are challenging times for social work with older people. New policy directions have highlighted numerous opportunities for creative collaborations between social workers, a range of health professionals and older people themselves. This chapter will argue that the social work profession should be central to policy for older people. This is not an argument that derives from professional self-interest: the chapter contends that social work's commitment to collaborative activity can improve the quality of services provided and hence the quality of care received by older people.

The chapter also recognizes that there are obstacles in the path of such collaboration. For example, where the notion of partnership is addressed in most policy documents, it is between health and social care in general terms, or between health and social services organizations, rather than between different professional groupings. However, better interprofessional collaboration is an essential part of policy for older people. As Hudson (2002) points out, problems at the interprofessional level can be the 'Achilles' heel' of partnership. Therefore, effective partnerships cannot be established without the creation of good systems of interprofessional collaboration.

The chapter begins by outlining the context of partnership working for older people, distinguishing the significance of interprofessional collaboration within this context. It focuses on a number of issues that potentially weaken the capacity of the various professions to work together effectively.

The chapter then engages with two key elements of collaborative practice: assessment and intermediate care. It concludes by arguing that the active presence of social work professionals within a collaborative framework will enhance the overall quality of services provided.

The context of partnership

Notions of improved partnership have been a consistent theme throughout the life of the Labour government, beginning with the *Partnership in Action* discussion document (DoH 1998), continuing through the Health Select Committee Report (DoH 1999) and having particular expression in the NHS Plan (DoH 2000a). The NHS Plan stated that 'the old divisions between health and social care need to be overcome' and that 'fundamental reforms' are required to address this issue (DoH 2000a, p.70). It further stated that there 'will be a new relationship between health and social care', which 'will bring about a radical redesign of the whole care system' (DoH 2000a, p.71).

The proposals to establish unified care trusts as an extension from primary care trusts are particularly significant in this respect. It is envisaged that the care trusts 'will provide for even closer integration of health and social services' (DoH 2000a, p.73), and would be established as single bodies to commission and deliver primary and community health and social care. Although the desirability of establishing care trusts through voluntary arrangements is emphasized, there is also a more coercive edge. For example, if effective partnerships cannot be developed voluntarily, the government reserves the right to *impose* integrated arrangements through the establishment of care trusts (see DoH 2000a, paragraph 7.11). As a result, most social services departments (SSDs) recognize that they must increase the extent of collaborative work, in part to protect their role in the commissioning and delivery of social care services.

The publication of the national service framework (NSF) heralded a further development in the process of collaboration and partnership (DoH 2001). As the cornerstone of its focus on person-centred care, the NSF proposed that a single assessment process for older people should be introduced. Its purpose is defined as follows: 'to ensure that older people receive appropriate, effective and timely responses to their health and social care needs, and that professional resources are used effectively' (DoH 2002a, p.1). It is required that the single assessment process should be introduced by April 2004 (DoH 2002a), requiring health and social care agencies to establish arrangements for inter-agency, multi-disciplinary and interprofessional collaboration – not just in respect of assessment but also in relation to commissioning and providing services. The role of the social worker is seen as central to this; indeed, the Department of Health has issued a specific document focusing on the implications of the single assessment process for social workers (DoH 2002c). Separate guidance has also been issued for other professions – nurses, GPs, therapists etc. – thus firmly establishing the interprofessional nature of the enterprise.

The NSF also extends the focus on intermediate care, first highlighted in the NHS Plan (DoH 2000a). Here it was stated that an extra £900 million would be invested 'to promote independence and improve quality of care for older people' (DoH 2000a, p.71). The NHS Plan is not prescriptive about the detailed arrangements to be established, but points to several possibilities, including rapid response teams, hospital-based rehabilitation services, recuperative facilities in residential or nursing homes and integrated home-care teams.

Specific targets are identified in the NSF for the different elements of intermediate care (DoH 2001, pp.42–3), representing an ambitious policy programme. Again, the government recognized that the creation of an effective system of intermediate care depended on the establishment of robust collaborative arrangements, as 'intermediate care cannot be the responsibility of only one professional group or agency' (DoH 2001, p.43).

Further detail concerning collaboration in assessment and intermediate care will be considered in later sections. At this point my attention will turn to the various difficulties that may be confronted when seeking to establish interprofessional arrangements for older people.

Obstacles to effective collaboration

Because effective collaboration is such a central part of the government's plans for health and social care, the obstacles that might obstruct its realization need to be carefully considered. For the purposes of this chapter, these have been broken down into several core themes:

- the connection between interprofessional collaboration and broader organizational and financial issues

- the tensions between organizations' need simultaneously to look outwards and inwards

- the literature that identifies the inherent problems in the development of closer collaborative working

- the continued marginalization of the needs, wishes and opinions of older people themselves, despite government rhetoric to the contrary

- the practical difficulties in involving older people in meaningful collaborative processes

- the lasting impact of community care changes, in particular the adoption of bureaucratic care management models, on social work practice with older people

- the relatively weak development of the social work role with older people.

Inter-organizational issues

Lewis (2001) demonstrates that there has been decades of what she terms as 'hidden policy conflict' between health and social care organizations, despite numerous calls to improve the quality of partnership working between them. She argues that the origin of this conflict can be found:

> ... in the way in which central government sought to define the nature of the responsibilities of the two services and, crucially, from the way in which the resource implications of this definition were never openly addressed. (Lewis 2001, p.345)

In her view, partnership working is most needed for those people who are not clearly the primary responsibility of either health or social care. Such people could be defined as requiring constant nursing care but not medical care, or alternatively needing regular, but not constant, medical or nursing care. Clearly, the majority of older people with whom social workers operate come under one of these categories.

Importantly, Lewis (2001) also identifies three broad levels at which partnership arrangements are located – financial, organizational and professional. From this, she argues that repeated failures to resolve the perverse financial incentives for both health and social care ensure that organizations act in ways that best suit their own financial priorities rather than the overarching goal of improved partnership. This is significant because the improvements to interprofessional collaboration have largely not been reflected in changed financial arrangements, despite the growing use of 'flexibilities' under the Health Act 1999 and cross-charging arrangements. As Lewis (2001) suggests, failure to resolve these financial issues could counteract many of the developments that are in train at the organizational and professional levels.

Inward- versus outward-looking organizations

The organizational emphasis on performance measurement in health and social care (Power 1997; Sanderson 2001) is one development which has forced organizations to look inwards, as has the major restructuring of primary health care – prefigured by the NHS White Paper (DoH 1997). One should not underestimate the upheaval caused by such changes and their impact on the development of innovative and creative responses to government requirements. These factors graphically illustrate what Charlesworth (2001) identifies as a 'paradox' at the heart of partnership working:

> It is a paradox that just as the government is asking organizations to collaborate more and to be more outward looking, they are also being forced to focus more on internal issues, particularly around monitoring and audit. (Charlesworth 2001, p.283)

While effective collaboration needs organizations to be outward-looking, the demands of audit, review and organizational change have forced health and social services organizations into a more inward-looking posture. It is difficult to reconcile these contradictory impulses.

Conceptual problems in interprofessional working

The development of improved interprofessional working should not be presumed to be unproblematic. Indeed, as Hudson (2002) points out, there is a strong tradition of critical literature on interprofessional collaboration that leads to negative conclusions about its potential. He argues that this 'pessimistic' perspective has focused on three elements:

- professional identity and territory
- relative status and power of professions
- different patterns of discretion and accountability between professions.

Indeed, the literature is crowded with authors examining these issues – particularly in respect of collaboration between social workers and doctors. Much of this material (see Dingwall 1982 and Huntington 1981 for classic accounts) focuses on the difficulties and problems that exist, emphasizing particularly inequalities of status and power. Bywaters (1986) went so far as to suggest that true collaboration between social workers and doctors was impossible unless it was predicated on the promotion of a social model of health.

There is also, however, a more optimistic academic tradition on which to draw (Hudson 2002). It is suggested that professionals can develop fruitful alliances when located with members of other professions (Dalley 1989). There is also evidence that effective interprofessional working can help to meet the goals of different organizations while providing better service delivery (Lymbery 1998b). Indeed, there is considerable recent research that highlights successful interprofessional working, although these studies often emphasize improved collaborative processes rather than demonstrate improved outcomes for service users (see, for example, Lymbery and Millward 2000; Ross, Rink and Furne 2000). However, the successes of individual projects do not entirely invalidate the potential problems, which represent major obstacles to be overcome.

The marginalization of older people

The place of older people within society, and their consequent marginalization by both health and social care services, is another critical factor. The experiences of many older people within the service system can be profoundly unsatisfactory, reflecting both societal ambivalence towards the existence of their growing numbers and the difficulty that agencies have in meeting the levels of need that are presented. As a result, many older people encounter social and health care services as oppressive and disabling. This can be experienced in many ways. Some service users complain of being given inadequate or incomplete information. In other cases, the complexity of their circumstances is often underestimated and their possible need for emotional support minimized (Thompson and Thompson 2001). Even in innovative projects, there remains a tendency to fit people into the services that exist rather than tailoring services to meet their need (Walker and Warren 1996). While the NSF (DoH 2001) does focus on the need to develop collaborative structures that fully involve older people, the precise mechanisms for achieving this are unclear.

Practical problems of collaboration

As Twigg (2000) identifies, there is an ambivalence in the way in which older people are perceived within community care. In the early documentation they were conceptualized as consumers, with the policy changes aiming to empower them more fully (see, for example, DoH/SSI 1991). However, it is not always possible for older people to express their wishes in consumerist terms (Lymbery 2000). A number of writers have focused on the importance of empowering older people (see, for example, Thompson and Thompson 2001), but efforts in this direction are seldom fully successful.

The practical difficulties of more active involvement of older people cannot be underestimated. By the time that many come to the attention of social workers they are in a position of crisis, often complicated by significant physical or cognitive impairments. The interests of older people and their carers or partners cannot be assumed to be identical, while the pressures on social workers – identified in the following sub-section – are considerable. All of these factors make meaningful collaboration difficult, although they should not be used to justify failure to engage with the issue.

Community care, care management and social work

The final points are closely connected. I have elsewhere discussed the impact of community care policy changes – particularly the introduction of care management – on social work practice with older people (Lymbery 1998a), concluding that the impact of 'new managerialism' within social services departments had forced social work as care management into a bureaucratized, proceduralized form of practice. Postle (2002) has echoed this conclusion in a more recent paper. In part, this can be explained by the form of care management practice that has come to dominate work with older people. Payne (2000) notes that a multi-professional model distinguishes high-risk mental health services and a model of service brokerage has been developed to meet the needs of adults with disabilities. Both of these roles have, he argues, a core professional role for social workers. By contrast, care management with older people is distinguished by the model of social care entrepreneurship, where the availability of services is tightly constrained by costs, and *professional* considerations are secondary to *economic* priorities.

The cumulative effect of operating within a financially dominated environment has had an impact on the working lives of social workers. As Postle (2002) demonstrates, they have to manage a complex set of tensions – juggling apparently infinite needs and finite resources: balancing the requirement for detailed financial assessment with relationship building and related work. As her respondents demonstrate, many practitioners believe that a reductive form of practice now dominates (Postle 2002).

A core reason why this has been allowed to develop is the professional weakness of social work with older people. Before community care, social work with older people was regularly reported as being among the least favoured areas of practice (see, for example, Rees 1978), a perspective confirmed by more recent studies (Litwin 1994). The lack of a clear professional identity has blocked the ability of social workers to resist the imposition of more restrictive, routinized forms of practice. While this is evident throughout social work, as Jones (2001) graphically illustrates, the lack of professional self-confidence is particularly marked in work with older people.

For interprofessional working these factors create a similar paradox to that outlined in relation to organizational priorities. Effective collaboration must be based on three elements:

- the capacity of all professions to enter into new sets of relations based on a professional self-confidence

- a clear understanding of each other's contribution to the process of joint working

- unequivocal support from employing organizations that allows practitioners to respond creatively to situations.

As can be seen, lack of professional self-confidence affects the capacity of social workers to function in accordance with the first of these principles. Further, the way that SSDs have responded to the demands of community care has constrained the autonomy and discretion allowed to practitioners. Neither of these represents positive auguries for the future of interprofessional work with older people.

The intention of the remainder of this chapter is to illustrate ways in which social work practitioners can contribute to more effective collaborative processes, despite the considerable obstacles outlined above. In so doing, it can be read as a contribution to what Hudson (2002) termed the 'optimistic' tradition of writing on interprofessional working.

Collaboration in practice: assessment

Assessment has long been acknowledged as the bedrock of effective health and social care. A concern to improve standards of assessment has also been long-standing: the current processes of care management were introduced to enable a move from service-led to needs-led assessments (DoH/SSI 1991). However, the introduction of a single assessment process is testimony to the fact that care management for older people has not wrought the changes that were anticipated. The NSF (DoH 2001) contains plentiful evidence of this. For example, there are major concerns about duplication of resources, about some categories of need not being properly assessed and of the failure of information systems to work adequately. Among particular concerns have been risk assessment and the need for skills and systems for the identification of abuse (DoH 2000b).

The government's intentions for the single assessment process are abundantly clear:

> All older people should receive good assessment which is matched to their individual circumstances. Some older people will benefit from a fuller assessment across a number of areas or domains...and some may need more detailed assessment of one, or a few, specialist areas. The single assessment process should be designed to identify all of their needs. For the older person, it will also mean far less duplication and worry – the fuller assessment can be carried out by one front-line professional and where other professionals need to be involved to provide specialist assessment this will be arranged for the older person, to provide a seamless service. (DoH 2001, p.31)

There has now been detailed guidance about implementation (DoH 2002a, 2002b), although many practical issues are still to be resolved (Ormiston 2002). The 'fuller assessment' can be carried out by a range of different front-line staff, including social workers, community nurses, occupational therapists and physiotherapists (DoH 2001, p.31). In some cases – for example, where there is cognitive impairment or mobility problems – a specialist assessment will be indicated. The NSF emphasizes the need for a full multi-disciplinary assessment where admission to long-term care is a possibility (which links explicitly to the focus on intermediate care, addressed in the following section).

For the purposes of this chapter particular attention will be given to the issues deriving from fuller, more detailed assessments, as these illustrate interprofessional concerns most clearly. The *Guidance for Local Implementation* (DoH 2002b) specifies four broad types of assessment – contact, overview, specialist and comprehensive. Comprehensive assessments would normally be indicated where the needs and circumstances of older people are particularly problematic, or where the level of support or treatment is likely to be intensive or prolonged. The NSF specifies that such an assessment would consist of exploration 'of a set of standardized domains' (DoH 2001, pp.31–3), which have subsequently been updated and amended (DoH 2002b). In the case of a comprehensive assessment all the domains should be surveyed and specialist assessment should be carried out in most of them (DoH 2002b).

If one examines the various domains and sub-domains, it is clear that no one professional will have the capacity to address issues equally well throughout. This is recognized by the emphasis on the need for effective joint working in the assessment process (DoH 2002b). In order to clarify how best social workers can contribute to assessments it is important to identify the unique features of the social work role. The fact that social workers are often less clear than other professions about the distinctiveness of their contribution to the assessment process is problematic. Unlike many health professions, social workers' abilities are not grounded in a discrete set of technical knowledge and skills. Indeed, the contributions of a social worker often appear to be encompassed within the repertoire of other professions, which makes it difficult to claim a unique role for social work within the single assessment process.

However, there are factors that lead towards a different conclusion. The first point to highlight is the fact that members of individual professions may have an inaccurate perception of their own strengths and limitations. Worth (2001) observed that social workers claimed to encompass more around health needs and functional abilities in their assessments than was justified by the outcomes. By contrast, district nurses claimed to include social aspects as an integral part of their assessments, but gave them much less priority than social workers. Therefore the claims of any profession – including social work – to encompass the core knowledge and skills of other professions should be treated with caution.

The second point is to assert that social work has distinctive characteristics that should place it at the centre of the new arrangements. The issue of values is a critical point here. Shared values are integral to the single assessment process (DoH 2002b and see Chapter 4), particularly person-centred care and independence. The terminology used is entirely consistent with the values of empowering social work; indeed, it is social work that has moved furthest in this direction, despite the limitations imposed by the dominant medical model of understanding old age (Thompson and Thompson 2001). The insistence that older people should be at the heart of assessment emphasizes the centrality of a holistic approach to their needs, based squarely on principles of empowerment (Thompson and Thompson 2001). In her research, Worth (2001) concludes that while there are shared values between district nurses and social workers, there are differences in the language that is used to describe them as well as differences in what is most emphasized in the value base. She observed that district nurses stress the values of care more than social workers, who emphasize values of self-determination and user empowerment. This finding was confirmed by a study examining shared practice learning for district nurse and social work students (Torkington *et al.* 2002). Here one of the district nurse students commented how a social work student's deployment of strategies of empowerment and advocacy placed the user at the centre of the assessment process, while ensuring that the overall assessment was better informed thus helping to minimize risk.

Both Worth (2001) and Torkington *et al.* (2002) conclude that there was no necessary conflict between the value bases of nursing and social work and that the perspectives of each helped to create a more rounded assessment. This leads to positive conclusions about the potential for collaboration within the single assessment process. In practical terms, the values on which the single assessment process should be based are arguably more familiar to social workers than they are to other professions.

In the view of the Department of Health, other distinctive elements of social workers' contribution to the single assessment process derive from their ability to understand the problems and needs of older people in a wider family, social, financial and housing context (DoH 2002c). By implication, therefore, social workers are well placed to assist older people and their families with any complex and painful decisions that may be required. In addition, the ability of social workers to co-ordinate and plan care services is also recognized, with the responsibilities of care co-ordination being best placed with those professionals who may have a long-term involvement with a person, either community nurses or social workers (DoH 2002b, Annex G). This co-ordinating responsibility is also cited in Annex H of the above guidance, specifying the particular role of the social worker when placing older people in care homes. It is envisaged that social workers will ordinarily be responsible for co-ordinating such placements, particularly where there is social services funding towards their cost.

There is another key dimension of social work activity that is less well recognized in the guidance. This connects to the social work concern with the *internal* resources of the service user. Reference to the Barclay Report (1982) helps to clarify this point. The role of social workers in assessment and care co-ordination was defined by Barclay as part of 'social care planning'; however, the report also insisted on a role for social workers in what was broadly defined as 'counselling'. In reality, since the implementation of community care, the 'social care planning' aspects of social work with older people have dominated the 'counselling' (Lymbery 2000); however, many older people do need assistance in helping them to adjust to their changed circumstances. As Wilson and Dockrell (1995) note, high quality services can only be achieved if the complexity and heterogeneity of older people and their needs is fully recognized. Of course, this point applies as much to the families of older people as to the older people themselves. The impact on an older person of entering residential care will be experienced by partners and carers as well: a social worker is well placed both to identify the extent of this impact and to respond sensitively and appropriately. The capacity to support and guide older people and their families through a series of major life changes re-emphasizes the sometimes forgotten role of social work in helping to address both the *internal* and *external* circumstances of service users (Butrym 1976).

Collaboration in practice: intermediate care

As noted earlier there are policy pressures that force health and social services agencies to develop new approaches to intermediate care for older people. Indeed, recent years have seen numerous research projects on this general theme (see, for example, Le Mesurier and Cumella 1999; Lymbery 2002; Shield 1998; Thomas and Means 2000; Trappes-Lomax and Ellis 2001; Trappes-Lomax, Ellis and Fox 2001; Younger-Ross and Lomax 1998).

Many of the projects are located within a discourse of rehabilitation. While there is continuing uncertainty about its precise definition (Mountain 2001), Nocon and Baldwin (1998) have argued that rehabilitation has three elements:

- It aims to restore an individual to a previous state.

- It involves some element of purposeful therapeutic activity.

- It can be achieved through a diversity of approaches.

Because the concept of rehabilitation has been central to intermediate care, considerable literature points to the centrality of therapists to its process (see Lymbery 2002; Shield 1998). By contrast there is little that has specifically explored the contribution of social workers, despite the fact that they are seen as a crucial occupational group in the NSF (DoH 2001). The purpose of this section is to make a case for the active involvement of social workers in intermediate care.

As Robinson and Stevenson (1999) have it, there are three locations in which some form of intermediate care can be provided: hospitals, including community hospitals (Vaughan and Lathlean 1999); residential care homes (Younger-Ross and Lomax 1998); and the community (Thomas and Means 2000). Irrespective of the location the tasks that need to be undertaken are broadly similar. Therefore, the roles of social workers within intermediate care are transferable between settings.

The first area has been prefigured by the discussion in the previous section: as with all social and health care, the initial assessment is the key to successful services. The assessment must be much more than simply a mechanical process that measures a person's eligibility for services. For intermediate care to be effective a number of different factors must be addressed; all of these point to the importance of an active multi-disciplinary process. First, the extent of an individual's capability to benefit from the services offered should be assessed. This is not simply a matter for physiotherapists, occupational therapists, nurses and doctors, significant as their contributions undoubtedly are. Other factors, which fall within the domain of social work's expertise, also must be addressed. The attitude of the person to rehabilitation and the prospect of regaining his/her independence is a key determinant of success. There are many older people who are physically capable of rehabilitation who do not, for various reasons, have the desire or the confidence to engage in rehabilitative processes. The external circumstances of individuals have a major impact on this, encompassing issues related to carers and other family members, the wider social networks of which older people are a part as well as finance and housing (Lymbery 2002). Again, this highlights the importance of collaborative arrangements for assessment.

Similarly, there are defined roles and tasks during the process of intermediate care that call for the involvement of social workers. These focus particularly on the role of social work in holding in balance the needs and wishes of individuals, their potential, their attitudes and response to their circumstances and the concerns of wider family and other networks. If rehabilitation is to succeed it cannot just be seen as a predominantly functional issue (Lymbery 2002); social and psychological factors are of equal importance. If these are not addressed it becomes probable that the benefits of rehabilitation will not last.

For example, the decline of an individual's physical capacities may be related to a range of factors, including depression and isolation. In addition, a person's attitude towards intermediate care will be affected by the concerns of their close family, who may have a desire to accentuate the need for 'safety', hence being unwilling to allow for the element of 'risk' that is inherent within the process of rehabilitation. Within the multi-disciplinary team it is the social worker who is best placed to help the older person and his/her family to manage these issues and tensions.

There are continuing tasks to be accomplished on and after the point of discharge from intermediate care programmes. Effective follow-up of people once returned to independence is critical; the social work role can be particularly found in the areas noted above – social, psychological and family dynamics. It is likely that some systems of formal and informal care arrangements will be needed to maintain the person independently; in addition, there will be a continued role in ensuring that any concerns of the family are addressed so that they do not destabilize the independence of the older person. Finally, the social worker will need to ensure that the older person's morale and confidence remains high, paying due attention to what that person perceives about his or her own situation.

Ideally, the work of the social worker in relation to intermediate care would not be the short-term task-focused work that has characterized much community care (Lymbery 1998a; Postle 2002). Enabling an older person's family to adjust to the demands of rehabilitation is not an activity that can be carried out quickly. Similarly, the work that would help an older person come to terms with changed circumstances is not of short duration. Older people's needs will change and it is crucial that these changes are captured through monitoring and review processes. Failure to recognize these realities would have two consequences. Most critically, it would weaken the effectiveness of the interprofessional working upon which intermediate care depends. In addition, it would ensure that social work has only a residual role in relation to intermediate care, not the central place that the NSF (DoH 2001) envisaged and for which I have argued in this chapter.

Conclusion

The material in the foregoing two sections outlines the distinctive contribution of social work in the single assessment process and intermediate care. However, a simple assertion of the need for good social work practice does not in itself overcome the obstacles to collaboration noted earlier. Effective interprofessional working can self-evidently be compromised by any failure to address critical organizational and financial factors. Of these, the preoccupation with performance measurement and short-term work are particularly significant. Equally, collaboration can be enhanced by sympathetic structural arrangements. The creation of multi-disciplinary teams for older people will go a long way to providing such assistance, particularly if supported by formal processes of shared learning.

Similarly, while this chapter belongs to the more optimistic tradition of writing on interprofessional collaboration, the relevance of the pessimistic tradition also needs to be acknowledged. This is exacerbated by the de-professionalizing tendencies that can be observed in social work (Hugman 1998), particularly in care management and social work with older people (Lymbery 1998a). It is important to insist on the *professional* nature of the social work tasks that have been highlighted, calling for the involvement of experienced, qualified and skilled practitioners. Finally, the absence of the older service user from more general debates about user involvement in social work is a key issue to be overcome.

The five distinctive roles for social workers that can be identified within the single assessment process and intermediate care do have the capacity to impact upon some, if not all, of the above points.

- In applying the values of social work, in particular the commitment to developing user-centred services and forms of empowering practice, there lies a genuine opportunity to place the older service user at the heart of all decision-making. Social work has a long history of being person-centred in its approach (at least in theory – there are many examples of user-focused literature that indicate where social work has failed in this respect; see Taylor 1993). Now that the NSF exemplifies a user-centred process, there is an opportunity for the person-centred values of social work to be central to its implementation.

- The distinctive contribution of social workers is also seen in their orientation to assessment and intermediate care, a reflection of the core values of empowerment (Thompson and Thompson 2001).

- Developing from these value-based issues, social work can contribute particularly effectively to some of the assessment domains – particularly 'user's perspective' and 'relationships'.

- In addition, as acknowledged within the guidance to the single assessment process, social workers have particular expertise and experience of care planning and co-ordination.

- The ability of social workers is also evident in work around a service user's response to his/her circumstances. In particular, a skilled social worker is well placed to help service users to gain insight into the nature and cause of their problems, offer support to them, and help them either to adjust to their situation or to act to change it. While this role has been undervalued in much care management practice (Lymbery 1998a; Postle 2002) it remains critical to effective collaborative practice.

Collectively, what these roles and tasks emphasize is that older people need more than the provision of practical tasks and that this must be recognized in the way services are planned and organized. The vision of social work that is outlined draws on the traditional notion of being responsive to the whole person within their social world (Butrym 1976). While this may have existed only on the edges of social work with older people, and been further marginalized in community care policies, this conception of social work should be an essential element of more effective collaborative care for older people. In addition, it should help to demonstrate the validity of the social work role and potentially draw it from the margins of work with older people to centre stage.

References

Barclay Report (1982) *Social Workers: Their Role and Tasks.* London: Bedford Square Press.

Butrym, Z. (1976) *The Nature of Social Work.* London: Macmillan.

Bywaters, P. (1986) 'Social Work and the Medical Profession – Arguments Against Unconditional Collaboration.' *British Journal of Social Work 16,* 6, 661–677.

Charlesworth, J. (2001) 'Negotiating and Managing Partnership in Primary Care.' *Health and Social Care in the Community 9,* 5, 279–285.

Dalley, G. (1989) 'Professional Ideology and Organisational Tribalism? The Health Service–Social Work Divide.' In R. Taylor and J. Ford (eds) *Social Work and Health Care.* London: Jessica Kingsley Publishers.

Dingwall, R. (1982) 'Problems of Teamwork in Primary Care.' In A.W. Clare and R.H. Corney (eds) *Social Work and Primary Health Care.* London: Academic Press.

DoH (1997) *The New NHS: Modern, Dependable.* Cm 3807. London: Stationery Office.

DoH (1998) *Partnership in Action: A Discussion Document.* London: Department of Health.

DoH (1999) *The Relationship Between Health and Social Services.* Cm 4320. London: Stationery Office.

DoH (2000a) *The NHS Plan.* London: Stationery Office.

DoH (2000b) *No Secrets: Guidance on Developing and Implementing Multi-agency Policies and Procedures to Protect Vulnerable Adults from Abuse.* London: Department of Health.

DoH (2001) *The National Service Framework for Older People.* London: Stationery Office.

DoH (2002a) *Guidance on the Single Assessment Process for Older People.* HSC2002/001: LAC (2002)1. London: Department of Health.

DoH (2002b) *The Single Assessment Process: Guidance for Local Implementation.* London: Department of Health.

DoH (2002c) *The Single Assessment Process – Key Implications for Social Workers.* (Consulted 2 July 2002.) http//www.doh.gov.uk/scg/sap/socialworkers.htm.

DoH/SSI (1991) *Care Management and Assessment: Practice Guidance Practitioner.* London: HMSO.

Health Act (1999) London: Stationery Office.

Hudson, B. (2002) 'Interprofessionality in Health and Social Care: The Achilles' Heel of Partnership.' *Journal of Interprofessional Care 16*, 1, 7–17.

Hugman, R. (1998) 'Social Work and De-professionalization.' In P. Abbott and L. Meerabeau (eds) *The Sociology of the Caring Professions*, 2nd edn. London: UCL Press.

Huntington, J. (1981) *Social Work and General Medical Practice.* London: George Allen and Unwin.

Jones, C. (2001) 'Voices from the Frontline: State Social Workers and New Labour.' *British Journal of Social Work 31*, 4, 547–562.

Le Mesurier, N. and Cumella, S. (1999) 'Enhancing Independence: The Effectiveness of Re-ablement Provision in South Worcestershire.' *Managing Community Care 7*, 4, 27–32.

Lewis, J. (2001) 'Older People and the Health–Social Care Boundary in the UK: Half a Century of Hidden Policy Conflict.' *Social Policy and Administration 35*, 4, 343–359.

Litwin, H. (1994) 'The Professional Standing of Social Work with Elderly Persons among Social Work Trainees.' *British Journal of Social Work 24*, 1, 53–69.

Lymbery, M. (1998a) 'Care Management and Professional Autonomy: The Impact of Community Care Legislation on Social Work with Older People.' *British Journal of Social Work 28*, 6, 863–878.

Lymbery, M. (1998b) 'Social Work in General Practice: Dilemmas and Solutions.' *Journal of Interprofessional Care 12*, 2, 199–208.

Lymbery, M. (2000) 'The Retreat from Professionalism: From Social Worker to Care Manager.' In N. Malin (ed) *Professionalism, Boundaries and the Workplace.* London: Routledge.

Lymbery, M. (2002) 'Transitional Residential Rehabilitation: What Helps to Make it Work?' *MCC – Building Knowledge for Integrated Care 10*, 1, 43–47.

Lymbery, M. and Millward, A. (2000) 'The Primary Health Care Interface.' In G. Bradley and J. Manthorpe (eds) *Working on the Fault Line: Social Work and Health Services.* Birmingham: Venture Press/Social Work Research Association.

Mountain, G. (2001) 'Social Rehabilitation: Concepts, Evidence and Practice.' *Managing Community Care 9*, 2, 8–15.

Nocon, A. and Baldwin, C. (1998) *Trends in Rehabilitation Policy – A Literature Review.* London: King's Fund.

Ormiston, H. (2002) 'The Single Assessment Process.' *MCC – Building Knowledge for Integrated Care 10*, 2, 38–44.

Payne, M. (2000) 'The Politics of Case Management and Social Work.' *International Journal of Social Welfare 9*, 2, 82–91.

Postle, K. (2002) 'Working "Between the Idea and the Reality": Ambiguities and Tensions in Care Managers' Work.' *British Journal of Social Work 32*, 3, 335–351.

Power, M. (1997) *The Audit Society.* Oxford: Oxford University Press.

Rees, S. (1978) *Social Work Face to Face.* London: Edward Arnold.

Robinson, J. and Stevenson, J. (1999) 'Rehabilitation.' *Managing Community Care 7*, 4, 39–44.

Ross, F., Rink, E. and Furne, A. (2000) 'Integration or Pragmatic Coalition? An Evaluation of Nursing Teams in Primary Care.' *Journal of Interprofessional Care 14*, 3, 259–267.

Sanderson, I. (2001) 'Performance Management, Evaluation and Learning in "Modern" Local Government.' *Public Administration 79*, 2, 297–313.

Shield, F. (1998) 'Developing a Therapy-led Community Rehabilitation Team.' *Managing Community Care 6*, 4, 160–168.

Taylor, G. (1993) 'Challenges from the Margins.' In J. Clarke (ed) *A Crisis in Care: Challenges to Social Work.* London: Sage/Open University.

Thomas, D. and Means, R. (2000) 'Getting Started: Early Research Findings on a Jointly Managed Community-based Rehabilitation Service in Bristol.' *Managing Community Care 8*, 6, 41–45.

Thompson, N. and Thompson, S. (2001) 'Empowering Older People: Beyond the Care Model.' *Journal of Social Work 1*, 1, 61–76.

Torkington, C., Lymbery, M., Millward, A., Murfin, M. and Richell, B. (2002) 'Shared Practice Learning: Social Work and District Nurse Students Learning Together.' Paper presented at the Joint University Council (Social Work Education) Conference, University of Derby, July.

Trappes-Lomax, T. and Ellis, A. (2001) 'Real Life Research: Implementing a Study on the Health/Social Care Interface.' *Managing Community Care 9*, 3, 22–30.

Trappes-Lomax, T., Ellis, A. and Fox, A. (2001) 'Real Life Research: The Ups and Downs of an Intermediate Care Study.' *Managing Community Care 9*, 5, 18–24.

Twigg, J. (2000) 'The Changing Role of Users and Carers.' In B. Hudson (ed) *The Changing Role of Social Care.* London: Jessica Kingsley Publishers.

Vaughan, B. and Lathlean, J. (1999) *Intermediate Care – Models in Practice.* London: King's Fund.

Walker, A. and Warren, L. (1996) *Changing Services for Older People.* Buckingham: Open University Press.

Wilson, G. and Dockrell, J. (1995) 'Elderly Care.' In P. Owens, J. Carrier and J. Horder (eds) *Interprofessional Issues in Community and Primary Health Care.* Basingstoke: Macmillan.

Worth, A. (2001) 'Assessment of the Needs of Older People by District Nurses and Social Workers: A Changing Culture.' *Journal of Interprofessional Care 15,* 3, 257–266.

Younger-Ross, S. and Lomax, T. (1998) 'Outlands: Five Years On.' *Managing Community Care 6,* 1, 37–40.

The Contributors

Christine Barton, who has personal experience as a service user, works with public and voluntary organizations to influence service provision. She was previously an education adviser for Leeds Education Authority. In 2000 her work in services to disabled people and equal opportunities was honoured with an MBE and in 2001 she was appointed as a lay member to the General Social Care Council.

Jean Davis practised for many years in NHS and local authority social work teams. She moved into education and training in the late 1970s, and was Principal Social Worker (Teaching) at Hammersmith Hospital. Since 1990 she has worked in interprofessional training, including the BSC Nursing and Social Work Studies course and the interprofessional programme for practice teachers at South Bank University.

Sonia Douek is the Manager of carers' services at Jewish Care. The service, which supports 1200 individuals, aims to enable people to live as full a life as possible within the constraints of their caring role. Following extensive experience in Jewish communal activities, Sonia obtained a degree as a mature student. Previous experience includes work with civil liberties, race equality and refugees.

Ruth Gardner is Senior Research Fellow at Royal Holloway College, University of London. She has researched and written extensively on child care and family support, her latest books being *Family Support* (Venture Press 1998) and *Supporting Families, Child Protection in the Community* (Wiley 2002). She has also been a practitioner and manager of children and family services.

Tony Leiba is Senior Research Fellow, North East London Mental Health Trust and South Bank University. His work embraces many aspects of evidence-based mental health practice, interprofessional learning, user and carer collaborative research and conflict management. He contributes to numerous interprofessional education and training initiatives within universities and with health and social care professional bodies.

Mark Lymbery is a lecturer in Social Work at the Centre for Social Work in the University of Nottingham. His research and teaching interests include care management and social work, social work in primary health care, social work with older people, interprofessional working and social work education. He has published widely in all the above areas.

Kirstein Rummery is a lecturer in health and community care at the Department of Applied Social Science, University of Manchester. Her research and teaching interests include disabled and older people's citizenship rights, access to health and social care and joint working between primary health and social care workers. Recent publications include *Disability, Citizenship and Community Care* (2002 Ashgate).

Dave Sims is Professional Lead for Social Work at the University of Greenwich. Previous roles in higher education include Course Director for a joint learning disability nursing and social work programme, and Head of Department managing community nursing, social work and practice teaching programmes. Dave is currently involved in development work for the new social work degree.

Tony Thompson is a former inspector of the General Nursing Council and advisor at The English National Board. Prior to being appointed as director of nursing to the Crown Lodge organization, he was Director of practice and Deputy Director of nursing at Ashworth Hospital. He is the author and editor of several textbooks and is associate director of Caring Solutions UK.

Jenny Weinstein's interest in collaboration began when she pioneered interprofessional practice learning as Dip SW lead at the Central Council for Education and Training in Social Work. She has written and edited a range of publications on collaborative practice in health and care and is currently Assistant Director at Jewish Care where she pursues her commitment to service user involvement.

Colin Whittington is an independent consultant (www.colinwhittington .com) involved in researching and facilitating collaboration and partnership. He also works with individuals and teams as a mentor/coach. He headed CCETSW's London and South-East Region, and led on partnership of social care and health for TOPSS England's national training strategy. His clients include national and local agencies and individual managers and professionals.

Subject Index

addiction, services for carers of people with, 132–34
Alzheimer's Society, 128
assessments
  attitudes to, 106–7, 108–10
  carer, 134, 135
  holistic, 115, 116, 117
  see also single assessment process
Audit Commission, 15, 18–19, 45, 55–56

Barclay Report (1982), 230
behaviour and education support teams (BESTs), 148
best values, 20
Better Services for the Mentally Handicapped (1971), 182
Better Services for Vulnerable People (1997), 20
black service users (mental health), diversity issues, 172–73
British Council of Disabled People, 105

care plans
  carers' contribution to, 134
  service user, involvement in, 65, 108, 196
care programme approach (CPA)
  care co-ordination, 164
  carers, 126–27, 163
  community care, 161–64
  failures of, 167
  integrated service delivery, 163
  managerial solutions, mistrust of, 164–65
  shared ideology, absence of, 164

uni-professional cultures, 164
  users, benefits to, 74, 77
Care Programme Approach for People with a Mental Illness Referred to the Specialist Psychiatric Services (1990), 163
Care Standards Act (2000), 23
care trusts, 22–24, 202, 220
carers
  advocacy for, 135
  care programme approach, 126–27
  community care, 123–24
  guidance for, 125–26
  health, impact of caring on, 129
  health services, changes in, 124
  information sharing, 121–22, 125–28, 134–35
  interprofessional team, inclusion of carer on, 135
  joint strategy, development of, 134
  multi-disciplinary working, 127–30
  national service frameworks, 125
  needs of, 123–24, 134
  numbers of, 121–22
  respite care, provision of, 128–32
  rights of, 124–25
  service access for, 132–34
  single assessment process, 131
  statutory sector, and crossing of boundaries, 130–32
  voluntary sector, use of, 135
  young, 123
  see also service users and carers
Carers and Disabled Children's Act (2000), 125
Carers' Compass for Primary Care, 128
carers' grant, 124–25, 131
Carers' National Association, 123
Carers Recognition and Services Act (1995), 125

Caring for People (1989), 17
Certificate of Social Service
    (CSS)/Registered Nurse Mental
    Handicap (RNMH), 189
child and adolescent mental health
    teams (CAMHS), 72
child protection *see* inter-agency
    collaboration; joint working
Children Act (1989), 144–45
Children's Fund, 145
Children's Task Force, 145
co-operation, versus co-ordination,
    141
Code of Ethics for Social Work (BASW
    1986), 87–88
Code of Ethics for Social Work (BASW
    1996), 88
Code of Ethics for Social Work (BASW
    2002), 85, 86, 88–89, 90, 97
Code of Professional Conduct (NMC
    2002) for nurses, 89, 90, 97
Code of Professional Conduct (UKCC
    1992) for nurses, 87–88
Code of Practice for Social Care
    Workers (GSCC 2002), 42
collaboration
    meaning of, 138
    model of, 39–58
collaboration, and partnership
    child and adult protection, 21, 31
    collaborative practice, 17
    critical application of, 30–31, 32
    dimensions of, in care services,
        23–26, 32
    distinction between and meaning of,
        15–17, 31
    evidence of effectiveness of, 30–31,
        76–78
    as fields of research, 29–30
    and global strategic analysis, 28
    as ideology, 28–29

as instruments of policy, 27–28, 31
    limits of, 29
    as mechanisms of workforce control,
        28
    in national policy, 17–23
    and professional competencies, 29
    promotion of (policy), 14–15
        see also New Labour
            modernization programme
    reflection, need for, 30
    and user-centred values, 29, 30–31,
        32
'collaborative advantage' concept, 142,
    154
collaborative practice, 17, 89–90
community assessment and
    rehabilitation teams (CARTS), 72
community care
    Better Services for the Mentally
        Handicapped (1971), 182
    care programme approach, 161–64
    carers, 123–24
    community-based services, failings
        of, 182–83
    Facing the Facts (1999), 182–83,
        186
    Griffiths Report (1988), 182, 184
    inter-agency collaboration, 18, 31
    Jay Committee (1979), 182, 189
    motives for, 182
    new managerialism, 225
    The New NHS: Modern,
        Dependable (1997), 182
    NHS and Community Care Act
        (1990), 182
    Percy Report (1957), 182
    professional self-confidence, lack of,
        225
Community Care, 74
community drugs teams (CDTs), 26

community mental health teams (CMHTs), 26, 73, 164–66
community nurses (CNs), 203–6
community psychiatric nurses (CPNs), 73
community teams for learning disabilities (CTLDs), 26
Crime and Disorder Act (1998), 21
critical language study (CLS), 28–29

Data Protection Act (1998), 76
Dementia Relief Trust, 128
Diploma in Social Work (DipSW)/Registered General Nurse (RGN), 189
direct payments, to carers, 108, 118, 119
Disability Discrimination Act (1995), 105
Disability Rights Commission, 105
disabled people, barriers experienced by, 104–5
diversity issues
    inter-disciplinary teams, 53
    interprofessional working, 172–73, 175
    service users and carers, 47
Draft Code of Conduct for Social Care Workers (GSCC 2002), 90
Draft Mental Health Bill (2002), 168–70

evidence-based practice, 67

Facing the Facts (1999), 182–83, 186
family group conferences (FGCs), 150–51
First Annual Report of the Learning Disability Task Force (2003), 7, 188

Framework for the Assessment of Children in Need (2000), 75

General Social Care Council (GSCC), 42
GPs, 70, 205–6
Griffiths Report (1988), 17, 182, 184
Guidance for Local Implementation (2002) (single assessments), 228

Health Act (1999), 21, 26, 113, 145, 156, 162
Health Act flexibilities, 21–22
health action zones, 21
health improvement programmes, 20, 21
Health Select Committee Report (1998), 220
Health Service Journal, 71
hospital re-admissions, reductions in, 77

identity, professional, 39, 40, 43, 49–50
institutional racism, 169
Integrated Care Network (ICN), 152
inter-, use of, 16, 45–46
inter-agency collaboration
    Audit Commission reports, 18–19, 31
    challenges for, 157
    child-centred approach, 149
    children and families, involvement of, 148–50, 157–58
    communication breakdowns
        assumptions about responsibilities, 76
        common understanding, lack of, 75
        confidentiality rules, 75–76

information, non-sharing of, 75
critical success factors for, 157
early years projects, 147–48
education-based projects, 148
family group conferences, 150–51
family support projects, 148–50
good practice principles, 149
infrastructure for
    agency, 146
    communication structures,
        152–53
    funding, 151
    Integrated Care Network, 152
    joint assessment, 151–52
manager expectations, 154
'multi-agency' initiatives, success
    factors, 55
organizational climate, effect of,
    154–56
PCG/T boards, social services
    representation on, 211–12
policy context for
    Children Act (1989), 144–45
    Health Act (1999), 145
    'joined up' strategy, 145
    policy versus programme
        approach, 146
Sure Start, 147–48
see also joint working
inter-disciplinary teams
communication, 52
directive philosophy, 51
diversity, valuing, 53
elective philosophy, 51
equality of status, 52
goals of, 191
innovation, 52
integrative philosophy, 51, 52
knowledge sharing, 73
operational collaboration, 25–26,
    27

outcomes as criteria for evaluation
    of, 190–91
professional difference, respect for,
    53
successful, features of, 51–53,
    191–92
team development
    forming phase, 193
    norming phase, 194
    performing phase, 194
    storming phase, 193–94
team management, 193
user involvement in, 116, 190
working definition of, 190
inter-organizational collaboration, 16,
    53–57, 58
see also inter-agency collaboration
inter-personal collaboration, and trust,
    48, 56, 57
intermediate collaboration, 25
interprofessional collaboration
    anti-discriminatory practice, 71
    barriers to, 221–22
    care programme approach, 164–65,
        176
    competencies, 29
    conceptual problems in, 219, 223
    conflicts, 173–74
    diversity issues, 172–73, 175
    education and training, 170–71,
        176
    factors for enhancing of, 71
    identity, professional, 39, 40, 43,
        49–50
    knowledge and skills required for,
        48–49
    mechanisms for promotion of,
        72–73
    need for, 69
    overcoming barriers to, 71

professional opinion, challenging,
    64–65
professionals' views on
    clinical psychologists, relative
        autonomy of, 165
    nurses, 166
    occupational therapists, as
        misunderstood and
        undervalued, 166
    psychiatrists, containment
        function of, 166
    scepticism, 165
    social workers, and discomfort
        with medical model,
        165–66
protectionism, 71, 76
record sharing, 71
roles, lack of understanding of, 71
shared learning
    disability service models,
        changes to, 189–90
    joint qualifications, 189
    nursing and social work,
        competition between, 189
    promotion of, 14
    pilot schemes for, 189, 197
social workers and nursing
    profession, differing approaches
    of, 70
status discrimination, 71
uni-professional education, 70, 71
see also values, shared

Jay Committee (1979), 182, 189
joined-up services, 15
joint investment plans, 20, 21
joint working
    benefits of, 140–41
    bilateral planning, 138, 139
    child protection guidelines, need for,
        144

Children Act (1989), 144–45
citizens' participation, levels of, 140
co-operation, 138
collaboration, 138, 139
communication, 138, 139
consultation, 138, 139
    and joint work,
        inter-dependence of, 143
difficulties of, 141
factors assisting, 153–54
family-centred approach, 143–44
joint planning, 138, 139
planned communication, 138
process improvements, 143
service users, collaboration with,
    143–44

Lawrence, Stephen, 91
learning disability services
    collaborative working
        agency rivalries, 192
        disadvantages of, 192
        foundations of, 190–92
        good practice guidance, 197
        impact on service, 196
        key points for development of,
            195
        professional and organizational
            barriers, 192–93
        service user involvement, 196
    developments in, 182–86
    failures in delivery of
        children's and adult services,
            poor co-ordination between,
            185–86
        collaboration, inadequate,
            184–85
        institutions, effects of, 183–84
        key issues, 183–86
        personal security and safety
            issues, 183

unequal distribution of services, 185
inter-agency communication, 197
local strategic partnerships, 186–88
service delivery improvements, proposals for, 196–97
Valuing People (2001), 181, 183, 186, 195
LEAs, and education-based projects, 148
Local Government Journal, 71
local strategic partnerships (LSPs), 186–88

mandatory partnership working, 15, 18–19
Mental Health Act (1983), review of, aftercare duties under the, 162
compulsory detention and treatment, extension of, 169, 176
'mental health professional', new role of, 170
mental health services
collaboration
as essential element, 176
inter-agency problems with, 168
policy context of, 162–63
service users' views on failures in, 167
legislation, appraisal of, 168–70
national service framework, guiding principles of, 161, 162–63
see also community care
Modern Local Government (1998), 20
Modernising Social Services (1998), 21, 123
multi- versus inter-, use of, 16, 45–46
multi-agency networks, 26, 27, 53–54
multi-disciplinary teams see inter-disciplinary teams

National Services Framework for Mental Health (1999), 23, 161, 162–63
National Services Framework for Older People (2001), 23, 213
national services frameworks, 20, 125, 150, 220–21, 227–28
National Strategy for Carers, 124–25, 128, 130
New Labour modernization programme, 31
Best Value, 20
collaboration, expectations of, 23
health and social care, relationship between, 20, 21–22
health improvement programmes, 20, 21
inter-agency strategies, 20–21
joint investment plans, 20, 21
'learning organization', 45
multi-disciplinary assessment, 20
national service frameworks, 20
NHS Plan, 22
partnerships, 20
primary care groups, 20, 22
Quality Protects programme, 21
'whole system' development, 19–20
New NHS: Modern, Dependable (1997), 182
NHS and Community Care Act (1990), 17, 124, 161, 163, 182, 203
NHS Plan (2000), 22, 26, 161, 162
nurse training, 189

older people, services for
collaboration, obstacles to
financial arrangements, 222–23
'hidden policy conflict', 222
marginalization, of older people, 224–25

organizations, inward- versus outward-looking, 223
integrated care system, 77–78
intermediate care, 230–32
partnership, policy context for
  care trusts, establishment of, 220
  Health Select Committee Report (1998), 220
  Labour government, 220–21
  national service frameworks, 220–21, 227–28
  NHS Plan (2000), 220, 221
  Partnership in Action (1998), 220
person-centred values, 233–34
rehabilitation
  elements of, 230–31
  social workers, case for active involvement of, 219, 231–32
see also single assessment process
one-stop shops, 143
operational collaboration, 25–27
organizational models
  co-operative models and the 'learning organization', 45
  'new managerialism' model, 44–45
  organizational measurements, criticisms of, 45
  performance management and efficiency models, 45

palliative care teams, 26
partnerships
  continuum of in social care and health, 23–24, 26, 27
  principles governing success, 18, 20, 25, 54–55
  'whole system' working, 18, 20, 25, 55–57, 58

see also collaboration, and partnership; primary health care, partnerships
Partnerships in Action (1998), 21, 220
Percy Report, 182
pooled budgets, 22, 25, 113, 116, 145, 156, 162
primary care groups (PCGs), 20, 22, 77, 202
primary care trusts (PCTs), 22, 202
primary health care
  collaborative projects
    community nursing, 203–4
    GPs and community nurses, 205–6
    health and social care managers, 204–5
    'liaison' workers, 204
    non-statutory workers, 204
    social workers, 206–7
    users and carers, 207–8
    see also primary health care teams
  NHS Plan, 202
  partnerships
    costs of, 213
    in current policy climate, 213–14
    inter-dependence as prerequisite for, 213
    lessons in for social workers, 214–15
    NHS and social services difficulties with, 202–3
    for partnership's sake, 212–13
    and reinforcing of power inequalities, 213–14
  social services representatives on PCG/T boards, influence of, 208–12
primary health care teams (PHCTs), 26, 73

Princess Royal Trust for Carers, 130,
    132–33
private partnership schemes (PPPs), 28

qualifications, joint, 83–85, 189
Quality Protects, 21, 145

racism, 91, 169
rapid response teams, 26
Report of the Committee on Nursing
    (1972), 189
research, on collaboration, 19
respite care, for carers, 128–32
Royal College of Psychiatrists, 169

'seamless service' ideal, 17, 19, 103–4
service users and carers
    direct payments to, 108, 118, 119
    diversity issues, 47, 64
    empowerment of, 65, 112, 114–15,
        115, 116
    at heart of system, 14, 41–42, 57,
        63
    impact, 47
    inclusion, 47
    information, provision of, 111–12,
        114, 116, 117
    involvement of
        and choice, 64
        in decision-making, 118,
            119–20
        ensuring, 46–47
        evaluating effectiveness of, 69
        policies for, 67–69
        professional opinion,
            challenging, 64–65
        records, access to, 66
        in research, 67
        in strategic development of
            services, 66–67

    user self-determination, 65
    key workers, 109
    location, 47
    person-centred approach, 115, 116
    professional attitudes, influence of,
        106–9, 110, 113–14, 118
    service provision, fragmentation of,
        110–11, 113, 114
    social approach, 115, 116, 118
    technical language, avoiding use of,
        66
    'whole system' working, 55–57
    see also assessments
single assessment process
    assessment types, 228
    carers, 131
    implementation of, 227
    interprofessional implications of,
        228–30
    national service framework,
        220–21, 227–28
    for older people, 72
    social work, centrality of
        care co-ordination abilities,
            229–30, 234
        counselling, 230
        shared values, 228–29, 234
        understanding of context,
            229–30
Social Exclusion Unit, 145
social inclusion, 197
social workers
    approved social workers, 170
    discomfort with medical model,
        165–66
    interpersonal skills for, 118–19
    and nurses, values of, 86–89
    rehabilitation, case for active
        involvement in, 219, 231–32
    role as care managers, 124
    training, 43, 48–50

staff selection, user involvement in, 68
strategic collaboration, 24–25
Sure Start, 147–48
'survivor movement', 67

teams *see* inter-disciplinary teams
Thatcher government (1980s), 17
trust, 48, 56, 57

values, shared
    accountability, to service users,
        89–90
    codifying of, 90, 97
    collaboration and partnership as
        professional, 29–32
    and different models of care
        'fair and equal treatment', clash
            over meaning of, 91
        interprofessional conflicts, and
            loss to service users, 91–92
        societal value shifts, 91
    ethics, definition of, 85
    and interdisciplinary degree, 83–85
    interprofessional practice, as good
        practice, 96
    nurses and social workers, values of
        discrimination, 86
        respect, 88
        risk/hardship/suffering, 88
        service user and carer
            involvement, 89
        state and society, relationship
            between, 87
    person and social context,
        relationship between, 86–87
    political correctness backlash, 83
    professional defensiveness, 97
    service users and carer involvement,
        86

social work values, exclusivity of,
    83, 86–89
values, definition of, 85
values and ethical practice case
    history, 92–96
values and ethics, distinction
    between, 85, 86
'values led' practice, 97–98
Valuing People (White Paper 2001), 7,
    181, 183, 186, 195
Victoria Climbié Inquiry, 7, 23, 74–75,
    76, 92
voluntary sector, strength of, 131, 135

whole-system approach, 18, 19–20,
    25, 54–57, 58, 156
Working Together to Safeguard
    Children, 75

youth offending teams (YOTs), 26

Author Index

Abrams, D., 40
Adams, R., 43
Anderson, J., 141–42
Anderson, S., 27
Arnstein, S., 140
Aspinall, K., 25
Atkins, M., 103, 115
Atkinson, M., 27, 28, 31, 55
Aymer, C., 83

Backmann, R.E., 48
Bacon, F., 121
Badger, F., 31, 64
Baldwin, C., 230
Banks, S., 87
Barnes, C., 105
Barnes, M., 19
Barr, H., 29, 140
Barr, O., 182, 193
Barton, A., 9, 16, 28
Barton, C., 103–20, 239
Baxter, C., 71, 184
Belbin, M., 44
Bell, L., 14, 49, 53
Bennett-Emslie, G., 203
Beresford, P., 14, 31, 47, 64, 65, 66, 67
Berger, P., 39
Biggs, S., 18, 27, 63
Billingham, K., 73
Birchall, E., 70, 75
Blair, T., 19
Blom-Cooper, L., 163
Boateng, P., 145
Bottomley, V., 17, 19
Bowl, R., 19
Bowls, R., 68

Bowman, A., 202
Boydell, T.H., 40
Braye, S., 42, 193
Brill, N.I., 190
Brockbank, A., 43
Brown, J., 189, 193
Brown, L., 204
Bullock, R., 75
Burgoyne, J.D., 40
Butrym, Z., 230, 234
Bywaters, P., 224

Callaghan, G.M., 205
Cameron, C., 64
Campbell, J., 104, 105, 114–15, 119–20
Campbell, M., 54
Campbell, P., 169
Carpenter, J., 77, 167
Carter, T., 47
Chamberlain, J., 67
Chambers, B., 67
Charles, M., 144
Charlesworth, J., 223
Child, J., 48
Clark, C.L., 85
Clark, M., 129
Clarke, J., 212
Clough, R., 124
Coleman, A., 208, 209
Craig, G., 213
Crow, G., 151
Cumella, S., 230

Dalley, G., 70, 224
Davis, J., 8, 83–98, 91, 239
Dearling, A., 44
Dingwall, R., 224
Dobson, F., 19
Dockrell, J., 230

Dominelli, L., 43
Douek, S., 9, 121–35, 239
Dowling, A., 77
Doz, Y.L., 28
Duncan, S., 75

Edwards, K., 172
Edwards, R., 97
Ellis, A., 230
Esterline, B., 146
Evans, C., 67
Evers, H., 64

Fairclough, N., 28
Farnham, D., 44
Faulkner, D., 48
Fenge, A.L., 67
Fisher, M., 19, 67
Flynn, M., 73, 184
Foote, C., 71, 77
Ford, R., 164
Forsgarde, M., 202
Fox, A., 230
Freeman, M., 27, 43, 44, 53, 73, 171
Freidheim, C., 28
Furne, A., 224

Gardner, R., 9, 137–58, 148, 149–50, 154, 239
Gask, L., 71
Geddes, M., 54
George, M., 45
Giddens, A., 28, 50
Giraud Saunders, A., 186
Glen, S., 70
Glendinning, C., 65, 205, 207, 208, 209, 212
Glennester, H., 17
Glisson, C., 155–56
Greig, R., 186

Grey, M., 75
Griffiths, R., 17
Gulliver, P., 53

Hadley, R., 124
Hallett, C., 70, 75
Hally, H., 163
Hamel, G., 28
Hancock, M., 19
Harding, T., 64, 66
Hardy, B., 48, 54
Hatfield, B., 77
Hattersly, J., 190
Hearn, J., 44
Heddell, F., 188
Hemmelgarn, A., 155–56
Hendry, E., 144
Henwood, M., 29, 208
Hickey, G., 67
Higgins, R., 173, 174
Hill, K., 168
Hogg, M., 40
Holzhausen, E., 122
Hopkins, G., 185
Horton, S., 44
Hudson, B., 1, 16, 20, 30, 45, 54, 71, 156, 202, 223, 224, 226
Hughes, L., 202
Hugman, R., 233
Hunter, D.J., 173
Huntington, J, 224
Hutchinson, J., 54
Hutton, W., 28
Huxham, C., 142, 153–54

Jacobs, S., 208
Jones, C., 226
Jones, R., 202
Jordan, B., 123, 124
Jordan, C., 123, 124

Kai, J., 71
Kasperson, L.B., 50
Keeley, B., 129
Khan, P., 70
Kipping, C., 67

Laming, Lord, 7, 31, 45, 74–75, 76, 92
Lane, C., 48
Larson, M.S., 89
Lathlean, J., 231
Lawler, J., 44
Le Mesurier, N., 230
Leathard, A., 182
Leiba, T., 8, 9, 63–79, 70, 161–76, 239
Levin, E., 30
Lewis, C., 202
Lewis, J., 17, 222–23
Littlewood and Lipsedge, 172
Litwin, H., 226
Lomax, T., 230
Low, H., 70
Loxley, A., 17, 71
Luckman, T., 39
Lupton, C., 16, 70, 76, 141, 150
Lymbery, M., 10, 203, 219–34, 224, 225, 230, 232, 233, 239

Macdonald, G., 67
Macpherson, W., 91
Makins, V., 147
Marsh, P., 151
Mathers, N.J., 71
Mayo, E., 44
McDermott, G., 167
McGill, I., 43
McGrath, M., 19
McIntosh, J., 203
Means, R., 230

Milewa, T., 77
Miller, C., 27, 43, 44, 50–52, 53, 73, 171
Millward, A., 224
Milner, J., 43
Molyneux, J., 52, 53
Mooney, A., 122, 124
Morgan, G., 146
Morgan, J., 152
Morris, J., 105
Mountain, G., 230
Murphy, E., 163

Nally, B., 182
Nocon, A., 230
Nolan, P., 31
Norman, I.J., 164–65, 165–66
North, N., 70
Nygren, L., 202

O'Byrne, P., 43
Oldman, C., 173
Oldman, H., 66
Oliver, O., 105
Onyett, S., 19, 164
Ormiston, H., 227
Øvreteit, J., 19

Parsloe, P., 44
Payne, M., 43, 44, 225
Peck, E., 53, 164, 165–66
Pedlar, M., 25, 40
Petr, C.G., 141, 143–44
Pierre, S.A., 172
Pollitt, C., 63, 64
Postle, K., 225–26, 232
Poulton, B.C., 71
Power, M., 223
Poxton, R., 186, 202
Preston-Shoot, M., 193

Quinn, C., 16
Qureshi, H., 208

Raine, P., 67
Rao, N., 123
Reder, P., 75
Rees, S., 226
Reeves, S., 175
Rehman, H., 64
Rendell, P., 84, 91
Revans, L., 23
Richardson, M., 192
Rink, E., 224
Robinson, J., 231
Rogers, J.A., 67
Rokeach, M., 85
Ross, F., 203, 224
Ross, N., 27, 43, 44, 53, 73, 171
Rummery, K., 10, 201–15, 202, 205,
    206, 207, 208, 209, 213, 240
Ryan, T., 184, 185

Sanderson, I., 223
Sbaraini, S., 77, 167
Secker, J., 168
Shaw, I., 30, 192
Sheilds, P., 172
Shield, F., 230
Shooter, M., 169
Simon, A., 122
Sims, D., 8, 83–98, 91, 240
Sinclair, R., 75
Sines, D., 193
Skjorshammer, M., 173, 174
Slater, J., 191
Solancke, A., 64
Stanners, C., 71
Statham, J., 71, 122
Steel, J., 182
Stevens, A., 182

Stevenson, J., 231
Stevenson, O., 44
Straw, J., 19
Swan, W., 152

Taylor, M., 213
Thomas, D., 230, 231
Thompson, N., 10, 224, 225, 229
Thompson, S., 224, 225
Thompson, T., 181–97, 240
Tissier, J., 203
Tjosvold, D., 173
Torkington, C., 229
Torkington, N.P.K., 71
Towell, D., 53
Trappes-Lomax, T., 230
Truman, C., 67
Tucker, C., 204
Tuckman, B.W., 193
Twigg, J., 225

Vagg, J., 182
Vanclay, L., 164
Vaughan, B., 231
Villeneau, L., 19

Waddington, E., 48, 54
Walker, A., 184, 224
Walker, C., 184, 185
Walker, E., 64
Walker, T., 184, 185
Wallcraft, J., 67
Walter, U.M., 141, 143–44
Walton, J., 44, 53
Warner, L., 130, 132
Warren, L., 224
Webb, D., 28
Weinstein, J., 8, 18, 63–79, 70, 71,
    73, 240
West, M.A., 71, 191

Westman, B., 202
Wexler, S., 130, 132
Whittington, C., 8, 13–32, 14, 26, 29,
    39–58, 44, 48, 49, 53, 240
Wilmott, S., 87
Wilson, G., 230
Wolfe, J., 167
Worth, A., 70, 228, 229

Yarrow, L., 120
Younger-Ross, S., 230, 231